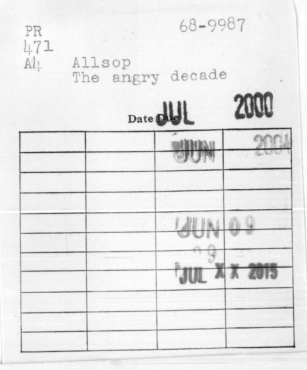

Date Due

JUL   2000

JUN   2004

JUN 09

JUL X X 2015

PRINTED IN U.S.A.

the angry decade

KENNETH ALLSOP

the angry decade

a survey of the cultural revolt of the nineteen-fifties

Distributed by
KENNIKAT PRESS
PORT WASHINGTON, N. Y.

FOR B

PETER OWEN LIMITED
50 Old Brompton Road London SW7

*

Third Impression 1964
© Kenneth Allsop 1958, 1964

Printed in Great Britain by
Lowe & Brydone (Printers) Ltd London NW10

contents

acknowledgements

I thank the following publishers for permission to quote from the books whose titles are in parenthesis: Weidenfeld & Nicolson (*Cards of Identity*), Chatto & Windus (*Under The Net, Flight From The Enchanter, The Sandcastle*), MacGibbon & Kee (*The Divine And The Decay, Mr. Nicholas, Happy As Larry, Summer In Retreat, Declaration*), Secker & Warburg (*Hurry On Down* and *Living In The Present*), Longmans, Green (*Prospects of Love*), Neville Spearman (*The Ginger Man*), Victor Gollancz (*Lucky Jim, That Uncertain Feeling, I Like It Here, The Outsider, Religion And The Rebel, Emergence From Chaos*), Faber & Faber (*Look Back In Anger, The Entertainer, Switchboard, A High Pitched Buzz*), Macmillan (*The Contenders, Preliminary Essays*), Eyre & Spottiswoode (*The World's Game, Room At The Top*).

The Angry Decade was written in the autumn of 1957 and was published the following Spring.

Looking back now over what I wrote then, about seven years ago, I do not find myself in remorseful disagreement with most of the judgements and opinions, although I gave too much prominence to some writers who rode through on the rush but fell out of sight in the scattering. However, they were conspicious at the time, and I think should therefore remain in the record. For whatever value *The Angry Decade* has is, I think, as a social bulletin, a "live" documentary from the scene of those quite exciting and interesting years, and it would be dishonest now to correct balances with the aid of hindsight or modify the immediacy in which the judgements were made.

Nevertheless, it may be worth a quick survey of what that outcrop of new break-away writing did amount to in the larger context, what affect if any it had upon its inheritors, and what those now almost middle-aged young men of that remote angry decade have achieved, or at any rate done, since.

First, it ought to be remembered that at that time a number of younger novelists and playwrights now famous—at least highly respected—had never, or barely, been heard of. Alan Sillitoe, Muriel Spark, David Storey, Stan Barstow, Harold Pinter, Arnold Wesker, Simon Raven, Henry Livings, Robert Holles, Keith

Waterhouse, Shelagh Delaney, David Caute, Alun Owen, John
Fowles—all were still unpublished or just making their debut, and
among them are several with greater talent than many of those discussed in the following pages.

What is striking about the later wave is how little trace there is
of the angry school of fiction that seemed in the middle Fifties to
cleave ahead into the far distance, inexorably decisive as the M1—
how abruptly it petered out in the mud of abandoned country.
Sillitoe, Barstow and Storey certainly deal in social-realism—but,
through the eyes and experience of their cobbly *lumpenproletariat*
characters, from a very different angle to that mockingly mutinous
jeering of the Redbrick boys of a few years earlier. What has also
almost disappeared is the desperately "contemporary" novel, with
its bright identikit trappings (up-to-the-minute inclusion of the
Twist, Chelsea boots and CND) which soon looks sad and wilted.
What has emerged again, like a seedling lily bursting through a
New Town's cement—and I doubt if anyone would have predicted
this as a serious possibility in the post-*Lucky Jim* days—is the
arrogantly snobbish, posturingly mannered upper-class novel done
by Auberon Waugh with a languid superciliousness and a kind of
poisoned distaste for all beyond the pale, but by Simon Raven
with a romantic stylishness which gives his preposterous melodramas
a melancholy lyricism.

Such novels as these may be a direct reaction against the bed-
sitter New Brutalism and the provincial picaresque that had gone
before—protests against the protests—but this cannot apply to the
mainstream of present-day fiction which does not even bear that
antipathetic relation to it. Both the brittle-giddy peregrinations of
smart young copywriters around the King's Road and the sullen
strugglings of insecure scholarship boys at the class barricades
dribble on. Yet there has recently been a departure from the genre
novel to individual imaginative work. This can be as barren as the
futuristic fantasies, *The Clockwork Orange* and *The Wanting Seed*, of
Anthony Burgess, who has rather mysteriously been enjoying a
vogue. It is to be seen more impressively in such diverse authors
as Muriel Spark, whose macabre comedy extends with equal
authenticity to an inspection of the aged (*Memento Mori*) and to an

inspection of well-bred war-time young women (*The Girls of Slender Means*); in John Fowles, whose first novel, *The Collector*, was a brilliantly original and distressingly frightening portrait of a humdrum psychopath, seen dually through his own mind and that of the young woman who is his victim; and in David Storey, whose *Radcliffe*, although working-class in setting and circumstances, was about human passion and compulsion—a book I disliked but which irresistibly moved over one like a black thunder cloud spitting lightning.

Those are but three random examples of the dissociation from the angry period novels that seems to have become mandatory. But this break has not happened in the theatre—indeed, the chain reaction set in movement by John Osborne's *Look Back In Anger* has spread and detonated in branching trails of gunpowder. There may not be much connection between Pinter's menacing *non-sequiturs* and the atmosphere of invisible lurking terrors he alchemizes through his non-relating characters, and the arguable naturalism but passionate emotional commitment of Wesker—yet, under the fairly useless label of kitchen sink plays, both Wesker and Pinter and the host of other gifted young dramatists who have come up through the Royal Court, the Arts Theatre and the Theatre Workshop have sparked from the same point, the spring of 1956 when Osborne's play was put on.

In a letter to the *Sunday Telegraph* about the new drama's failure to establish itself commercially in the West End, Lindsay Anderson last November spoke bleakly of the staunch middle-browism of the London theatre. The grim truth is, he wrote, that the London theatre public remains a Church of England Congregation. Agreed that the long runs and gilt-edged investments continue to be Agatha Christie and brassy musicals. Nonetheless, while few of the new-comers' plays caused traffic-jams of coach parties, for the past eight years the London stage has been aboil with experiment and noisy with rough hectoring accents not heard before when the frontier was a french window deluged with buttermilk sunshine and the action confined to lighting an Abdulla and swinging a tennis racket.

The indolent and conventional middle-brows, as Mr. Anderson accurately pointed out, are still there, solid, unmoved and immovable, occupying most of the seats in the other theatres, but there has grown enough enthusiasm for the new wave to give employment, perhaps capricious and not always of long duration, to more than thirty young dramatists who are insistently thrusting upon the stage slices from the underparts of life and vigorous, vulgar language hitherto thought not fitting in the preserve of philistine niceness. And, of course, by now the new drama has developed its own cliches and stereotypes—reality overdone to a pitch of theatricality, ordinary speech reproduced to an extreme of incoherence, identifiable human problems pushed to the point of nagging self-pity.

Still, wherever else it may have fizzled out, the anger that erupted in the Royal Court eight years ago begat a generation of writers attracted to a medium they would previously have regarded as invulnerable and who have made free use of it with the roistering boldness of the beggars holding their ball at the mansion in *Viridiana*.

But what of the innovators themselves? What became of them when kissing had to stop? As I remarked earlier, a number whose work is discussed in these pages did not sustain their start, or, to put it another way, they confirmed one's suspicions that there was really nothing there to start with by collapsing into obscurity with the collapse of the angry cult. Most of course, have continued writing professionally and seriously—yet, and I say this with reluctance and regret, it is impossible not to feel disappointment at the dullness that overcame much of the talent that seemed so bright in the early sunlight of welcome.

Osborne, himself, after flashing erratically in the works that followed *Look Back In Anger*, in 1962 put on his *Plays for England*, a double bill consisting of a hobnailed burlesque of a Royal wedding entitled *The Blood of the Bambergs* and *Under Plain Cover*, an uneven but startling Genet-like interior view of a fetish-fixated couple, happy in their kinky little cocoon until exposed by a Paul Slickey journalist. His *Luther* radically altered the concept of Osborne as a playwright: for here was an expertly carpentered and polished piece of stagecraft, but without the railing eloquence and spontaneous savagery that put the electricity into *Look Back In Anger*. It may have been an indication of the future Osborne, professional but tamed.

About Kingsley Amis I feel the kind of worry that a mother might for a son with a rare flair for the science of the stock market who fritters away his time at gin rummy. After the novels discussed here, Amis produced the not wholly successful but, beneath its flippant comedy surface, serious morality story, *Take A Girl Like You;* a monograph on science-fiction, *New Maps of Hell;* a collection of not more than average short stories, *My Enemy's Enemy;* and then, last autumn, his latest novel *One Fat Englishman.* This had a mixed reception, and some critics, it is fair to say, thought it splendid. I must repeat that I thought it a failure, sour, tired, scamped and rancorous, even more depressing when Amis's weakness for elaborately wordy humour was being flogged along with wet towels. The reason for my glumness is essentially because of my admiration for Amis: second wind coming, I'm sure—I hope.

Somewhat the same must be regretfully be said of Iris Murdoch. Since I considered her work here, she has published four more novels. *The Bell* with ambiguous symbolism but dry humour, examined a cranky utopian community in the Cotswolds. *A Severed Head* brought the first really hard questioning Miss Murdoch had received—this intricately rigged plot of musical beds, in which adultery and incest were the theme tunes, was praised for its cleverness; but also remarked upon was its artificiality, the glossy magazine writing and the rather donnish archness with which the phoney characters were given Greek mythological significance.

On the whole I personally enjoyed the intricate meshing of the puzzle, but was disappointed by *An Unofficial Rose*, in which symbolism seemed more obtrusive and self-indulgent as she moved her marionettes around in their Ivy Compton-Burnettish interlockings. Then last autumn, came *The Unicorn* which seemed to me—and, I think, to most other critics—deplorable. This was a plunge down to Daphne du Maurier—murky Gothic doings in an Irish Castle, where everyone was odd, not to say queer, described in banal prose, and now with the symbolism thick as sludge upon meaning and action. But, as with Kingsley Amis, one staunchly feels that Miss Murdoch is having an off-period, that her true talent is recouping.

About John Wain there is practically nothing to say. It is generally accepted that he can no longer be taken seriously as a novelist. He continues his journalism and recently published a collection of pieces, *Essays on Literature and Ideas*, a mixture of sensible criticism and air-beating diatribes against the enemies he espies under the bed he has made and must lie upon.

John Braine followed *Room at the Top* with *The Vodi*, the story of a tubercular weakling haunted by the symbolic malevolent gremlins (the Vodi) who are out to get him. Although this novel lacked the drive and dash of *Room at the Top*, and contained careless slips of fact and of logic, it had good writing and genuine feeling in it, and was an interesting try. Yet its comparative flop seemed to scare Braine back to the security of *Room at The Top* formula, and in 1962 in *Life at the Top*—the most recent novel he has published—he returned to his original hero, Joe Lampton. It was a poor pot-boiler, both coy and crude, and prefabricated with the sex and success ingredients that were certainly in *Room At The Top* but which there were controlled by a muscularity of purpose; here was flabbiness, contrived drama and a wallowing in a sentimental sympathy for the hero the author seemed trapped in but which did not ensnare the reader.

Colin Wilson continues to make reviewers fret and fume, and ask peevishly why he was ever published at all. Wilson, undeterred, barnstorms on through his private Grand Guignol. Black magic, rape, sex-murder, hypnotism, satanism, and unspeakable jollifications in darkest Notting Hill, surge prolifically from Mr. Wilson's typewriter. He has published ten books since *The Outsider*, including a study of the place of imagination in literature (*The Strength to Dream*) and a digest of applied perversion in vomiting detail (*Encyclopaedia of Murder*). His last novel, *Man Without A Shadow*, was presented in the form of the sex-diary of an amateur Nietzsche in quest of an orgasm like a launching-pad count-down that will project the happy cosmonaut into the orbit of existentialist consciousness. What can be said of Mr. Wilson is that, impervious to critics' anti-missile missiles, he stays consistently on course, and doubtless his books sell—but he seems to have pulled off his announced objective, to change the thinking of man, only as regards what is thought of him.

In fact, it seems not to be the star names of that earlier period who have maintained or enlarged their reputations, but the then minor figures. Hugh Thomas turned from novels to produce his definitive and major *The Spanish Civil War*. Correlli Barnett similarly has developed, with an incisiveness not obvious in his novel *The Hump Organisation*, into a military historian, the author of *The Desert Generals* and *The Swordbearers*, both provocatively individualistic and masterly in their interpretation of the complexities of warfare.

Of them all I would say that Thomas Hinde has most truly held to the vision and technical skill revealed in *Mr. Nicholas*, and matured, quietly and consistently, as a novelist of firm distinction. His last two *The Cage* in 1962 and *Ninety Double Martinis* in 1963, explored with even finer subtlety the slide-area at the edges of the reality we believe we dwell in—the first that of the white settlers and African nationalists in the bad dream they shared, the second the actual nightmare world (like filming a TV screen) of a neurotic schoolmaster, in which the baleful spiralling of terrors is conveyed not by muzzy shadow-and-light effects but by plain narrative writing.

But this prologue is the postscript: how did it all begin?

author's note

I think I should state at the outset that I know personally—some well, some only slightly—most of the writers whose work and attitudes are discussed in this book.

With many of them I have talked or corresponded about the problems and the patterns of writing in the post-war period, and these privately expressed opinions are quoted with their permission.

Personal acquaintance has not, I hope, affected my attempt at an objective examination of their work.

KENNETH ALLSOP

Before Seymour Glass, a character in J. D. Salinger's short story *A Perfect Day for Bananafish,* goes up to his hotel room to shoot himself, thereby eluding the new wife he has nicknamed Miss Spiritual Tramp of 1948 and life altogether, he has been on the beach with a friend. The friend is a little girl named Sybil whom he escorts into the sea.

To Sybil he says: "You just keep your eyes open for any banana-fish. This is a *perfect* day for bananafish."

"I don't see any," Sybil says.

"That's understandable," replies Seymour. "Their habits are very peculiar."

There is an interesting similarity between bananafish and the generation of new writers who in the Nineteen-Fifties have been named the Angry Young Men. It seems that this is a *perfect* day for them, but it is difficult actually to see any. In fact I have come to that phrase Angry Young Men with some circumlocution and reluctance. The gloss has gone from its pile from being chased too hard and too long through the headlines. It has been classified as vermin and I hope that we shall be able to riddle it with buckshot and, after this first section, leave it lying in the hedge-bottom for most of the time during the rest of the book.

Yet it would be tortuous to attempt a survey of the British intellectual landscape of the Nineteen-Fifties and deliberately to avoid the phrase Angry Young Men. It would also be wrong, because although its validity in a collective sense may be dubious, although whatever meaning it originally had has been smudged over by promiscuous use, it does signify. For a variety of oddly mixed reasons which I want to investigate, the Fifties are of consequence because it has been in this decade that a new chorus of voices has broken through the mumble of the stale, worked-out cultural tradition lingering on from the Forties. Although chorus is hardly accurate because it implies a concord that is not present. Clamour may be better, for the opinions, philosophies, arguments, complaints, accusations, exhortations, tomfoolery, laments and bickering (backed, one can hardly overlook, by rhythmic reverberations of chest-beating and rolling logs) is full of all the dissonance to be expected in a modern concert. The generic title for the protagonists of all these divergent and often conflicting attitudes is, in the mind of the general public, like it or not, Angry Young Men. That starting point must be accepted and questions asked on that basis.

Is the Angry Young Man label wildly off the mark? Certainly all who have been herded together under the banner, while perhaps finding the advertisement not without value and the accompanying fame not unpleasant, individually hotly denies that that has any connection with *him*. But it does ring a response in most people today. The names Kingsley Amis, Colin Wilson and John Osborne peal out like a treble bob, cracked with discord to those with more sophisticated ears, but there they are, the Three Musketeers of the revolutionary army, all for none and none for all. They do not conceal their mutual distrust, dislike and disagreements.

Amis: "I don't like these glum chums."

Wilson: "Jimmy Porter [the hero of Osborne's play *Look Back In Anger*] is a pseudo-Outsider. He doesn't possess the strength of mind to create anything."

Osborne: "I must read *The Outsider* [Wilson's first publication]. I'm told it is a very good reference book—such a wealth of bibliography."

There is not, it can be seen, any grand design of amity and

16

purpose here. They have widely disparate outlooks on modern problems and modern solutions: Amis, flippant and facetious, the grin on the face of the garrotter, but whose political purpose has dwindled with disillusionment; Osborne, whirling words like a meat cleaver; and Wilson, a sort of philosophical steeplejack scaling sickening heights with untested equipment.

However, they and their supporters do share a quality which has been misread and misnamed anger. I think the more accurate word for this new spirit that has surged in during the Fifties is dissentience. They are all, in differing degrees and for different reasons, dissentients. I use that word in preference to dissenter, because that implies an organised bloc separation from the Establishment, whereas dissentient has a more modulated meaning— more to disagree with majority sentiments and opinions.

That is what has happened in the Fifties—a generation suddenly made up its mind. Not so much to rebel against the old order of authority and standards, but to refuse to vote for it. Some of the dissentients are in fact working for the overthrow of the exhausted but tenacious ideas, a little band of spiritual bomb-throwers led by that guerrilla philosopher Colin Wilson who campaigns against the present high priests of Western civilization.

Some, who are the emotional actionists, are all for reform and revolution, for whipping up fervour for political causes and such dashing melodramatic measures as, say, disbanding the monarchy forthwith, and these are represented by—he would, I suspect, refuse to lead anything—John Osborne.

Then there are the others, by far the biggest group who share with Kingsley Amis a cynical, mocking, derisive disgust with authority and the "shiny barbarism" (as Richard Hoggart in *The Uses of Literacy* called our present mass culture) but who, out of either laziness or despair, opt for an inert neutrality—or even conform enough to loot some of the good things still left in the "residential" middle-class bondbox.

The new dissentient writers seem to me to fall quite clearly and naturally into those three groups, and I want later to discuss in detail their outlook, methods, intentions and differences. But first let us review some of the characteristics that all the groups share and which immediately distinguish this new generation from their literary progenitors. The predominant characteristic is a tough, ruthless, hell-with-it approach to their particular undertakings that is utterly uninhibited by the blood-thinning refinements of the old upper-class *rentier* overlord they are trying to evict, the tentativeness, the subtle qualifications, the tolerant reservations, and perhaps, the final deliquescence into ambiguous mist.

The phrase Angry Young Man carries multiple overtones which might be listed as irreverence, stridency, impatience with tradition, vigour, vulgarity, sulky resentment against the cultivated and a hard-boiled muscling-in on culture, adventurousness, self-pity, deliberate disengagement from politics, fascist ambitions, schizophrenia, rude dislike of anything phoney or fey, a broad sense of humour but low on wit, a general intellectual nihilism, honesty, a neurotic discontent and a defeated, reconciled acquiescence that is the last flimsy shelter against complete despondency—a wildly ill-assorted agglomeration of credos which, although without any overall coherence, do belong to this incoherent period of social upheaval.

A perceptive comment was made about this situation by Professor Leslie A. Fiedler, of the University of Montana, in an article "The Un-Angry Young Men", an examination of the current state of mind of the U.S. college student, in the January 1958 *Encounter*. Remarking that although two of the literary redoubts—the journals *Encounter* and *London Magazine*—are "presided over by two of the chief surviving representatives of the Thirties, Stephen Spender and John Lehmann", the change in Britain is deep and violent. Later in the article he says: "The young British writer has the inestimable advantage [comparing him with the young American writer] of representing a new class on its way into a controlling position in the culture of his country. He is able to define himself against the class he replaces: against a blend of homosexual sensibility, upper-class aloofness, liberal politics, and avant-garde literary devices. When he is boorish rather than well-behaved, rudely angry rather than ironically amused, when he is philistine rather than arty—even when he merely writes badly, he can feel he is performing a service for literature, liberating it from the tyranny of a taste based on a world of wealth and leisure which has become quite unreal."

When and where did the phrase Angry Young Man originate? Leslie Allen Paul, the religious philosopher, contributed a letter to one magazine's correspondence columns in which was proceeding a ding-dong exchange of flippancies about the phrase, rather plaintively reminding everyone that in 1951 he published a book with Faber entitled just that, *Angry Young Man:* it was an autobiography, the story of a Marxist's personal class-warfare during the Twenties and Thirties, and his eventual conversion to Christianity. Indeed it would be surprising if such an obvious grouping of ordinary words had *not* been used before May 8, 1956. However it was then, when *Look Back in Anger* by Osborne (who up to that time had been a hard-up repertory actor with long 'rests') was put on at the Royal Court Theatre, Sloane Square, that it suddenly came to have specific significance and wide use. I shall be discussing this later, but the point to be made here is that the hero of *Look Back In Anger,* Jimmy Porter, quickly became a character genus. Articles in the weekly reviews began talking about "the Jimmy Porters and the Lucky Jims" including the hero of Amis's novel *Lucky Jim* (which had then been out just over two years) as another contemporary prototype.

On May 26 *The Times* carried one of its facetious "sarky schoolmaster" leaders, which now seems generally accepted as the source of the phrase. In fact, although the subject was the anger of today's young men, the word anger wasn't used. It said:

"People who like to leave the theatre in an argumentative mood will go to the Royal Court Theatre to see Mr. John Osborne's play *Look Back In Anger.* They will not necessarily argue about the merits of the piece, but they will remember those reviews in which it has been put forward as an expression of opinion valid for the generation of those in their late twenties. They will see a thoroughly cross young man, caught into an emotional situation where crossness avails nothing. And they may well wonder whether the young men of today are really as embittered, as prompt to offence, as the hero of the play.

"Most young men, in every age, are probably much alike. They turn the world, as far as they can, to their own account, in order to become old men as painlessly as possible. Mr Osborne, however, is dealing with that inconvenient phenomenon, the clever young man. It is he who sets his stamp upon a generation, he who sets the level at which the men of his own age will be remembered by posterity. Are we, then, to think that those who are now in their late twenties are likely to be known above all for their touchiness and their rages? . . . A Cinderella spirit, quite alien to the pre-war generation, is abroad, and a closing-time admitted before ever the revels begin.

"Indeed, the young sometimes put on almost too serious a face. There is about the young men a suspicion of a whisker, about the girls a common-sensical forthrightness. Where the prodigies celebrated by Mr Evelyn Waugh in 1930 or thereabouts organized parties in balloons and swimming baths, the youth of today visits prisons and reads Kierkegaard. Exceptionally, perhaps, the young people of Mr Osborne's play can be found, just as the heroes of Mr Kingsley Amis ring true in a limited setting. But it is likelier that the real tone of our age will be found much closer to that of a century ago. Already our didactic writers are getting back to Samuel Smiles; it is only a matter of time before the evil old men of the day flinch uneasily from the start of some youthful Thomas Arnold."

Jimmy Porter does not visit prisons or read Kierkegaard. He is a tough dead-end kid intellectual hunched like a killer spider in the middle of his emotional web. He is certainly cross, with an hysterical, nagging, hyperbolic bitchiness about pretty well everything. Examined objectively, there is little that is constructive or organically developed in Jimmy Porter's invective, but the dialogue Osborne laces through the play like a spluttering gunpowder trail is authentic modern talk, and aroused excitement in critics and audiences. Whacked all around the head, they came away dazed and in a masochistic ecstasy from the sheer *anger* of it and after wading through years of theatrical cold rice pudding it's easy to understand this.

It should in fairness be stated here that Osborne, with the upset loathing you might expect in a dowager waking up from a champagne night in bed with her butler, has vehemently denounced the Angry Young Man vogue. While admitting that he wrote a play with a title and a character that has stimulated the idea, he

blames the press entirely (and not quite honestly when you see*
how often he has gratuitously used the phrase himself) for falsifi-
cation of the phrase.

It is fascinating to look back over these past two or three years
at the way the old literary Establishment has been hopping from
one foot to another in a nervous tizzy about the inrush of the new
denomination. Of course *Lucky Jim* when it first came out in
January 1954 was welcomed with delight. So were a few other what
then appeared to be isolated novels in the new genre, such as
Thomas Hinde's *Mr. Nicholas* and John Wain's first novel *Hurry
On Down,* and no wonder, because for some time before that
The Times Literary Supplement and other literary organs had
been deploring the deadness of the cultural scene. There had been
a long correspondence in the *Literary Supplement* about "the
death of the novel" and desultory discussion had been bombinated
about in the letter columns of *The Times* and *The Observer* on
the economic plight of the writer, the general implication being
that no-one nowadays was going to slave away at a novel when he
could get £25 a week at the coalface or £10 for driving a bus.
There was, in fact, a growing atmosphere of concern about the
literary wasteland, a growing agreement that, somehow, it must
be irrigated with new talent. Even the more mandarin prose-
producers, who had never previously displayed anything but
benign contentment at their long and happy reign, began to
glance over their shoulders at the empty horizon (and I almost
gave that horizon a capital H). After all everyone likes to have an
heir.

So every work of promise, containing a mere hint of originality,
was received with generous warmth, culminating in the hosannas
of praise for *Look Back In Anger* and the even more delirious enthusiasm for Colin Wilson's *The Outsider* when it appeared in
May 1956.

It was after this that the enthusiasm began to ice over a little.
Misgivings began to spread beneath the floppy bow ties and the
rumpled cardigans. A note of chiding reproof began to infiltrate
the ninepenny weeklies and the serious Sundays. In broadcast critic

*See page 131

21

circles and on television discussion programmes elderly jowls began to droop with disapproval, and through the pipe smoke came the first gruff words of criticism. The new note was one of reproach and admonition—these youngsters weren't kissing the hand that had patted them; easy success; bit big for their boots; also big heads. The sweeping statements began to sweep. In *Books and Bookmen* Malcolm Elwin asked: "Surely this insistence on youth as a condition necessarily interesting suggests a symptom of an insecure society's pursuit of novelty?" In *The Spectator* Iain Hamilton remarked: "Your average New Hero is egocentric, of course . . . He gorges his way through life like a worm, instinctively contracting and relaxing his muscles . . . He is also, of course, for a large part of the time an Angry Young Man—without knowing, naturally, what he is angry about." In *The New Statesman* Colm Brogan wrote: "Lucky Jim is a loafer, a sycophant, a vulgarian who has taken advantage of State bounty to secure a university post when he is mentally and morally unfit to be a school janitor." "The danger that confronts the contemporary English novelist", lectured *The Times Literary Supplement* leaderwriter, "is not that of biting off more than he can chew. It is that of relaxing into the small humours of a grumbling, self-enclosed cosiness." J. B. Priestley referred to "a somewhat loutish style of sullen acquiescence, found in some younger novelists," and then really tore loose on Wilson's book: "If the Outsider is poisoned by an embittered egoism, if he wants to hurt and not to heal, if there is more hate than love in him, can he bring us nearer to a solution?" he demanded, and concluded obscurely: "We are waiting for God, not for Godot." There was the dramatic mass recantation when Colin Wilson's *Religion and the Rebel* appeared last October, and the emotional scenes of reformed Wilson fans publicly repenting were reminiscent of the confessional orgy at a Soviet treason trial. In *Punch* A. P. Herbert contributed a 58-line poem entitled "Angry Young Men", which trumpeted to its end:

> No British young, since British young were new,
> Have had such boons and benefits as you.
> The talk of war "unsettles" you, I see:
> I've served in two, my lads, and suffered three.

We did not whine and whimper at our doom:
We did not cry "Frustration!" in the womb.
We saw, and shared, some grandeur in the grime.
Cheer up, my lads—you'll understand in time.

And, of course, Somerset Maugham intervened with his famous succinct pronouncement on the Lucky Jim type of hero: "They are scum."

Eyeing gossip column items about Osborne's £20,000 a year, about Wilson's vast treble-chance reward, about John Braine's £15,000 profit from his first novel *Room At The Top,* the old guard seemed increasingly regretful that they had opened their arms so impulsively in the beginning. Now that the newcomers had been admitted to the inner circle they were treacherously making rude and frightening threats to take over control.

There are two major reasons why they so promptly made contact with a big, attentive public. First, they filled the vacuum in that great echoing museum where the arts used to be kept in Britain—and their very presence, even before the quality of their offerings had been examined, seemed a heartening thing. Second, some of them, and Wilson especially, immediately displayed an acute appreciation of the publicity techniques of this modern age, and systematically and ruthlessly employed them to blazon their names in headlines. Stopping short of Wilson's lurid vaudeville acts as the centre of a horse-whipping attack and as vilifier of Shakespeare, some of his contemporaries' methods have been more subtle but have achieved strikingly effective results.

They have deliberately sought the advantages that there are in being known to the enormous public served by the *Sunday Pictorial,* commercial television, and the monster women's magazines. (*Good Housekeeping* of January this year presented "A short directory to Angry Young Men". Clearly it had been decided at an editorial conference that by now the Angry Young Men had reached the *Housewives' Choice* public and that a sink-side guide should be provided. The page was topped with a fresco of thumbnail pictures of Osborne, Wilson, Amis, Bill Hopkins, Stuart Holroyd and Wain. With that stern detachment that popular

23

journalism assumes when being censorious about popular journalism, and which fills me with warm affection, the writer, James Gordon, began: "The popular newspapers, for lack of better copy, have invented a new legend, the Angry Young Men. . . . Forget all this nonsense invented by the newspapers and exploited for its sensationalism," and he settled the whole matter with: "After all, the Angry Young Man movement is a passing post-war phenomenon—the result of delayed shock.") They have also offered themselves for collective consideration in such symposiums as *Declaration.* So it ill becomes them to be churlish about being grouped together.

Osborne, and some others, understandably embarrassed and irritated by the custard pie usage of the phrase Angry Young Man, are at liberty to deny affiliation. Yet a news story usually evolves from a certain chemical process: the desire of the journalist to make a news story and the desire of the other party concerned to be made into one.

It may well be that the general public have two rather hazy and limited impressions—that the Angry Young Man lashes out and the Angry Young Man cashes in. The important thing is that, with justification, the phrase illuminated for large numbers of people a new state of mind in Britain of the Nineteen-Fifties. *Look Back In Anger,* arriving at that particular moment, caught and crystallised a floating mood. It was as if the pin-table ball that many young people feel themselves to be today, richocheting in lunatic movement, had hit the right peg. Lights flashed. Bells rang. Overnight "angry" became the code word.

But can all of the new arrivals, the novelists, critics, philosophers and playwrights, and those who just give television interviews, be said to be angry? Certainly they feel strongly enough about the situation they find themselves in—articulate citizens of Britain in the Nineteen-Fifties.

In the Forties, apart from the wounded resentment of the white-collar class against the rapine of Labour Government and the daily Nineteen Eighty-Four style hate programme conducted by the Conservative Press against the Enemies of the People (Laski,

Strachey, etc.) there was little genuine strong emotion abroad. Battered by the war and ten years of filthy food, worn-out clothes and austerity, with grime and drabness rubbed into the pores, the British public was in what GPs call a "run-down condition". It hadn't the energy to support or the appetite for new intellectual brainwaves or banner-wagging movements. Also there was a conscientious but laborious social revolution in progress. The attempt was being made, with clapped-out industrial machinery, no money to spend and little enthusiasm for it, to redistribute the national income. It was a low voltage revolution in which the Labour Party, always quick on the draw with a compromise, bent backwards to be respectable and constitutionally correct. I suspect that we should be thankful for timidity and the slurred movement in politicians. Nevertheless it was not a period that lit the populace with a white fire. Most people, while grateful (noisily or furtively) for the National Health and the new security of life, seemed to find a drab self-righteousness in the system and existence under it like living in a giant Welsh tin chapel. Consequently in 1951 the voting was for self-interest and faster living. Meanwhile Britain was producing, as well as the Welfare State, Jimmy Porter.

He and his generation are those aged between twenty-five and thirty-five—that is, who were born between the early Twenties and the early Thirties. It has been a lifetime incessantly criss-crossed by catastrophe. From all directions, roaring and lurching like tanks over a battleground, the crises have never stopped coming. Being autobiographical for a moment, when I glance back I see down my thirty-seven years the symbols of disruption set close as a picket fence, individual memories starting with a child's view of the General Strike, the cold grey shadow that the Depression threw into even a 'disengaged' suburban household, the fear that was communicated to a disinterested teenager by the flickering menace of Hitler and Mussolini in the newsreels, the first physical encounter with real suffering when, as a junior reporter, I met hunger marchers trudging up from the coalfields, the friends who were killed in Spain, then the major black-out of the war and its epilogue of dreary years, and the dawning of the H-bomb era.

Set all this against the experience of countless thousands of

25

Europeans and Asians, with their horizons of barb-wire, slave-camps, obliteration bombing, DP trains, fragmented families and first-hand knowledge of atom-bombs, and the British citizen's history looks tame as Winnie the Pooh's. Nevertheless the background of anyone under forty is lacking something that those over forty have known.

It is difficult to prove this sort of statement, but I personally have, and I believe a great many men and women in my age group have, an intense nostalgic longing for the security and the innocence that seems to have been present in Britain before the 1914 war. It has become almost a tribal ancestral memory. While being aware that I am romantically glossing it all over into a sunny simplicity, for me that period is a montage of striped blazers and parasols in Henley punts, tea on the lawn with spotted flycatchers hawking from the tennis net, and Ernest A. Shepard London squares with autumn fires glinting on the brass fenders in the drawing rooms. I know that there was grinding poverty, and hideous living conditions too, yet I am sure that the Victorians and Edwardians had an inner confidence that we shall never know. On the other hand, perhaps a more accurate picture of even the pleasanter aspect of pre-1914 was the one George Orwell gave in *Such, Such Were The Joys,* his blood-chilling account of his prep-school which has never been published in Britain because of libel-threats. Recalling the "sheer vulgar fatness" of that period, of champagne parties in rococo houseboats on the Thames, Saki's novels, *Where The Rainbow Ends,* and scrumptious teas at the Troc, he distilled it in this wonderfully and comically evocative sentence: "From the whole decade before 1914 there seems to breathe forth a smell of the more vulgar, un-grown-up kinds of luxury, a smell of brilliantine and crème de menthe and soft-centred chocolates—an atmosphere, as it were, of eating ever-lasting strawberry ices on green lawns to the tune of the Eton Boating Song." Still, Jimmy Porter and his older brother have been taught brinkmanship since they were let out of the play-pen—the technique of extracting satisfactions in a sort of compensatory spirit while your toes inch back from the crumbling edge.

26

This is where we come to the paradoxical knot in all their lives. Within this larger sense of futility and doom in Britain since the war there has been a dead centre, the theoretical motionless hollow at the centre of a whirlpool. The new dissentients are mostly working class or lower middle-class clever boys, grammar school or perhaps minor public school, spending most or perhaps just the tail-end of the war in uniform, or at any rate a couple of years of National Service, then university (red brick, or even white tile, most likely) on a scholarship or a Service grant. In a time of calamities they have had the protection of collective security; their course has been convoyed through to the safe harbour of the Welfare State. Gertrude Stein called her contemporaries of the Twenties the Lost Generation. This one might be described as the All Found Generation. And are they grateful, this plebian elite who have been creamed off from the admass for higher education and managerial duties? Not in the least.

To the chagrin and deep hurt of their fathers who worked doggedly for—or at least voted for in a spasm of nervous idealism in 1945—the moderate Trade Union socialism that has spread education and opportunity, the ingrates do not think a great deal of the new deal. They display neither enthusiasm for their elevation nor comradeship towards the idealists who put them where they are. One point of view seems to be that the education and the opportunity have been spread too thinly, like prole margarine of the bad old days. The larger result is that the new dissentients feel unassimilated. They are a new rootless, faithless, classless class—and consequently, because of a feeling of being misplaced and misprized, also often charmless—who are becalmed in the social sea. They are intelligent and, beneath the cocky Brando cynicism, sensitive, so they cannot wallow in lumpish contentment. They are acutely conscious of lacking the arrogant composure of the ruling-class line: they are strangers to their own sort. They feel a mixture of guilt about renegading from their hereditary background and contempt for the oafish orthodoxy of their families. Success, meaning money, is judged to be the safest measure—and there doesn't seem enough of that to go round.

The outcome of this conditioning is the dissentience that is in

27

the air today—the "anger" which has been gratuitously credited to many who are either only disgusted or coldly critical. For the moment it is those who are angry who concern us. What precisely are they angry about? That would have been an easy question to answer in any other decade. In the Twenties people were angry about the "Land Fit For Heroes" confidence trick, about the slashing of the miners' rates, about the gaudy goings-on of the Bright Young Things. In the Thirties people got angry about the murder of Jarrow, about the air assault on Guernica, about appeasement. In the Forties, even amid the welter of woe brought by the war, an extra bubble of anger could force up to the surface at the Germans' massacre in the Czechoslovakian village of Lidice, as well as blitz-anger and patriotic anger.

But what is there to get angry about in the Fifties?

Plenty, I would have said, ranging across a whole keyboard of cases, from bass notes of gravity to the tinkle of snobbish irritations—from, say, the card-sharp use of nuclear power in diplomatic poker to the march of the concrete lamp-post men who are putting the mutilated carcase of Britain in a chalk-stripe suit. Yet the Jimmy Porters are not even angry about the dominant problem of our time, which soaks invisibly like fall-out into every minor problem and contaminates it—the unresolved struggle between capitalism and communism. Not only are the Jimmy Porters not angry about this: it bores them deeply. In *Look Back In Anger* the original Jimmy, grinding away like a tooth-drill at the nerve ends of all around him during that Sunday limbo in the provincial flat turns briefly away from his class obsessions and shouts: "There aren't any good, brave causes left. If the big bang does come and we all get killed off, it won't be in aid of the old-fashioned grand design. It'll be just for the Brave New Nothing-thank-you-very-much".

The Jimmy Porters are not interested in mankind's political dilemmas such as the ideological and economic contest between East and West, and even their concern with the deeper plight of the pervading loss of spiritual direction is utterly introspective. Their anger is a sort of neurological masturbation, deriving from the very problems they cannot bring themselves to confront. It is a textbook psychotic situation: the emotional deadlock in a person caused by a general conviction that certain major man-made problems that man is facing are beyond the capacity of man to solve. That is part of the spreading sense of loss of liberty and identity that I will return to later. So the Jimmy Porters simmer and lacerate themselves with self-doubt. They are angry at having nothing they dare to be angry about.

The objection raised to this sort of contemporary "anger" is that it is oblique, petty, pyrotechnic with irrelevancies, neurotic and, in the end, dishonestly meretricious. But of course the Osborne-Porter "anger" is not the unique manifestation of dissentience of this period. It was necessary first to define that type of dissentience. There are graver symptoms.

One of these is the delink, an American slang abbreviation for the "delinquency notice" of withdrawal a defaulting student receives from the college dean, and a word which I think can usefully be broadened and extended in meaning to apply to the creative artist who has allowed himself to be pushed beyond the far reach of despair into severe personality disorder. Lucky Jim, in his most thick-ear emanation (and caricature versions of Lucky Jim dot the new novels like daisies in May) is a cheerful delink. He is the man in the frayed flannel bags standing well back from the edge to scoff and jeer. No lout at heart, he won't risk taking a look at "the perception of complete terror" that is Wilson's definition of the reality of the world. Lucky Jim's attitude is guilt-tinged, defiant but candid. His instincts are sensitive enough to detect the yawning tragedy (his antennae 'pick up' the abyss ahead) but he is unsure whether he has the integrity and the courage to walk forward and examine it. Instead he 'plays safe' with what he sees to be "a sort of stodgy, stingy caution . . . you can't even call it looking after number one." Life is made into comic Commando warfare against the slobs. He thinks it's all hopeless, but all the same he's still in the human race.

The extreme delink has resigned, opted-out, withdrawn to the narcissistic twilight in which Samuel Beckett's dustbin creatures exist. The heroes of some novels—Thomas Hinde's *Happy As Larry*, William Camp's *Prospects Of Love*—have gone through the process of disengagement and emerged at the further end into medical schizophrenia. Their gyroscopes have failed. They have lost track of their own misery and live in inert inaction, in nothingness. They have become empty slates upon which experience chalks itself up and is wiped out by the side of a hand— "a single sentence will suffice for modern man", remarks the main character in Albert Camus's *The Fall*: "he fornicated and read the papers."

No anger where these zombies live, for here the emotional temperature is cold and static. Once Cocteau, describing what it was like for the addict to be without opium for eight days, wrote that when he placed his ear to his own arm he heard: "Catastrophe, riots, factories blowing up, armies in flight, flood—the ear can detect a whole apocalypse in the starry night of the human body." The extreme delink has lost all capacity for such suffering and starry delirium. He is a speiaeologist of the spirit.

A second symptom is the Outsider. He is over on the far right wing, out of the darkness in his own self-generated dazzle. I wouldn't call Colin Wilson's disposition an angry one, but what he writes is fried, like fish in batter, in a fanatical ardour of dissentience. Wilson and his small group of followers, or perhaps associates is a better word, seem to be trying to dynamite their way out of a dilemma and not to care how much damage is done in the detonation. They—Wilson, Stuart Holroyd (who published his *Emergence From Chaos* last May), Bill Hopkins (whose first novel *The Divine and the Decay* had an antagonistic reception last autumn) and a few others recruited since *The Outsider* came out are, in a more organised manner than is generally recognised by the public, propagating their Religious Existentialism which they say requires a higher type of man, a superman, to thrust humanity through to safety out of civilization's big crash. It is probably unnecessary to add that they see themselves as the supermen, the law-givers. So far the western world has not dropped everything and rushed to canonize them, which may be because the western world is just being as obtuse as usual, or on the other hand perhaps it is not quite the bovine telly-shackled admass that the Outsider sees. In the meantime, while we are finishing off our inspection of the new troops, let me just add that there is some hot mistrust felt towards the Outsider faction, the neo-Nietzscheians.

They are openly and militantly anti-humanist in the steps of T. E. Hulme. This peasant army (all the group, I think, grew up in provincial industrial towns) have had the temerity to clump into the academic closes where the trainee priests are learning their catechism from A. J. Ayer and Bertrand Russell, and break in with a loud errand boy's whistle. "Throw your logical positivism out of the window and stick up your hands," they shouted. They have irritated and offended the orthodoxy. "The Outsider is NOT anti-rational," Wilson has said. "It is not Reason he objects to: it is the tiny area of existence that 'rational thinkers' apply their reason to." J. B. Priestley has depicted the world as "already dangerously divided between intellect without feeling and feeling without intellect", and a reflection of this might be seen in the new writing.

Nevertheless some non-combatant leftists ("I'm a socialist in an abstract sense, but I'm not a Labour party-liner. How *can* you be nowadays?") have been shaken out of their detachment by the impact of the Outsider faction, and by the spreading of right-wing religiosity through the universities. I would like to think that there was a flame or two of real political controversy licking up, but I'm not yet sure whether that noise that we at first thought was the steely clash of ideologies wasn't just the clatter of poses being struck. There is more than a sniff of fascism about the outlook of the Outsiders — the disinterest in the gentle and the warm things of human life, their contempt for compassion, their dismissal of social reform as effete sentimentality, and their salivating reflex at the glimpse of approaching power. In *Declaration* Kenneth Tynan, the drama critic, too slickly dismisses the Outsider faction as just hot gospellers in the Norman Vincent Peale cast. Whatever they are up to, it is not hawking bromides for the Establishment. Still, when Tynan goes on to say: "One must be impatient with these young fuhrers of the soul, fantasy-Leopolds and fantasy-Loebs, who declare that Hitler, for all his faults, was after all an outsider and who commit themselves to stating that 'the most irritating of the human lice is the humanist with his puffed-up

31

pride in reason'," I know what he is feeling. Yet it is the period of nervous, half-hearted leftism that produced the Outsider—the time when Cyril Connolly wrote in the last issue of *Horizon*: "For it is closing time in the gardens of the West and from now on an artist will be judged only by the resonance of his solitude or the quality of his despair."

Many of that generation were sad synthetics, those culture disc-jockeys of the Thirties and Forties, those collective-farm fetishists with their etiolated sensitivity and their penthouse patter. They cared about fine writing and fine things, and they never let each other down in print even if they hated each other at Eton, but when you look back ten years at the exhaustion and inbreeding of that fag-end of a cultural period, it is not astonishing that the new dissentients came in with a rush—and that many of them were Angry Young Men.

Before looking at the writers and their attitudes in detail, and examining their origins, both social and intellectual, I want briefly to talk about some writers I am *not* talking about—those who cannot be omitted from anything purporting to be a survey of post-war literature but who lack—or, as they themselves might say, are uncorrupted by—the special characteristics of the Fifties.

I am thinking here of two distinct categories of 'quality' writers—perhaps three if we allot one to Graham Greene all by himself, with his important pessimistic insight and his absorption in univeral problems of regeneration, expressed in the bleak, de-nuded, snack-bar style that is no less effective for its dated mood (redolent of Studio One in the mid-Forties and afterwards by bus home with an autumn rain falling on the bomb-sites).

The others seem to me to be immediately distinct. There are, first, those for whom Connolly's "gardens of the West" have closed, and who are indeed in a state of sad solitude. I mean the Sitwells, the Ivy Compton-Burnetts, the Henry Greens, the Stephen Spenders and the John Lehmanns. Rather like the American Republicans who, Adlai Stevenson once said, had been "dragged kicking and screaming into the Twentieth Century," the survivors of the old *literati*, the candelabra-and-wine *rentier* writers have taken the Fifties on sufferance. Wincing with distaste, mournful and puzzled, they have withdrawn to a remote and musty fantasy life among their woodland temples. Their considerable talent is absorbed into the construction of elaborate, private languages, elegiac remembrance of things past, reveries that are passed like an empty parcel around an ever diminishing circle. Their writing becomes more and more heavily wrought with convoluted scroll-work, or more and more allusive, quivering with *nuance*, gauzy with conversational subtleties that taper off into the raising of an eyebrow.

"The post-war period has not yet established itself. . . . A kind of miasma, a dullness, still obscures the imaginative life of many," wrote Rose Macaulay in *New Writing and Daylight* in September 1946, discussing 'The Future of Fiction'. "A young man who has spent his adult years at high tension, among perils, discomforts, fears, adventures, will not see or write of life as if he had lived at ease; he will be either toughened or sensitized," and she added with great perspicacity—this was twelve years ago, before any of the new dissentients had begun publishing—"No new *style* is even faintly to be seen on the horizon. . . . There has been in fact a flight from style . . . the novel of the future will be in plain, un-coloured English, with no frills; the Max Beerbohm period is dead, those laurel trees are cut, and we shall go no more (for the moment) into those elegant, aromatic and verbaceous woods. Those who write mannered English are all of older generations; the future of the novel is not with them." Symbolic of these cast-aways on the rugged rocks of the Fifties is Evelyn Waugh, not strictly belonging to the high-born but who has so long lived among them, physically and artistically, that their adversity is his, as he would wish it to be. And with a candour that his like have so far flinched from, Waugh described with chilling, night-mare clarity what it is to be a sort of aristocratic dinosaur in *The Ordeal of Gilbert Pinfold,* an admittedly autobiographical novel which appeared last August. Here is Pinfold, fiftyish, fastidious, Catholic, Tory clubman, a novelist who has assumed the part of "a combination of eccentric don and testy colonel", living in a hunting shire with his wife and big family of handsome, well-mannered children. There are all the traditional ingredients, and a fine English game pie they appear to make—until Waugh removes the crust. Pinfold "abhorred plastics, Picasso, sunbathing and jazz—everything in fact that had happened in his own lifetime". He is shocked by "a bad bottle of wine, an impertinent stranger, or a fault in syntax". Winter (October onward) is a gruesome experience at Lychpole, with polar draughts whistling round the screens at the arthritic, gouty Pinfold, inducing him to multiply his doses of sleeping draughts, bromide, chloral, crème de menthe, wine, gin and brandy. Pinfold plunges deep into near-psychosis, in which he experiences all the horrors of a plagued imagination—he 'hears' people calling him a homosexual, a Jewish refugee, a swindler, a satyr and womaniser, a dipsomaniac, a literary fake, a bankrupt, a blackmailer, a Communist, a neurotic with suicide compulsions, a Blackshirt, a capitalist adventurer, and a sham Old Etonian. But the point is that the torment of the mental illness he goes through is really no more hallucinatory than the squirearchal life he stubbornly continues to live.

Are the *ancien regime* pathetic in their refusal to adjust, to come to terms with a world that is hostile, strange and terrifying to them? Or are they well off out of it?

There is another category of established, serious writers who have to some extent come to terms with post-war Britain, and who have, as novelists, taken up the position of observers. They are at least *looking*, even if their vantage point is essentially that of an unreconciled adult who knew the middle-class world before the bottom fell out in 1945. In this category come excellent novelists such as J. D. Scott, C. P. Snow, L. P. Hartley (and how significant are those curtly dignified initials, as to be found on inter-departmental memoranda, just as significant as books now by *Bill* Hopkins and the dedication "*Al's*" in Wain's *Preliminary Essays*), William Cooper, William Sansom, Angus Wilson, V. S. Pritchett and Anthony Powell. Now that I have written down those names I see what an interesting and specialist field of experience they illuminate. L. P. Hartley, the marooned Edwardian, looks with intense sympathy at his graceful human beings—but through the wrong end of a telescope so that they are seen at an enormous distance, bright and separate as a day-dream. C. P. Snow is deep in his long series of novels which are becoming a topography of the modern areas of power, the managerial world of Whitehall and Belgravia, with outposts in the New Towns and the atomic energy stations, where top civil servants, government committee experts, dons, Treasury manipulators and scientific planners conspire in their toneless, cautious voices, the New Conservative elite ruling from anonymous ministerial small back rooms. J. D. Scott in *The End of An Old Song* wrote a definitive study of the contemporary go-getter careerist (more than likely a Scot), the sort who heads like a guided missile for the high stakes, up to that stratosphere of World Bank conferences and the corporate bodies within which our manner of existence is controlled as finely and as arbitrarily as the knobs on the radiators. William Sansom parts the suburban privets like an etymologist probing grass stems with his tweezers. picks out his Surbiton and Welwyn Garden City specimens, and encases them in an amber of hard-gloss prose. Anthony Powell in his Widmerpool series of novels starting with *A Question Of Upbringing,* is interpreting with an oblique brilliance the pre-war cabbala of snobbery, caste marks, behavourism, internal scales of measurement, and the permissible eccentricities of the public school, that malleable system that can now supply industrial executives as efficiently as it did district commissioners. The three remaining authors come nearer to the Fifties: they are almost participants. V. S. Pritchett's *Mr. Beluncle* was placed in the Odeonised dormitory land, and he beautifully revealed the mingled fears and frivolities of this remote everyday life. William Cooper (a civil servant colleague of C. P. Snow) was the pathfinder for the provincial school. His first novel, *Scenes From Provincial Life,* published early in 1950, was in its laconic, episodic, throw-away style an authoritative piece of social anthropology, beautifully underplayed and deadpan, about the group of clerk-class mild bohemians in a market town caught between despair and nonchalance as the last peace-time months of 1939 slip away—and Cooper returned to this sort of sharp portraiture of the society that starts where London ends in his novel *Young People,* published last

35

February, with its setting in a Midlands university college. Angus Wilson continues to develop his unique gifts for spiking the idioms and types of today and yesterday, but those that he jabs on his skewer like a *kebab* and lightly grills, are the misfits and the class casualties of the social upheaval, the lost, the anomalous and the phoney, the invert who carefully knots his Winchester tie for his appearance in the dock, the genteel dispossessed in the South Kensington hotel reservation. Yet wonderfully accurate and authentic though he is, Wilson watches from outside, from the liberal-humanist viewpoint of someone born in 1913 and brought up in a home where there were servants and music and bank accounts.

What is absent in all these writers, all of whom have published books in this decade, is participation—they aren't *within* the psyche of the Fifties. And that is in no sense at all meant as a criticism of their work. An artist, broadly speaking, is for or against civilization, but he does not have to be embroiled in it. The new set of writers who have got the Fifties named the angry decade *are* involved. Some are deliberately so, some hate it. But they are coloured by the period and they colour it, just as reciprocally as Bix Beiderbecke jazz and the Capone speakeasies of the Loop, or Scott Fitzgerald and his time of collegiate golden girls and hipflask parties, or Lorca and chromium glare of the sun beating upon the last bullfight before the insurgent guns began bellowing, or that determined self-willed legend Richard Hillary and the lovely summer days of 1940 when to die in a Spitfire had the allure of sainthood. Those were their inextricable moments. ("At certain moments," Fitzgerald wrote in notes for *The Last Tycoon,* "one man appropriates to himself the total significance of a time and place.")

So it might be advisable to take a step back for perspective and size up this decade that is now in its last quarter, this loud and dislocated jumble of years which has produced the new dissentients and which they have helped to produce.

The Fifties might be said to be summed up in the close juxtaposition of Marilyn Monroe and Arthur Miller. A great many cultural frontier fences have been ripped up and class attitudes and tastes have mingled and cross-bred in a way that would have been impossible only ten years before. Yet some of the resulting paradoxes are stranger by far than the marriage of an eminent American body to an eminent American egg-head, an event which in itself reflected the period by producing little sense of incongruity. The major underlying paradox is the re-forming of the old class system under new management.

One of the major causes for the preliminary artistic desegregation is, of course, the influx of the new intelligentsia, the strongest force of fund-educated ever to perform an Arnhem operation upon the entrenched traditionalists. This happened in the late Forties and early Fifties because it was then that the bottled-up rush happened. They were at last settled down in jobs, marriage, flats and self-confidence after hectic mobility from school into temporary jobs, a year or two in Germany as Occupation troops, probably away again on a grant-supported sweat at a university, then the zig-zagging approach to a career. Finally they found that they had been provided not only with scholarships and travel, but with voices. A new class was articulate. The old gang had entered a state of intellectual menopause. What were the new dissentients waiting for? The typewriters began to shudder. What were they banging out? Strangely little in celebration of their own emancipation, or about the more distant horizons.

This, I think, is the first difference that strikes you when you take a panoramic view of the creative work being done in the Fifties. It is intensely introspective. It is almost indifferent both to the furniture and fittings, and the unhappiness and doubts, of present-day life except in the sense of their immediate use or their relation to the writer. I remark upon this with comparisons in mind.

Past authors who were partly emanations of and partly the shapers of their particular periods seemed to draw conscious stimulation from them, never to lose the sharp sense of being surrounded by those especial years.

Looking back on his first decade in New York, Fitzgerald wrote in *The Crack-Up:* "It had all the iridescence of the beginning of the world". It is precisely that quality of childlike wonder which pulses and shimmers through even the most facile, banal writing of this provincial whose first novel, *This Side of Paradise,* was taken by the youth of the Twenties as their manifesto, who became a folk hero at twenty-four and was forgotten at forty. How many of the new writers of Britain will look back with similar sentiments about their first professional decade? Most, I suspect, are not sufficiently conscious of it in an objective sense.

It does seem that before the war the artist was attentive to the wide realities around him. . . . Henry Miller in *Tropic of Cancer:* "The river is still swollen, muddy, streaked with lights. I don't know what it is rushes up in me at the sight of this dark, swift-moving current, but a great exultation lifts me up, affirms the deep wish that is in me never to leave Paris. New York is cold, glittering, malign. . . . When I think of this city where I was born and raised, this Manhattan that Whitman sang of, a blind, white rage licks my guts. A whole city erected over a hollow pit of nothingness." D. H. Lawrence, revisiting the North of England in 1925: "The utter negation of the gladness of life . . . the stacks of soap in the grocers' shops, the rhubarb and lemons in the greengrocers! all went by, ugly, ugly, ugly . . . the great lorries full of steel-workers from Sheffield. Ah, what has man done to men? . . . They have reduced them to less than humanness; and now there can be no fellowship any more! It is just a nightmare."

The Berlin of the Thirties fertilized Isherwood's imagination. Addressing a financier, W. H. Auden wrote in *Consider This and In Our Time:*

> The game is up for you and for the others
> Who, thinking, pace in slippers on the lawns
> Of College Quad or Cathedral Close . . .
> It is later than you think . . .

Auden was wrong as a prophet, but he was subjectively right about his time. Look at books by, say, Rex Warner, or Orwell, or the poems of C. Day Lewis or Louis MacNeice, with their imagery of commercial travellers, arterial roads, slump and slum, saxophones, their *feeling* of Hitler and Mussolini in the headlines, and you see that these, like those books of Lawrence and Miller and Mansfield, and Michael Arlen even, could not possibly have been written if the authors had not been accessible to, and receptive to, their periods. Think back to the sort of material you read in *Penguin Parade* and *New Writing,* and *Lilliput, Bugle Blast* and *Modern Reading,* the pieces such as Fred Urquhart and J. Maclaren Ross, Rayner Heppenstall, Laurie Lee, Henry Reed and G. W. Stonier, and of course Orwell, were writing during the war, which had a siren running all through them and the staccato look of being written in exercise books in NAAFIs and ARP centres, which were utterly of the Forties.

I do emphasise here that I am speaking of the *spirit* of these writings—not the lobbed-in symbol and metaphor of the deliberate up-to-dateness which particularly characterized a lot of the poetry of the Thirties, the sort cited by Wain in his essay on William Empson, where, quoting lines from Auden, he points out: "the bit about the instruments is just there to look chic and contemporary".

But I can't, drawing back to see the current writing against that background, detect the same sort of sensibility towards the age, and that is not a hinted reproof against the lack of social reporting, which is not what I mean at all. The Fifties appears to me to be the most profuse and *excited*—in a neurotic and superficial sense—I have lived through. So many oddly arraigned forces are at work. There is, first, that enormous umbrella fact at which hardly anyone does more than sneak an occasional glance, and which it seems almost brash to mention, the H-bomb, a solitary enormity which, like Sir Winston Churchill's "giant outlines and harsh structure of the twentieth century", is emotionally too big to see.

Leaving that out of it (and somehow we all seem to do exactly that) the central spectacle of our broken-winded economy is the extraordinary stubborn effort that has been made in the Fifties to revive the meaningful panoply of the pre-war Establishment. We are, let it not be forgotten—and there seem to be few reasons to remember it—the New Elizabethans. These words were projected at the time of Her Majesty the Queen's coronation as an incantation, and it looked as if some hard-faced romantics expected instant results—say, a spontaneous dismantling of the Trades Union Congress, and much whistling and hoeing all the daylight hours on the nation's land, and perhaps privateer jet airliners.

The ceremonial came back, the careful rapture, and all the commercial machinery of favours, circulation stunts, ritual, the Season and the marriage-market clicked smoothly into motion again, as if it had been kept ready oiled and polished. As it probably had been. The rich, who had taken to the hills while Attlee's hunting party amateurishly stumbled about, came out of hiding, nervously sniffed the air, then scampered back to the old water-holes, where the society-columnists were waiting to welcome them.

Kaleidoscope is the word that will probably be used in bumper "scrapbook" programmes of the future to describe this period, but it is not that at all, for beneath the skitter and thresh of surface movement, like the flash of dragonflies and water-boatmen upon a summer pond, there is fearful stagnation.

I have just been jotting down, in a sort of factory psychology test way, the immediate word-associations set off in my mind by the phrase "The Fifties". I do not put this forward as a typical sensory-pattern for anyone in Britain, but merely that of someone who spends most of the week in London and who by nature of his job is close to the manufactured ferment of a degenerate entertainment industry and the money-making drives of a metropolitan day. The Fifties—these are the flashbacks as they come to me. . . .

Television and the TV 'celebrity', espresso bars, skiffle, the boom of the pop-singer, indoor plants, Samuel Beckett, *The Threepenny Opera*, Louis Armstrong's visit and jazz becoming 'smart' as well as widespread, capital punishment, Actor's Studio, James Dean, Marlon Brando, jeans, full employment, *The Boy Friend* and *Cranks*, jukeboxes, new playwrights, the Sack, Bloody Marys, return of, and then the surprising extinction of, the deb, brighter shops and more consumer goods, cult of the bust, Monroe, Mansfield and Dors, Audrey Hepburn and the gamin vogue, New Towns, the Festival of Britain, Margaret and Townsend, Elvis Presley, Tommy Steele and the build-up boys, rock 'n' roll, Billy Graham, the Cold War and the detergent war, TV commercial jingles, Gilbert Harding, closing down of cinemas and newspapers, the Stately Home conducted tours, Suez and Hungary and Cyprus, the flight from Communism, Burgess and Maclean, the 'provincial' novel, the Goons, *The Catcher In The Rye*, nylon shirts, McCarthyism, strikes, Trades Unionism's rise to full power, West Indians, Brixton and the new Harlems, rising prices, inflation, the lung cancer panic, the Dockers and the gold Daimler, panel-games, hi-fi, the Comet, Mike Todd, wide-screen cinema, the four-minute mile, the pools, the death of Orwell, Shaw and Dylan Thomas, the teen-age industry, horror comics, *My Fair Lady*, expense account high-living, the sputnik just slightly ahead of Foster Dulles in his encirclements of the globe. . . .

If you run your eye across that list quickly, as you ruffle through one of those little coloured books that produce the illusion of cinematographic movement, what a sombre picture it gives of a sick and meretricious society, with instability endemic and the values of a corrupt bobbysoxer. The most frightful thing predominant there is the desperate avoidance of thought, with the intellectual and cultural influences sandwiched thinly between the rubbish. It looks, mostly, like an inventory of the contents of a dope-addict's cupboard. It dismays me to see so starkly before me the physical characteristics of the society *I* live in. But then, perhaps, I live on the lunatic margin of reality, in the arena where the manipulators and the hucksters work. That is so. It is additionally so that among that welter of cross-purposes and confused attitudes there is a greater fluidity of ideas than has been known in previous decades. But one shouldn't be too blithe about that. *Waiting For Godot* may have caused palpitations of conjecture in the Kings Road, but the argument did not penetrate much farther north than Hampstead Garden Suburb. It is the vista of Hoggart's "shiny barbarism" that stares at you, the forces of modern mass entertainment that do not so much debase taste as "over-excite it, eventually dull it, and finally kill it . . . they 'enervate' rather than 'corrupt' in de Tocqueville's phrase. They kill it at the nerve."

When I first read Hoggart's book, I felt that important though it was as original and authoritative research into the changing character of working-class life, he was unduly melodramatic about

41

the conditions now forming—"the monstrous regiment of the flat-faced", the new workers gliding through their leisure in a television twilight and in the jukebox arcades, "a sort of spiritual dry-rot amid the odour of boiled milk".

Yet now, looking at the aesthetic breakdown reflected in that word-association picture, I think Hoggart may not have been very much overdoing it. A few years ago *Time*, the American news magazine, reported a diagnosis undertaken by Dr. Robert Lindner, a state prison consulting psychologist. Lindner took the overall but not highly novel view that in the twentieth century world mass man is in a mess. His more detailed analysis, however, was interesting. I am now quoting *Time* of December 6, 1954:

"Dr. Lindner has reached the startling conclusion that the youth of today is suffering from a severe, collective mental illness. 'Until quite recently,' Lindner told a Los Angeles audience, 'the rebellion of youth could be viewed with the detachment usually accorded anything so common and natural. The brute fact of today is that our youth is in a condition of downright active and hostile mutiny.

"Both the basic tendencies of modern youth—to 'act out' and to drift into herds—are symptoms of a psychiatric condition worldwide in scope, related directly to the social and political temper of our times. There is only one mental aberration in which these two symptoms coexist: in the psychopathic personality, essentially anti-social, conscienceless, inclined to violence in behaviour, and liable to loss of identity. The psychopath is a rebel without a cause—hence, in a chronic state of mutiny. He strives solely for the satisfaction of his moment-to-moment desires. Raw need is all that drives him. . . .

"The youth of the world today is touched with madness, literally sick with an aberrant condition of the mind formerly confined to a few distressed souls but now epidemic over the earth.'

"One of the major factors producing psychopathy is damage to the ego. *He sees a loss of individuality and consequent damage to the ego in the 20th century's mass political movements, social and industrial giants, wars and economic upheavals.*" (My italics.)

I don't know if all that is true, and I don't see that there is any accurate way of proving it to be true, and my immediate reaction is to reach for *Miss Lonelyhearts* and quote Nathanael West's hero: "As soon as anyone acts viciously you say he's sick. . . .

No morality, only medicine." Nonetheless, most of us have an uneasy feeling that it probably is true, and when we focus down to Britain in the Fifties and extract some of the violence that always seems overheated in the United States, the terrifying contention seems supported. The younger population are largely non-political, and this is a new alliance that runs right through Western Europe—the party of the non-partisans, the a-political who are almost enthusiastic in their refusal to respond to stimuli. They have seen the bloody-nose results of political zest, and they have with a natural pendular movement swung away from both political activity and political faith. Today in Britain the general current of feeling is that politics is a racket, a stylised shifting around of different interest blocs like a crap game with two blank loaded dice, and that, as Kingsley Amis concluded in his Fabian pamphlet *Socialism and the Intellectuals* "the best and most trustworthy political motive is self-interest". I would say that the sentiment of most intelligent non-party people in Britain today is the cynical and sophisticated one that they are being taken for a ride, but so far the ride has been fairly comfortable considering the abyss of economic disaster beside which we are steering.

Despite this mistrust and disillusionment, the leaning is towards the Right, with all that means in attitudes of caution, blandness, conformity, and the strengthening of the administrator's hand. In the universities the mocking, snook-cocking irreverence towards the Labour Party's endeavours that was prominent in the late Forties seems to have intensified—perhaps ossified would be the better expression—into a refusal to take politics seriously. The line is that politicians are self-seeking, vain and fundamentally dishonest and that, anyway, Britain's only conflict is the make-believe in the House of Commons between two sides both equally ineffectual and irrelevant in a world context, while the real economic situation is expressed in a cartoon sketch of labour and capital obstinately locked in a death grip, like two muscle-bound Cumberland wrestlers, not really moving much or hurting each other much, but with their faces hidden in each other's flesh and their bottoms stuck up in the air. There does seem to be the beginnings of a new leftism (see Lindsay Anderson and Tynan in *Declaration*) but it is doubtful if it can have much practical application. It is essentially naïve. It shies away from the tough, tangled problems, both ethical and tactical, that democratic socialism must solve, and gets its kicks from emotional utopian generalities, a return to a Fabian fairyland. As yet, it has not touched the overall political condition of the nation.

So, in this society of sluggish public emotions, with an endemic cageyness about falling for political trickery, reconciliation and passive hedonism blow like a humid wind. A Beaverbrookian get-fairly-rich-quick philosophy is about the only easy excitement, like piracy on Lake Windermere. What do you do? You become a good organization man, a Man In a Sports Club Blazer. You integrate. While perhaps scoffing at the Old School Tory, impatient of his snobbery and his quaintness, with no sympathy for his part in the class struggle (which he had in a very positive form), you become a New Conservative. I would just mention here — because I shall go into this in more detail later — that it has a fascination for me to see how, despite the simplified, arty new leftism of political thrill-kids, the only positive action to take over comes from the extreme Right, the Wilson will-power movement, who have appropriated the Brechtian view:

Truly I live in a dark period.
To speak calmly is stupid. A smooth forehead
Is a sign of insensitivity. The man who laughs
Has merely not yet been told
The terrible news . . .

This cannot truly be said of such excellent comic radical novelists as Amis and Gwyn Thomas, for they know the bad news all right, but, especially in the case of Amis, they hang on to a studied neutral flippancy. Leftism in its emotive, protoplasmic state, a quivering transparent blob of indignation, is seen most dramatically in Osborne. It is not the despair itself that is necessarily unjustified in the British pessimists, it is their misreading of its nature and the personalising of its effects, deliberately reducing the larger issues to a local symptom. If this needs emphasising I think we have only to make a few comparisons with Continental voyages into these dark seas of the human soul.

When Jimmy Porter arrived there was a fair amount of fast identifying, but the suddenness with which that dropped away shows that, despite his trenchant turn of phrase which enlivened the ear, there was nothing of any size or depth to identify with (you can't transplant Jimmy Porter out of that attic—it is impossible to think of him drinking with a group of men in a bar, or laughing at Chaplin in a cinema, or walking in the country). Despite the smallness of the audiences there was, I'm sure, much more lasting and influential identifying in that highbrow horror-comic *Waiting For Godot*.

The world of Samuel Beckett (incidentally an Irishman resident in Paris) is the precise upending of *Over The Rainbow*. This is the real Never-Never Land, a space journey to the other side of the moon—and all done within the universe of a man's skull. Against a shattered, leprous landscape Beckett strips his specimens—two tramps, a puffed-up tyrant and his servant—down to the bones of disgust and despair. Nothing happens: nothing can. Godot never comes: he never will. Yet this twilight of negation, where all hope, self-reliance and springs of joy and aspiration are forever extinguished in desolation and futility, is not without humour. There is a kind of tormented slapstick comedy to be discerned when the grey wind stops fluttering their rags and rattling through the nothingness of their words. I assume that Beckett is saying that it is pointless taking the death of man too seriously, because there will be no living thing to mourn him when he is gone from Earth.

This is despair extended into the dark recesses of a delink's thoughts. *Godot* is a hymn to extol the moment when the mind swings off its hinges.

The two things that have struck me about Beckett's work are first that he is in his technique an obsolete writer and second that his standpoint is a surprisingly orthodox one in the environment of the Fifties. Both these points are understandable when you remember that although his novels *Watt, Molloy, Malone Meurt, L'Innommable,* and *Murphy,* his two plays, *Godot* and *Fin de*

Partie, and the play he wrote for the Third Programme last year, *All That Fall,* have all burst on us in the past few years, Beckett is no tyro. He is fifty-one, he has been writing around in the little-magazine outback for years (he published his first poem *Whoroscope* in 1930) and although the bulk of his work did not reach publication here until the Fifties (*Murphy* went unnoticed when it appeared in England in 1938) much of it was written before and during the war. He is not, in France where he has lived and been known about for years, thought of as being a particularly 'daring' experimental writer. His harsh, desolate, denuded style is entirely and unmistakably his own, but his literary 'form', the stream-of-consciousness device which most young British writers wouldn't dream of using nowadays for fear of being thought quaint, derives from his years as secretary to James Joyce. That is only a partial explanation. He is in a monolithic way the last of the Left Bank Mohicans of the Twenties; the others of the *avant-garde* died or deserted or prospered, but Beckett was a loyal expatriate. He may now along the Boulevard Saint-Germain look a bit like a lace-fronted old lady who has stubbornly stayed on in her laurel-hedged house in Ladbroke Grove despite the way the district has gone down, but he is a traditionalist, whose thinking follows a clear artery of desperation through Kafka, the French nihilists like Jarry, Ionescu and Artaud, to such rogue-existentialists of the present as Jean Genet.

In *Molloy* the crippled, degraded tramp hero says: "I have no reason to be gladdened by the sun—and I take good care not to be," and elsewhere: "I have been a man long enough. I shall not put up with it any more, I shall not try any more." In *Malone Meurt* the hero, another cripple who is clubbed to death in an insane asylum, says dully: "I tried to live without knowing what I was trying. . . . Now, neither hot nor cold any more, I shall be tepid. I shall die tepid." In *All That Fall* a blind woman cries: "I was so plunged in sorrow I wouldn't have heard a steam roller go over me", and again: "Christ, what a planet!" In *Murphy* the name-part, who also is found seeking sanity among lunatics and who dies from burns after a gasfire blows up, says: "Any fool can turn the blind eye, but who knows what the ostrich sees in the

46

sand?" In *Fin de Partie,* the distorted ape-like Clov says: "Enough, it is time that it finishes—and in the meantime, I hesitate, I hesitate—to finish."

Is it surprising that *Godot,* the first taste most British people had of Beckett, came as a traumatic shock? Here, at least, was someone presenting himself for judgment on Connolly's terms of "the quality of despair". *Godot* produced some extreme reactions. It was denounced as a sly intellectual hoax—worse, a confidence trick. It was called boring. It was called "amusing". It was also, with great determination and at considerable length in writing and on the BBC, interpreted as being an affirmation of the Christian faith.

But of course most people knew it wasn't. Without performing an elaborate autopsy on it, they knew that this was the work of a mind at the end of its tether, in which all the aches of mankind had become an enormous numbness. *Godot* is a drama of the stasis. The world is a wasteland and man is dying in a void from which even pain has drained, for God is dead—if he ever existed.

Colin Wilson in *Religion and the Rebel* describes how when he was seventeen, making tea in his mother's kitchen, he had a blackout, and "had an insight of what lay on the other side of consciousness. It looked like an eternity of pain." Beckett the arch-defeatist has seen further. He has seen the closing down of the last dusk.

Beckett is unconcerned with writing requiems for humanity, for he sees life as polluted and pointless: he merely scrawls its obituary, without bitterness or compassion because he cannot really believe it is worth the words he is wasting. His characters are extreme schizophrenics, lost in their own dark aphasia within the larger cavity of a running-down world. I find it surprising by the way that Wilson has done no more than give Beckett a passing mention in either of his books, for the Beckett men are Outsiders of the most acute kind, who have made the last rebellion, not just against the ennui of existence, but against existence itself; suicidals who cannot even see the point of bringing the razor to the wrist.

Is it any wonder that despair on this scale was found hair-raising by London? Alongside that the grizzling of native pessimists looked like Rebecca of Sunnybrook Farm stamping her foot. The point I want to make here is that Beckett's attitude, although severe and uncompromisingly poetical, is not exceptional in the climate of thought he knows. Just as Orwell pointed out nearly twenty years ago, what people are up against—the crushing of individuality, by politics or tanks—is more *real* and probable and comprehensible across the Channel, thus Beckett is merely expressing a universal feeling, as he has experienced it, about the liberal *angst* that has been for a long time the prevailing frame of mind in Western Europe.

If we in Britain supposed that Beckett's was a solitary anomalous voice, we were quickly corrected. Within months, plays by Bertholt Brecht and Jean Genet had crashed into our awareness. Again, both of these men (Brecht died in June 1956 at the age of fifty-eight) were seasoned, mature craftsmen, whose work was charged with a depth and force of revolutionary feeling, a violence, a knowledge of evil, and moral strength.

The Threepenny Opera was the first to arrive—thirty years late, which seems to be the time it takes for Great Britain reluctantly to accept that a foreigner can be a genius—and for many, certainly for me, there was the electrifying, euphoric sense of being present at a significant occasion. Brilliantly staged, it was what Brecht and Kurt Weill had made out of John Gay's *The Beggar's Opera* by setting it in the early Nineteenth Century and turning it into a ferris-wheel of all the vice, stinks, gaudiness and brutality of a metropolitan asphalt jungle, with the accompaniment of Weill's raucous, corny, Tin Pan Alley ragtime music. Of course it is *Das Kapital* turned into a pop-song. It is Brecht the Communist growling through the mouth of Mac the Knife, his bedizened mobster: "What is a pick-lock compared to a debenture share? What is the burgling of a bank compared to the founding of a bank? What is the murder of a man compared to the employment of a man?" His characters, in their shoddy finery and scatological rags, swirl about like a colony of cannibal rats, their only ethic an undeviating amorality, *The Threepenny Opera* is bottled essence of the malaise of the big city, the slickness and the poisoned sick look that you can see all around you any late night between Shepherd's Market and Leicester Square.

48

How does Man live? By throttling, grinding, sweating
His fellows, and devouring all he can! . . .
No, gentlemen, this truth we cannot shirk:
Man lives exclusively by dirty work.

This is Brecht's basic tenet—but, although he has like Beckett
the measure of man's anguish and prescience of a coming holo-
caust, he reacts quite differently. Beckett shrugs: Brecht the
moralist and mentor utters his huge denunciation and then declares that human free will can deal with the situation, if human
beings rouse themselves to use it.

His power of pity and anger became even more vehemently
evident in two more plays, *Mother Courage* and *The Caucasian
Chalk Circle*, and then one began to get full sight of Brecht's
genius. The sometimes oversmart revival of the expressionist,
picaresque theatrical style was forgotten. He indicts, in language
that can hurl right down the register from pathos to supreme
tragedy, the mixed cynicism and sentimentality, the ruthlessness
and the muddle, the hypocrisy and yearnings, of a rotting society.
"Scepticism moves mountains," he insists, but you see developing
out of his social protest and venomous irony a Shakespearean
rejoicing that man inhabits the earth, and might even inherit it
if the anti-lifes are evicted.

And then in came Jean Genet, the conscientious Wild Man
from Borneo of French drama, who in *The Balcony*, which had its
world premiere at the Arts Theatre in May 1957, presents *his*
parable of living in the present. He takes as his microcosm a
fetishist brothel. The machine guns are stuttering in the streets,
for outside a rebel force is cutting the old guard to confetti. In
this peripheral fantasy, criminals and perverts, in their fetishist
guise of queen, bishop, judge and general, appear on the brothel
balcony as the new regime and give the mob the ceremonial that
will please and stabilise them. Around that small kernel of plot
are wrapped successive layers of symbol and metaphor, and an
undercurrent of demonic horror is never absent. By normal
theatre standards *The Balcony* is a heaped sundae of ritual,
whipped-cream rhetoric and crystallised emblems representing
abstractions such as Authority, Power, Sex, Religion and so on.

49

Nevertheless, you realise that here is an artist looking with a single eye at a world whose only brief respite from the deadly boring ritual of everyday life is to plunge into deeper illusion.

Camus, Brecht, Beckett, Genet, and, of course, Arthur Miller — and Sartre, now writing his autobiography which may be helping him to resolve his own deep dilemma of his committal to Communism: what all these writers have — and what is such a rare power among our own writers — is a sense of that epidemic "damage to the ego" that Lindner diagnosed. I have not out of malice recalled the advent of all these great writers to try to cut our younger creative artists down to size, but if any value is going to be derived from this survey, the proportions must be right.

Now let us consider particular cases and see what our native cultural revolt of the Fifties amounts to, what the individual dissentients are saying: for that, and not by repeating the manifesto of a Movement as a slogan, is the only way in which we can judge the "quality of their despair" — or the hope that their anger may contain.

Of all the dissentients the one who has most cause to complain of misrepresentation, but who, unlike several of his more voluble and less violated contemporaries, rarely troubles to, is Kingsley Amis.

Amis published *Lucky Jim* on January 25, 1954, and it has since gone into twenty impressions and has been translated into nine languages. It must be one of the most hugely successful first novels in the English language. It has been 'turned into' a film, which was mostly a skimming of the slapstick, with the book's mild acidity drained off or watered down. When the picture came out the London *Evening Standard* also further disseminated the adventures of Jim Dixon by serialising 'the story of the film'.

In view of its wide circulation in these various forms it would seem logical that a large number of people, including critics, have become acquainted with the character of Jim Dixon—which makes it all the more peculiar that he has become the symbol for almost precisely the opposite kind of person.

For the first eighteen months or so of the book's life the appellation Lucky Jim came into gradually wider use to apply to a post-war genus of cocky university graduate who had scholarshipped his way out of the working class but was still rather truculently with them in spirit. It was after Osborne's play dramatised the snarling Jimmy Porter that the two Jameses began to be confused

51

in a most complicated way. It was Lucky Jim who suffered, who began to be coloured by the slightly sinister reputation of his artistic relative, and the earlier alleged devil-may-care sunniness of his personality was overshadowed and then forgotten. It became a routine piece of slander upon luckless Jim to be described in literary reviews, articles about Angry Young Men, letters to editors, Rotary luncheon speeches and television argybargy programmes as an emblem figure of all that is discerned by older observers as malevolent, sombre and menacing in Young England.

Amis's second novel, *That Uncertain Feeling,* which came out in August 1955 was rarely taken into account in these gaily portmanteau definitions, despite the fact that it had been received with stentorian approval for being "brilliantly funny", "lewd and rollicking", and "broadly farcical and Rabelaisian". By the following year Amis himself had merged personalities with the character he had created and Lucky Amis had been firmly fixed in current mythology as one of the provincial hyena pack who had suddenly been identified as prowling around the cankered body of the upper class, a rancorous 'kitchen sink' novelist, hunch-shouldered from the weight of his chips, endlessly beefing about his discontents and envies.

This Jekyll and Hyde alchemy has been commented upon here and there, Philip Toynbee on one occasion remarking that "the discrepancy" is yet another sign of "how little attention most people pay to what they read". He added, revealing a further level of confusion: "it is like Jim Dixon to claim that he is thoroughly satisfied with his lot". Amis himself in one of his rare utterances about his famous but misunderstood book brushed aside suggestions that it might have "sociological implications", stating flatly that the chief thing was that he had intended it to be a funny book. It has been elsewhere and often stated that Lucky Jim wants the privileges of the old ruling class without its responsibilities.

To decide exactly what Lucky Jim does think, feel and want, it might be illuminating to take the almost unprecedented step of referring to the book. This is what can be discovered about Jim Dixon from Amis's sparse and scattered detail of biography: he is in his early twenties, fair and round-faced and wears goggle-like spectacles that constantly mist over in emotional sweats. He is short and has an orang-utang breadth of shoulders. He attended a local grammar school, saw service in the RAF—as a corporal in Scotland—and speaks with a northern accent.

When the story opens he is nearing the end of his probationary year's engagement as a junior lecturer in medieval life and culture at a provincial university. Throughout the book Dixon is dominated by the fear of getting the sack from the job for which he feels only a bored loathing. His efforts "on behalf of his special subject, apart from thinking how much he hated it, has been confined to aiming to secure for it the three prettiest girls in the class". Asked by a friend what had led him "to take up this racket", he explains that the medieval papers were "a soft option in the Leicester course, so I specialised in them". He says: "Good God, you don't think I take that sort of stuff seriously, do you?"

Dixon is and always has been hard up. When he rips his trousers on a protruding spring in the Professor of History's car, he reflects bitterly that, apart from a pair belonging to a suit "much too dark for anything but interviews and funerals", his only other trousers are "so stained with food and beer that they would, if worn on the stage to indicate squalor and penury, be considered ridiculously overdone". He rations himself with cigarettes and reflects at one point that he has never all his life been able to smoke as much as he wants. When he decides to break it off with Margaret, the dirndl-skirted hysteric with whom he has been having a tense, unconsummated affair, the first words of abuse that leap into her mind are, naturally: ". . . a shabby little provincial bore like you."

The inference is that it is Dixon's background of shabby provincialism, the scrimping and saving that higher education means for working-class parents even with the bestowal of scholarships, that has created in him the living terror of poverty. We meet him at the beginning of the book possessed with the necessity of ingratiating himself with his professor, at least until his contract has been renewed—"until then he must try to make Welch like him"—despite the fact that he thinks Ned Welch is a pretentious, drooling fool.

To work this he runs library errands for him, writes a piece of gobbledygook entitled *The Economic Influence of the Developments in Shipbuilding Techniques, 1450 to 1485*, submits to arty weekends of part-songs and recorder music-making at his house, and agrees to deliver a lecture on 'Merrie England' during College Open Week.

This sounds to be an extreme state of abject degradation, and so it would be if Dixon was a sold-out time-serving hypocrite, prepared to lick any boots for material gain. In fact he isn't. His acquiescence is badly done. His sucking-up to Welch and his other superiors tends to break down the moment it is put under strain. Dixon reacts to fakery and humbug with the infallibility of a traffic light turning red at pressure on the cross-road contact pad. His false humbleness is hurled aside by the gale of irresistible derision.

Dixon has such a sensitive nostril for the phoney that, out of sight of authority, a bumptious irreverence bursts forth towards practically anything, genuine or false, that is labelled culture.

His policy is "to read as little as possible of any given book". Guzzling his customary pints of beer in a pub, and shovelling seven cocktail onions into his mouth at once, he says: "Look, Margaret, you know as well as I do that I can't sing, I can't act, I can hardly read and, thank God I can't read music." He "read, heard and even used the word scholasticism a dozen times a day" without knowing what it was. When he is considering having it out with Bertrand, the bogus artist son of Welch, he has no doubt that he can beat him, although Bertrand is taller and heavier, for "he was confident of winning any such encounter with an artist"— Dixon's instinctive assumption being that anyone who has anything to do with the arts must inevitably be effeminate, cowardly and fraudulent. He recognises a song as some "untiring facetiousness by filthy Mozart". Merely to stand in Welch's office, with its rows of superseded books and examination paper files and teaching timetables, induces in him "overmastering, orgiastic boredom and its companion, real hatred".

This aggressive barbarianism is part of a total condemnation of upper class attitudes. At the suggestion of anything tainted with

54

sensitivity or refinement Dixon's two fingers jab the air to the accompaniment of a raucous Bronx cheer. (There is a similarity here, incidentally, between the resentment Jim Dixon feels towards "his betters" and the salivating fury that that caste-word "mummy" arouses in Jimmy Porter in *Look Back in Anger*.) When Bertrand splutters that he's "a lousy little philistine", and a "nasty little jumped-up turd", it can be nothing but a tribute to his integrity.

In fact Dixon's integrity is of more concern to him than he is willing to admit. He makes up to himself for his outward sycophancy to boss-rule by a concealed guerrilla warfare. He has a battery of mocking funny faces—his Eskimo, crazy peasant, Evelyn Waugh, sex life in Ancient Rome, Edith Sitwell, lemon-sucking and ape faces—with which he expresses his true feelings about situations in which he has to pretend interest or agreement, and behind his back his hands twist into obscene gestures while he talks to the people upon whose favours he depends for a living.

He goes much further. His concealed contempt for the privileged, despite his anxiety to "keep in", bursts out in nervous, impulsive bouts of aggression. While a guest in Welch's house, he writes on the steamy mirror in the bathroom "Ned Welch is a ℨoppy Fool with a Fase like a Pigs ℨum". He absconds from the musical fest to sink bitter in the local, creeps back into the house and swigs half a bottle of port, and burns his bedclothes with a cigarette. His surreptitious blows for the underdog take the form of a sort of social hit-and-run buccaneering, drawing moustaches on the cover girls on the enemy's magazines, writing them frightening letters, burning their insurance policies, making hoax telephone calls and hijacking their taxis—behaviour which is, of course, loutish, but which results more from ungovernable spasms of disgust and insane boredom than from premeditated spite.

His more extreme tendencies towards destruction are sublimated in violence-fantasies. When Margaret asks histrionically: "Do you hate me, James?" he is flooded with the desire "to rush at her and tip her backwards in the chair, to make a deafening rude noise in her face, to push a bead up her nose". When he is being driven by Welch, inextricably trapped within range of his waffling discourse, he has the sudden thought of picking up a spanner from the dashboard pocket and striking Welch in the back of the neck. "Scratch 'em," he whispers to the Welch's cat, Id, as he tickles it under the ear, "pee on the carpets."

Beneath this Keystone Cop class-warfare there is however a political conviction stronger than Amis either realises or admits when he says that he just wanted to write a funny book. Without ever making such a specific declaration, Jim Dixon is plainly Labour. There are occasional hints of idealistic reasons for this. Deep inside enemy territory, at the cultural bunfight at Welch's house, when Bertrand makes jibes about the "lads at Transport House" (this is during the Attlee Government) and their "soak the rich policy", Dixon for once doesn't bite his tongue. "Well, what's wrong with that, even if it is that and no more?" he demands. "If one man's got ten buns and another's got two, and a bun has got to be given up by one of them, then surely you take it from the man with ten buns."

The clearest statement of the Dixon-Amis political outlook comes near the end of the book when Bertrand, who is abruptly adapted from a footling snob into a jackbooted power-boy, invades his digs to warn him off Christine, the girl both want.

"Just get this straight in your so-called mind," Bertrand grates. "When I see something I want, I go for it. I don't allow people of your sort to stand in my way . . . I'm having Christine because it's my right. Do you understand that? If I'm after something, I don't care what I do to make sure that I get it. That's the only law I abide by; it's the only way to get things in this world. The trouble with you, Dixon, is that you're simply not up to my weight."

And Dixon, suddenly clad in the radiant white habit of a democratic St. George, makes in reply his longest speech in the book which reveals hitherto unsuspected depths of feeling about the individual's rights and egalitarianism. "You're getting a bit too old for that to work any more, Welch," he says. "People aren't going to skip out of your path indefinitely . . . You're a twister and a snob and a bully and a fool."

Yet most of the time throughout *Lucky Jim,* Dixon's social sentiments seem much earthier and less worthy. He has a peregrine's keenness of eye for uppishness. The fact that the Welches' breakfast is served from hotplates on the sideboard seems curiously offensive to him. He reflects that he finds repugnant "any notion of anyone having any special needs for anything at any time, except for such needs as could be readily gratified with a tattoo of kicks on the bottom".

Fundamentally his outlook seems to be even more subjective, often nakedly a matter of personal envy and spleen. Even the girls he gets seem to him to be second best, as when he first sets eyes on the luscious Christine, who has been brought down to the Welches by Bertrand: "The notion that women like this were never on view except as the property of men like Bertrand was so familiar to him that it had long since ceased to appear an injustice". Later, when he hears that the Welches' younger son Michael, a pseudo-writer, has his own flat in London, he experiences "a small rage at the thought of a little louse like that having a flat in London. Why hadn't he himself had parents whose money so far exceeded their sense as to instal their son in London? The very thought of it was a torment. If he'd had that chance, things would be very different for him now. For a moment he thought he couldn't think what things; then he found he could conceive the things exactly, and exactly how they'd differ from the things he'd got, too."

In those words there appear to be confirmed all the accusations that have been made against Lucky Jimism as being an ooze of self-pity and egotism. Although instantly attracted towards Christine, he hangs back from a feeling of inferiority. "She's a bit out of my class, don't you think?" he says gloomily to a friend. He thinks it should be possible for the right man to stop, or at least hinder, her from becoming a refined gracious-liver and arty-rubbish-talker. But he is quick to reprove her: "Don't you try to queen it over me", and there is a subtle but significant change in his attitude to her once he has detected in her voice "a faint Cockney intonation".

There are moments when he disentangles himself from his own

farcical class-conflicts and sees in himself a "stodgy, stingy caution. . . . you can't even call it looking after number one." When Bertrand shouts: "Everyone hates you, Dixon," Dixon obviously never doubts the veracity of it. It is axiomatic that when his world is divided into "the two great classes of mankind, people I like and people I don't", the Welches and their sort must be his enemy. Yet the bristling inadequacies and inferiorities which would have produced a steel-jawed Communist twenty years ago have now produced Jim Dixon, one whose only ferocity is that he won't hear a word against the Welfare State and whose ultimate philosophy is that "nice things are nicer than nasty ones".

Yet it appears to Dixon that despite the argument and fury over the Welfare State, it has turned out to be damned little different when all the gas has cleared away. Luck is still the most valuable thing to have—when it seems that he has lost Christine he reflects: "It was luck you needed all along; with just a little more luck he'd have been able to switch his life on to a momentarily adjoining track, a track destined to swing aside at once away from his own."

Of course he has the luck. When it seems that all is blackest, job lost, girl gone, character thoroughly assassinated, his sorbo texture works again: he bounces into the almost middle-class job he has always wanted and into the bed of the almost middle-class girl he has desired. His technique seems to be justified, for he has got the job by showing no deference—only the 'cheeky honesty' that after a few pints of bitter vanquishes his timidity— to the tough industrialist, and he has got the girl by talking in his broadest northern accent and shovelling fried egg and bacon into his mouth with his fingers—by 'being himself'.

I think that all the foregoing is a fair portrait of Lucky Jim Dixon—except that it only scrappily conveys what is most important in the book, its funniness. Although it is facetiously prolix in parts, it is a very funny book and some of the crises in which Dixon is submerged deserve to have a long life in comic literature. It is possible to select evidence to prove that Dixon is craven, dishonest, toadying, oafish, shifty, temporising, philistine, crude and juvenile—yet that is not the man who emerges from the pages of the book. Despite his flaws and his foolishness, Lucky Jim is likeable, good-hearted and sympathetic, and you know that he is essentially a decent chap.

It seems to me that Amis, whether or not he had that specific intention, accurately defined and explained many of the grudges of the post-war fund-aided, who believe that although they are being permitted to undergo an educational process hitherto much restricted, it is only on sufferance. It can be done, they point out, only by putting up with being hideously short of money for all the years of training and by respecting the ramparts that the rich and well-bred have constructed about themselves within the new social territory—a position similar to that of the Negro in the north of the United States, who can live a 'desegregated' life as long as he does not try to edge over too far into white areas.

This is not exactly drawn from personal experience. Kingsley Amis was born in 1922 in Clapham, London, of Baptist lower middle-class stock. Both his parents came from Denmark Hill, another inner London suburb, and he grew up in a third London suburb, Norbury. His father was an export department clerk in a big City office. He potted this period for me in this way: "Up-bringing similar to parents, minus the chapel-going: fortnight's annual holiday near Cromer—no car, but maidservant; father's friends virtually without exception other white-collar commuters; musical evenings; whist, becoming bridge by say 1939; tennis and cricket club; Conservative, Ratepayers' Association; neither parent any artistic interest—unless you count father's Gilbert and Sullivan—though not actively philistine."

He attended the City of London School from 1934 to 1941, was at St. John's, Oxford, between 1941 and 1942, and returned there in 1945 after military service, finally coming down in 1949. He went straight to University College of Swansea as a lecturer in English, where, despite toying with the idea of coming to London to take up full-time writing, he still remains. He lives with his wife and children in Swansea, in comfortable financial circumstances with his combined earnings as lecturer, author and free-lance journalist.

This appears to be a picture of a secure, rather shielded life for these times and reveals no obvious collisions of class and political passions. Was *Lucky Jim*, then, just a piece of comic invention into which has been read social significance which it does not possess, was its class-consciousness entirely the emanation of the character and not of the author? On the contrary, Amis's second novel, *That Uncertain Feeling*, published in August 1955 emphasised this condition of the Fifties even more heavily.

It is told in the first person by John Lewis who is an assistant librarian in a Welsh industrial town. (John Braine, incidentally, the author of *Room At The Top*, was himself a librarian in Yorkshire—immediately it is a recognisable environment.) Whereas Jim Dixon was short and round-faced, John Lewis is tall and round-faced, rubicund and cheerful also, which seems effectively to mask the mixture of cunning and laziness that is so often the make-up of the small-town small-time official.

This time Amis came out into the wide world. Lewis, at twenty-six, is married with a child. Their income is paltry. They live in a 'flat', that is in the upstairs rooms of a villa. This is home, where Lewis reads his *Astounding Science Fiction* magazines among the airing nappies and the rickety shelf with its few dog-eared Penguins: "I sat down in one of the ripped and peeling leather armchairs by the empty fireplace and looked round the room in search of something to engage my attention . . . the matchwood shrine painted black which discharged some of the less important functions of a sideboard with its tiny square shelves, tinier inch-deep drawers with what looked like old-fashioned pendant ear-rings attached in the middle, and mirror mounted on bamboo scaffoldings; the gate-leg table whose gate-leg, like any gate, was liable to swing to without warning; the unlicenced, crackle-ridden wireless, surmounted by a cereal-bowl full of nasturtiums stolen from the front garden; the tall box-like couch, said to turn into a bed when the proper forces were applied, and stained with the activities of children. These formed a job lot which was oddly unreal and unconvincing, like a murderer's sitting-room reproduced in the Chamber of Horrors."

His wife Jean is a sturdy, slangy girl, her attractiveness a bit stained by nappy-washing and shabby clothes, with a militantly 'ordinary folk' manner, who prickles at the least whiff of uppishness.

So does Lewis, come to that, but the dreariness of his routine life combined with the nubile attractiveness of a local bigwig's wife who smokes gold-tipped black cigarettes (a sure brand of sin, it seems) flatten the class barriers while his marriage goes reeling against the ropes. The story of *That Uncertain Feeling* is, in fact, that of the temporary sexy madness that can drive a man into situations which he knows can bring only disaster and ruin, but which he cannot resist. The moral outcome of the novel is that Lewis disciplines himself to abjure the allure of the local monied rackety life and also the promotion fixed for him by his mistress.

Although that is the ostensible plot, the deeper central issue of the book is again the class one. The first thing that strikes you is the curious misnomer that runs all through the book—the assumption by Lewis and his wife (and presumably by Amis) that this circle into which he is briefly sucked is upper class. It is actually the shoddy-smart roadhouse set of well-heeled vulgarians that can be found in the golf clubs and American bars of any town—the group who drive big Jaguars, have the latest LPs of New York musicals, and bet on the dogs, and which always includes a few car dealers, hard-eyed women in suits, and a rather dated type of twenty-nine-ish man with a bushy moustache, a blazer and an RAF tie. The second thing that strikes you if you read *Lucky Jim* is that, although this novel is just as funny in places, it generally has a rather drabber and deadlier atmosphere, and that now, with life under a Tory Government, the class-enemy outlook has lost Jim Dixon's zany irresponsibility and taken on a much more grey, grousing sound. Even so, there is never any doubt in your mind that this is the accurate sound of the setting.

At the very start, when Lewis is told that the lady who is being rude in the Reference Library is "well-dressed like. Plenty of money", he remarks grimly: "Yes, I know the kind of lady."

When he finds that she is Elizabeth Gruffydd-Williams, "one of the biggest Aberdarcy names", he remains deliberately unimpressed. He realises that the hostility he instantly feels arises from his "familiar embarrassed defensiveness at talking to a member

61

of the anglicised upper classes." When Elizabeth invites him and his wife to a cocktail party, Jean warns him to behave, because "I've seen you with these upper-class types. Showing off all the time, honest Joe making no bones about what he thinks of them, that's you. . . . All the bloody horse-riders and yachters and golfers and aeroplane-fliers and what-not. You know 'em all right. I can never think what to say to those types."

"Neither can I," replies Lewis. But it is not an intellectual hiatus he feels—just the same old class thing, that they are 'better' than he. He regards himself as "a sworn foe of the bourgeois, and especially the anglicised Aberdarcy bourgeoisie".

He goes to the party in the spirit of a Salvation Army man attending a black mass, and after a brush with a phoney Welsh bard considers making "a renewed effort to be marked down as 'impossible', bawl a defence of the Welfare State, start undressing myself or the dentist's mistress, give the dentist a lovely piggy-back round the room, call for a toast to the North Korean Foreign Minister or Comrade Malenkov."

Soon after he has slept with Elizabeth for the first time he is able to look round the saloon bar at the fish-shop proprietor or cinema manager ordering two double brandies and forty cigarettes and reflect that even if "those chaps represented the new privileged classes in 'our society', you could console yourself with the thought that there was a lot to be said for them compared with the old privileged classes. At least this crowd had enough bad taste to drink brandy before 'dinner'."

Finally after a rather grubby necking and boozing party on the beach, Elizabeth tells him that she has 'organised' the job he wants. "You can take it from me," she says, "that nobody ever gets any kind of job or position in this world completely on his merits. There's always something else that enters into it. It may be politics, it may be having the right kind of face or education or background or whatever you like to call it, it may be, well, doing someone a personal favour."

In reply Lewis says: "One of the things I feel rather strongly about is fiddles," and he proceeds to mend his morals and his marriage. The final chapter shows him happy again with his wife, with a clerical job in a colliery office, saved from the pollution of the quasi-English upper class and back safe among his own folk, the miners, in a mucky town.

When he remarks to his wife how glad he is they're back, she says: "Yes. Don't you feel you're running away, though?"

"Yes, I do, thank God," Lewis answers. "You want to forget about 'running away' being what people say about armies retreating and deserters and so on. This isn't like that. Our kind of running away was a stroke of bloody genius. It's always the best thing to do in that kind of situation."

Running away is precisely what Amis and his similarly-minded group of dissentients are often accused of doing. The question is, are they? Amis has told me that he was "a callow Marxist from 1940-42", served on a local anti-hanging committee and took part in demonstrations about the hanging bill and against the Government's Suez policy. But apart from those sporadic spasms of ardour he remains rather cynically mistrustful of political action or even political alliances, although his general viewpoint is evident from his novels.

It is again that symptom of the Fifties, the stubborn disenchantment and insistent lowbrowism, that runs through all Amis's work. Certainly one of the freshest and sharpest critical minds now writing, he can undermine his own authority with a silly piece of bravado such as his introduction to the page review in the *Spectator* of *The Outsider*. "Here they come," he wrote, "tramp, tramp, tramp—all those characters you thought were discredited, *or had never read, or (if you are like me) had never heard of:* Barbusse, Sartre, Camus, Kierkegaard, Nietzsche, Dostoievsky, George Fox, Blake, Sri Ramakrishna, George Gurdjieff, T. E. Hulme. . . .". My italics.

His jazz criticism in *The Observer* suffers from the same defect— the terror of being called a dirty egghead, so, in the same way that he had "never heard of" any of the above, it seems he has never heard of any jazz musician since the death of Fats Waller, and his musical writings are confined to the constricted, monotonous and 'unintellectual' field of New Orleans and Revivalist bands.

His third novel, *I Like It Here*, which came out in January of this year, lumbered along most of the way at this boggy level, with rare, brief flights into the old roaring comedy. This book was the outcome of a visit to Portugal on the prize money of a Somerset Maugham Travel Award, and it was at first written as a personal account of the trip and later transformed into 'fiction'.

After *Lucky Jim* and *That Uncertain Feeling* it is a sad slump. Throughout it seems to me to groan with desperation, as if Amis wishes he had never taken it on and is flogging himself forward, paragraph by gruelling paragraph, to the end of the dusty trail. It has the thin plot of the mission undertaken by a prosperous free-lance, Garnet Bowen, to Portugal to solve the mystery of the identity of an old-school novelist. Along with Bowen go wife and children. Bowen hates Abroad, because there you find foreigners, bull-fights, and "all those rotten old churches and museums and art galleries". The book proceeds at that level of slightly tipsy 'awfulness'—like a small boy determined to win a reputation for himself by shouting rude words at the half-shocked, half-delighted girls in the class. The philistinism is remorseless and grindingly boring on the do-away-with-architecture and fleas-and-smelly-lavatories line, with a regularly recurring mother-in-law joke and, when the fun seems to be flagging, the rapid interjection of the word bum.

Some of the writing is almost like Jerome K. Jerome in his 'lyrical' passages between the joke-parts in *Three Men In A Boat*—dictionary-pillaging padding, such as: "He had thought in the past that a binary system of laziness and conceit accounted fully for all the motions of his life, but of late its orbit had shown perturbations from a third component. This additional body seemed to be fear, and abroad, of course, was what took him to perihelion."

I Like It Here can most charitably be put aside as a slip of the pen, an interim mistake between Amis's good start and what should, from the sound of it, be an interesting continuation—a long novel about middle-class life in the Home Counties which he is now completing. *I Like It Here* caused general dismay among the critics: "A comic strip from *Blighty*", said Penelope Mortimer in the *Sunday Times*, and Toynbee in *The Observer*, remarking that "this writer's cloacal tendencies have here got quite out of control", thought that the reason for the novel's failure was that Amis, whom he presented as the successor to P. G. Wodehouse, "has not been aware of his true kinship and has mistaken the nature of his talents".

What is apparent in *I Like It Here*, badly sewn together though it is, is the far more direct and explicit political 'placing' than the previous two novels had, and Bowen (who is really stage three in the gradually ageing version of Dixon-Lewis) condenses his outlook into capsule form when he recalls his wife once accusing him of "pretending to like beer because he thought it was working-class, British, lower-middle-class, Welsh, anti-foreign, anti-upper-class, anti-London, anti-intellectual, British and proletarian".

But there is really no need to ferret about searching Amis's political views and motives when he has put them flatly down on paper. In January of last year he wrote a pamphlet for the Fabian Society entitled *Socialism and the Intellectuals*. Here he states with a frankness that he tends to shy away from elsewhere that "on the whole I may seem to have shown a certain amount of acrimony towards the intelligentsia which is rather unfair, because some of my best friends are intellectuals. Nor can I ever pretend that I am not one myself."

This was an altogether odd production, more commendable for the honesty of its puzzlement than for either deep political intuition or clarity of thought. He is quite frequently right, as when he remarks that during the masochistically happy reign of the left wing intelligentsia in the Thirties, it was the done thing anyway to be left. "A man who was not, and further was not active in the movement, was often regarded with much the same mixture of contempt and unbelief as nowadays, I am told, greets the Oxford undergraduate who wants to be in the swim but fails to go to church."

What does emerge with clarity is Amis's fastidiousness. For him a leper-bell clangs at the approach of anyone with a firm mouth and the obvious determination to perform good deeds. Do-gooders, people with a mission, and especially the power-driven upward-striving, the jacks in office and the authority-lovers, make his blood run chill. One gets the impression that, although he

C

feels he must officially regret the passing of the stirring causes of old, Spain, fascism, mass unemployment, he would not really wish to be faced with that sort of intellectual barnstorming. For two reasons. He sees dispassionately much that was sham and smart in the 'revolutionary' hot-gospelling of the Thirties. He quotes an Auden stanza (from *Spain 1937*):

Today the deliberate increase in the chances of death,
The conscious acceptance of guilt in the necessary murder;
Today the expending of powers
On the flat ephemeral pamphlet and the boring meeting.

About this attitude he says: ". . . we had Mr. W. H. Auden, the idol of the young, talking about the glories of working for the overthrow of capitalism by force. The great point is that it was not only politically desirable, it was also a form of spiritual salvation."

Arising out of that is the familiar fearing refusal to take the risk of being bamboozled. Amis states that he has always and presumably always will vote Labour, that he supports a social conscience, yet his conclusion is a defeatist one. At the end of these thirteen pages he owns up that he is a disgruntled romantic who has to take the only safe and available principle: that he has no political interests to defend and therefore the only repository for trust is self-interest.

That is a cheerless point at which to complete the circle of self-examination, and although it may be more stubborn to say this, I suspect that it may be John Lewis braggadocio, the defiant jutting underlip of the 'little monkey' who *won't* please his teacher by reciting the proper declension, although she knows jolly well that he knows it and he knows she knows. The point is, of course, that despite all the tough jocularity, the pasting for Orwell for so depressing the educated reformers, and the rather smart-aleck flippancies about the "irrational capacity to become inflamed by interests and causes that are not one's own", his loathing of snobbery and oppression, his warmth, his liking and respect for his fellows, combine to leave a deeper and more influential impression than the surface arguments.

This two-level impression also applies to John Wain but for

different reasons. Wain is three years younger than Amis, the son of a prosperous dentist in Stoke-on-Trent. He attended a local school and then went up to St. John's College, Oxford. From there he went to Reading University as lecturer in English Literature, from which he resigned in 1955 to write full-time. He published his first novel *Hurry On Down* in 1953, his second *Living In The Present* in 1955, and his most recent *The Contenders* this Spring. He has also published poetry and two volumes of criticism.

As a writer should, Wain takes himself seriously and was able to reply to my question about his upbringing: "Same social and educational background as Shakespeare", and to say that as far as problems of this age are concerned he is "as engaged as Chaucer, less than Aristophanes". In his essay entitled "Along The Tightrope" in *Declaration** he quotes Christopher Isherwood reflecting that he wants a place in society and that until then "my writing will never be any good; no amount of talent or technique will redeem it; it will remain a greenhouse product; something, at best, for the connoisseur and the clique." With no evident hesitation, Wain sees himself included in this situation of wry exclusiveness, a sort of cerebral golden eagle, rare and shot at. He comments that he finds Isherwood's reflection "immensely sympathetic. Especially that bit about not wanting to be a greenhouse writer, admired by 'the connoisseur and the clique'. How one agrees! Better no reputation than the kind of reputation that accretes and clings to a Corvo, a Firbank, a Lautreamont even!"

The contributors to *Declaration* were invited to express their view on the state of our civilisation and "their role in society". It is, I suppose, logical in light of his above remarks that Wain should spend a good deal of his space discussing and explaining his novels and cantankerously reproving critics who do not appreciate what he is doing.

"All artists who do not see themselves as mere entertainers are

---

*It is of interest here to remember that Amis refused to contribute to *Declaration*. "I hate all this pharisaical twittering about the state of our civilization," he was quoted in the Introduction as writing to the Editor. "This book is likely to prove a valuable addition to the cult of the Solemn Young Man." Amis told me later that he also said it was a piece of "dismal self-advertising" but the Editor omitted that.

engaged in grappling with the problems that face the society they live in," he writes. ". . . Thus, when I wrote *Hurry On Down* the main problem which had presented itself in my own existence was the young man's problem of how to adapt himself to 'life'. . . . So naturally I wrote a novel about a man who had been given the educational treatment and then pitchforked out into the world. . . . When the mixture was stirred up and cooked, the central thing that emerged was a moral point—something to do with the nature of goodness—but nobody, except myself, saw this, so there is no point in bringing it up now."

He then turns to *Living In The Present*, "a novel that was meant to be constructive, and to attack fashionable despair and nihilism; the man decides to commit suicide on the first page, and on the last he looks back and wonders how he could have been so misguided; life intervenes and teaches him the necessary lessons. The failure of this book was so spectacular that I can only assume that everyone found it literally unreadable; certainly very few of the comments it received were any use to me, because they all seemed to be by people who had not read further than the first ten pages: e.g. one journalist quite recently attacked the book as 'hysterical', because it gave a picture of contemporary young manhood as seedy, despairing, self-lacerating, etc.: he should have made it clear that he was taking the first chapter and letting it stand for the whole, a procedure which, if generally adopted, would revolutionise criticism. There is nothing one can do about this, except admit that the book failed to reach an audience, and write it off."

There is so much arising from all the foregoing that it is difficult to know which flower of self-esteem to pluck first. I have no recollection of the particular attack upon *Living In The Present* Wain refers to, so perhaps he is justified in accusing the unnamed journalist of basing his criticism on the first chapter. On the other hand it seems not to have occurred to Wain that the journalist was applying the description 'hysterical' to the book as a whole.

Later in the essay he speaks, certainly not without reason, of the danger "when *every* book is reviewed by some charlatan whose only concern is to leave the reader with an impression of *his* cleverness, his personality, his graceful style."

Hurry On Down appeared a few months before *Lucky Jim* and at that very juncture which I talked about earlier, when the first urgent ripples of anxiety were running through the welcoming committee because no young contestants seemed to be hoving into view. *Hurry On Down* was delightedly received, by charlatans and all. It was praised in the *Spectator* for being "inventive, impulsive, cogitative and often very funny". J. B. Priestley in the *Sunday Times* did not begrudge saying that he liked it "for its brave attempt at the picaresque". The *Manchester Guardian* applauded "a sharp eye, an economical pen". There was a general glow of goodwill and encouragement.

Far more, I fear, than the book deserved. It is an almost fascinatingly bad novel. In his retrospective survey in *Declaration* Wain adds: "In my first two novels I made a fairly rough-and-ready attempt at the presentation of serious issues through the medium of very broad comedy, not to say outright farce." I don't think Wain knows what either comedy or farce is, which may explain his bewilderment at the failure of these novels to strike the public response he expected. His idea of comedy is a crude, gross and (to borrow a word from the unidentified journalist) hysterical exaggeration. For example early in *Hurry On Down* Charles Lumley, the nomadic *déclassé* hero, has met an old university acquaintance and they go into a pub for a drink. While they are talking a labourer sitting on the bench beside them lights "a clay pipe". The following scene ensues:

"Dense blue smoke gathered around Froulish and forced its way into his eyes, nose, throat, and lungs. Charles started back before he too should be overwhelmed. Getting up, he took his drink and stood about six feet away from the evil-smelling volcano.

"You say to yourself," came Froulish's voice in a strangled shout, " 'What a spineless swine he must be to let a woman keep him.' . . She really cares, I'm going to faint any minute, whether the Novel—whether Literature lives or not! Damn this filthy smoke! Lumley! Where are you? I can't see anything!"

"Froulish dragged himself to his feet; his figure could be dimly made out through the fog. 'This way!' shouted Charles. . . . Clawing the air in front of him, his face green and soaked in perspiration, Froulish emerged; and Charles, swiftly catching his swaying figure, seized him by the arm and dragged him out into the clear air."

All that arose out of someone lighting a pipe. Humour depends for its existence on having its roots in reality, and this sort of grotesque extravagance, improbability piled upon absurdity, is done with boring frenzy around all the caricatures which people the book. *Living In The Present* is not as bad, but it is not good. The central hypothesis—that Edgar Banks intends to kill himself—is quite unacceptable. Because Wain has made no attempt either to understand or describe the personality of a potential suicide, the whole structure of the book collapses. Everything in the novel, the 'tension', the actions of the characters, particularly the 'obsession' of Banks, rely upon the credibility of this central situation. As from the outset it is impossible to feel that Banks, this dull creature with no sense of desperation, will kill himself, Wain is from then on trying to peg washing on a broken line. Even if that could be accepted, the story has a remarkably unpleasant cast of characters, and I do not mean by that that some are not 'nice' people. On the contrary, several, such as Tom Straw, the amiable, stolid art-historian, who appears to stand for responsible, quiet authority, and Catherine, the reason Banks abandons his suicide-plan, for "sanity could be mirrored in her grey eyes and nowhere else", are no doubt meant to be normal, balanced, decent human beings, yet most are poisoned by malice. Despite the fatuously all-black Mosleyites, whose facial expressions are described in Tod Slaughter terms, there are more believable people in *Living In The Present* than in *Hurry On Down*, which is a fresco of gargoyles. Yet both books have a repellently cold and scaly feel about them.

The first few pages of Wain's third novel, *The Contenders*, published in March of this year, seem to promise a big improvement in characterisation, and there is a *closeness* to human beings that is missing entirely from the previous books. The starting point has impact and importance in this time of grammar school sweat-shops and the intensely competitive structure of State education. We meet the three main characters, Joe Shaw (the narrator), Robert Lamb and Ned Roper as sixth formers, and the grim rivalry between Lamb and Roper has already eaten deep into their relationship which has the superficial guise of friendship. Unfortunately the early relevance, the *rapport* between reader and the scene and events which Wain unfolds, soon disappears. The blight takes hold again. The reader is wrenched into the peculiar bilious Wain world.

The odd thing is that he does not examine violent situations—these are 'normal' relationships between people within the framework of 'normal' society. Lamb and Roper are not 'ordinary'—one is supposed to be a brilliant artist, the other a brilliant businessman—but at least they are not presented as the psychopaths that their brutal dehumanised conduct would suggest they are. Again, in *The Contenders* I was struck, almost fascinated, by the unvarying hostility with which everyone behaves. No one in Wain's world ever *says* anything to anyone else: they shout or jeer. I again found myself depressed by the battering of ill-feeling. His favourite words are sneer, bitter, murderous, splenetic, snarl, nastily, bullying and peevish. The human emotions he writes about are charged with violence and loathing; people snap and yell at each other; they are constantly feeling 'savage contempt' or 'cold ill-nature' towards each other.

Indeed it is difficult to see why Wain of all people should object to being called an Angry Young Man when he and his books are gripped by a permanent bad temper, and although he is clearly concerned with modern problems, the result is opaque and blurred, as if he has steamed up the glass by panting too near to it.

Why then is Wain worth considering seriously in the context of the new writers? Because, in a way, he is more interesting than Amis as an example of someone who has been produced by the curious conditions of the Fifties, because despite immature overwriting and freakish unreality of characterisation Wain genuinely cares about and genuinely wishes to work out his relationship with the society he lives in, and finally, because his voice, arrogant and peevish much of the time, is being raised on behalf of the verities that are on the defensive, and at the sight of which Amis and many others seem to think that running away is "a stroke of bloody genius".

First of all Wain as a writer has probably suffered from being too promiscuously used as a symbol. Since it appeared, *Hurry On Down* has always been placed in the list by trend-charters as a significant and major work. In his "Along The Tightrope" essay, Wain says this very thing: "The minute any kind of artist attracts attention he is treated as a spokesman for his generation, his nation, his class, and what not. We have all seen, and deplored, the absurd results of the widespread journalistic habit of making *Lucky Jim* a symbol for anything that happened to be going about in search of a symbol."

We have also seen the absurd results of someone who can describe on paper his disappointment that his books have failed to obtain the right reaction without it occurring to him to trace the break in the circuit back to himself. This is a not uncommon critical astigmatism—a writer's inability to understand why the public ear can't catch the voices which chime so clearly in his head, and which he has even gone to the bother of jotting down to make it easier for the dullwits.

And, of course, Wain, as does any writer, wishes to influence—and, logically, to be a spokesman for—his generation. In that same essay he states flatly: "Authors fall into two categories, broadly speaking: those whose concern with humanity is analytical and enquiring, and those who are out to recommend something positive. . . . The artist's function is always to humanise the society he is living in. . . . Today the adversary is the machine. . . The job of humanising our environment has to be taken more seriously than ever. *And he that is not with us is against us.*"

That could not be plainer. It is for these reasons, his determination to communicate, that he writes in a sort of colloquial bad-temper, a forceful slanginess. "Meanwhile we want a little less gas about Thomas, and some criticism that really talks turkey and gets down to particular instances," is a fair example of Wain's style and his belligerent 'brass-tacks' pose, this being from his "Review on Dylan Thomas's Poems". This literary style which has come to be a weapon of the revolt, the anti-stuffed shirt, hob-nailed boot approach (the more sensitive and subtle the subject, the more boorishly you clump across it) has already fossilised into a cliché in its more affected form—Graham Hough, reviewing Wain's *Preliminary Essays* in last December's *Encounter* asked why, if you care about poetry and consider it important enough to be worth discussing, "discuss it in terms that suggest the advertising of detergents? The ghastly clichés, meant I suppose to show how commonsense and down-to-earth one is, produce a similar effect. . . . Of course Mr. Wain is anxious to avoid the *cher maitre,* defence-of-Western-values pomposities of the official literary manner; but they are not best avoided by deliberately talking in a vulgar and trivial manner of things one really cares about. Academic writing does not become any the less academic for trying to ape the jargon of the travelling salesman." Through the hotchpotch of contrived burlesque in *Hurry On Down* comes some seriousness and sense. It is the iliad of a modern displaced person, for Lumley, just down from university, skitters through a bazaar of odd jobs, from window-cleaning to radio gag-writing, in an attempt to find which class level to slot himself into. At the outset he expects nothing but further disillusionment, for "the blunt, simple reason that his problems did not really admit of any solution . . . his predicament was not one that could be improved by thinking." Lumley feels himself to be imprisoned in his class yet not one of them. He is not trying to do an Orwell, to crash-dive into the *lumpenproletariat,* for he had always despised the "idiotic attempts" of the idealists of the Thirties "to enter, and be at one with, a vaguely conceived People". What Lumley is trying to do is to be outside the class structure altogether, to take life as it comes—he wants for the rest of his life "to travel without a passport".

Now all this is valid, interesting and proper subject matter for a novelist writing about the world he moves in. Unfortunately, as with Banks's suicidal urges, Lumley's rejection of society carries no conviction—in neither situation is a case built up, or even produced ready-made, for convincing the reader of the truth of these extreme plights. Yet, somehow, through all the farrago of "tasting life", of seeing how the other seven-eighths live, there is reached in the final pages some real sort of synthesis. Lumley is telling

Blearney the show-promoter: "I never rebelled against ordinary life; it just never admitted me."

Blearney says in correction that was because it hadn't got what he wanted, and Lumley says: "What do you think I want?"

"Neutrality," said Mr. Blearney calmly.

This comes as something of a revelation to Lumley and later, when he is alone he thinks: "Neutrality; he had found it at last. The running fight between himself and society had ended in a draw."

Banks in *Living In The Present* is portrayed as starting off in a far worse quandary. "There was no sense in trying to blink the fact that modern life had got out of hand. . . . Wherever he went, whatever he did, there would always be the insupportable ennui and pointlessness of human life." As I have already said, he is in the end rescued from "the plague-ridden jungle" by the love of a good woman, and there is a general increase in hope and confidence. The last page perks up like a Debbie Reynolds film. "The best way to make a present to life was to be happy," Banks philosophises, and when Catherine whispers: "Put your arms round me," obedient to the new simplicities of cosy romance, Banks gives "a long, silent shudder of laughter at his own happiness as he thought of the bad yesterdays and the wonderful tomorrows."

In the *London Magazine* for November 1956 Wain contributed a piece entitled "A Writer's Prospect", which had the look of being the fork in the road. It had the air of a *Times* announcement stating to whom it concerned that John Wain would no longer be responsible for any spiritual debts incurred by John Wain in the past.

It was written in his customary impatient, brusque, post office counter clerk style, and fairly early on got going again with how impossible it is for the writer to be appreciated nowadays—there is "the really extraordinary lack of intelligent comment on what is going on" and continuing: ". . . so however hard you try to avoid being misunderstood and travestied, you find it useless," most critics "do not—to be frank—possess even ordinary competence," and so on.

The only point in recalling this further bout of inculpation is the curious twist it takes at the end, where, while berating Mr. Hilary Corke for "silly impertinence" in reviewing Dr. David Daiches's *Literary Essays*, Wain remarks "Tradition is a pretty big thing not to believe in", and concludes: "If you must be a man of letters it is not a bad plan to get yourself born in England. There are many snags about writing primarily for English people; lack of a critically intelligent public one of them; but, after all, an author needs some things even more than he needs intelligent criticism, and one of them is a liberal atmosphere. The freedom of the English writer from bullying officials and hysterical witch-hunters, the generally good-tempered attitude of people towards him, is worth a cart-load of critics. Examples of this good temper abound; there is *nothing* this people will not forgive. Let me end as I have gone on, in thoroughly bad taste. At the end of the 'thirties, when this country was about to be attacked with a strong chance of being defeated, our two most gifted young writers left our shores and became citizens of another country. Good luck to them. But if they had been Frenchmen or Italians, would they be honoured guests today in their rejected country? Would one of them occupy a traditionally honoured academic chair? I doubt it. Here is something that we might well boast about; as long as the innate English gentleness of spirit is still so much in evidence, it is at least possible to build a future for literature."

Wain seems to be the first of the new dissentients to display signs of readiness to conform, to opt for orthodoxy after all; the hoarse rebel yells that were briefly voiced now seem, in his mid-thirties, to be modulating to those familiar gruff admonitory tones of the junior Establishment, a sort of trainee Priestley. Which raises the fundamental question whether the dissentience of the Fifties has any genuine revolutionary essence, or whether it is just a cyclic take-over bid—a question which I want to discuss at more length in the final chapter.

The other two reasons why it has seemed to me worth discussing Wain at some length are these. First because he typifies the star-building system of the Fifties. Of course, this is far less organised in the literary field than in the 'TV personality' and pop-record fields, in which plugging and persistence can create national glamour-heroes, but writing 'names' can also be produced from a talentless vacuum. That of course does not apply to Wain, but, apart from displaying some fresh and interesting, although often undeveloped ideas in literary criticism, his accomplishments as a novelist are too minor and too faulty to be taken into serious account. Yet Wain's self-confidence combined with the climate of acceptance into which he first appeared have created a curiously freak reputation. In a way it is far more inflated than Colin Wilson's, yet because it has mostly been done in deliberately high-brow terms, within the *Encounter* and Third Programme poetry-reading reservation, it is less vulnerable than Wilson's mass-circulation caperings at which every gossip-columnist and *Daily Sketch* letter-writer can have a stab. Wain is undoubtedly the most over-rated writer of the Fifties, and stands as a lesson in present-day careerism—how, if he is aggressive enough about it, a writer can get himself accepted at his own evaluation, irrespective of talent.

But a far more important reason for examining Wain's work closely is because of the influence it has had on other new novelists. However clumsy and contrived *Hurry On Down* was, it did move out of the conventional environments. Instead of public school Young Woodleyism, up-dated Oppenheimer society scatter-braining around Mayfair and Menton, classy but coura-geous war (the Rupert Brooke spirit revived at Alamein), and Dr. Miniver bravely holding out against the National Health Service, Wain struck out into unimaginable territory. His mixed-up wrongly-educated bourgeois hero tried his hand as a hospital orderly, a dope-runner, a chauffeur, a window-cleaner and a TV script-writer—hardly routine ground in English novels—and he zig-zagged from one to another, never adjusting, never assimilating.

This journeying with a central character through a sequence of picaresque events, with the staccato omnivorousness of a cinema newsreel, stimulated a fashion that still continues. Of course it did not start the fashion, because Joyce Cary was doing similar things with Gulley Jimson years ago and so was Linklater, and before that a whole chain reaction of picaresquerie. But *Hurry On Down* certainly set a new cycle in recrudescence, of the intellectual

76

rebel without a cause wandering through the deserts and jungles of the post-war world trying to find somewhere to pitch his tent.

One of the more unfortunate results was the case of Thomas Hinde. Hinde, whose real name is Sir Thomas Chitty and who works as a public relations officer in Shell, published his first novel, *Mr. Nicholas,* in 1953, the same year Wain published his. There was no similarity between them, either in subject matter, treatment or quality. *Mr. Nicholas* is by the highest standards, a brilliant and beautifully written book, controlled, exact and illuminating. It is set in outer exurbia, the Surrey stockbroker belt, where the pines and heather maintain a distant illusion of country in what is really a superior housing estate, gorse hills carved up into private-drive three-acre plots containing their mullioned villa apiece, golf courses, tennis courts, filling stations and tarted-up 'taverns'.

The Nicholases—Mr. Nicholas, Mrs. Nicholas, and their three sons Peter, David and Owen—occupy one of the villas. The dominant character is Mr. Nicholas, a retired barbarian business-man who feeds on other people's timidity, bullies relentlessly in a team-spirit way ("I won't stand being insulted in my own house, old boy"), starts a Defend Britain Club and organises local cricket. *Mr. Nicholas* is our equivalent of *Baby Doll* or *Tobacco Road.* In the American version of living hell you have violence, lust and degeneracy carried to their extremity. In *Mr. Nicholas* you have a particular British middle-class incubus affecting a family of strangers imprisoned under one roof, strangled by their inhibitions and compulsion towards correctness, all trying to act out their conception of a hearty mummy-and-daddy-and-the-boys ideal. The action, which is mostly an internal shift of prisms, occurs during Peter's long vacation from Oxford. It is a 'lovely summer'—weeks of chromium sun that singes the clock golf lawn and brings out everyone in Aertex shirts. The heat encloses them like a glass bell under which there is a curious state of trance, in which meals are served, drinks mixed, tennis played, and the deep conflict between Peter and his father, and the intricate permutations of conflict that exist between all, stretch to an unbearable tension.

The drama, which is Russian in its dreadfulness—the bolting

of David with the queer retired Army officer, their manic-depressive father's capitulation to a depression state—barely ripples the surface of the suburban lily pond, and the tragi-comedy is elegiacally developed to the final irony of the tyrant's survival.

Mr. Nicholas, although confined in its scope, is because of its acute discernment and the understated power of its prose one of the few really distinguished post-war novels, and was an arresting though lonely cry of dissentience when it came out five years ago.

Last year Hinde published his second novel *Happy As Larry.* During the intervening years *Hurry On Down* and *Lucky Jim* had appeared, with them a new sort of hero far less genteel, well-bred and good-mannered than Peter Nicholas, a hero who had never even visited in the rich sham-rustic dormitories. Perhaps that was why in *Happy As Larry* Hinde came through the wattle curtain.

The title had the new ring. The setting, if not the provinces, was similarly disembodied: the Earls Court hinterland, the vast transit camp of the rootless, where coloured students, lower-paid trade paper journalists, and feature photographers live in either basement or attic flats. Larry Vincent and his wife Betty live in one of the back streets, four floors up. He is a neurotic failure, an out of work schoolteacher who would write if he could persuade himself of the point of it. He is tall but walks "with his shoulders bent". His hair is thin and suggests "something of poor quality".

He does not mind the shabby, pointless penury in which they live, for really he feels that tidiness wastes time and a regular job is a failure, not success. But Betty makes him doubt the certainty of his own mind.

The story opens on a monstrous note. Betty has persuaded him to shave and put on his best suit and go off and meet someone who may help him to find a job. As he is walking up the road he hears her call but deliberately ignores it. He has no wish to go back to hear what she has to say. "He understood now that it was better not to talk. Talk led to dignity and consistency, things of no value." She calls again but he doesn't stop. Then he hears the car and he looks round just in time to see it enveloping her with screeching brakes.

But he doesn't stop. A few minutes later he is standing in a pub

78

thinking that Betty, his wife of two years whom he is fond of and wishes he was kinder to, is no doubt dead. He buys some beer.

The vomit begins to splash. The drift begins through the phantasmagoria of marginal London, ostensibly in pursuit of a pornographic photograph, but which becomes a Kafkaesque groping into his own schizophrenia. The unreality intensifies. It is a landscape of tube station entrances glaring into the early hours, lamplight in cold, wet streets after all the cafes have shut, the blazing Bayswater Road when the commuters' cars are scrambling home, Kensington when the winter night of fog falls at four-thirty. Larry is dunned for rent, pushes a dud cheque, is kicked down the stairs of the BBC, wanders zombie-like in his absurd search. Early on he tries to make sense of it all. In a Fulham Road pub, where there is the usual crowd—a man-lesbian, duffle coats, a girl with prefrontal leucotomy, young underwriters in bowlers, Tiger a wizardprang BOAC pilot—he says to his acquaintance Paul: "Sometimes for a short time I seem to understand. More often it's just a sense of the importance of struggling."

"You're a victim," says Paul.

At a party he meets Sasha. She is pretty, with long brown hair and big warm breasts. "She made him feel that life was hopeful. He was again sure that he could mean to do things and succeed." The hope withers pretty fast.

He is by now homeless, dossing down during the snow period in a friend's attic, and some days he does not get up until evening, then just to walk around the emptiness. "The city of eight million people was round him and there was no one he particularly wanted to see." He is, occasionally, eating in Lyons. He is thin with malnutrition, coughs all the time through his grey twilight of mind.

When he briefly walks with Sasha through the streets bright with Christmas windows the surrealism admits a trickle of happiness. But Sasha is a psychopath. She is an art teacher "in between jobs", and has been for two years. She lies and steals compulsively, and is afraid because she believes she smells. She does too. She does little but sit on her bed in her room among the piles of menstrual-stained clothing and empty cosmetic jars.

When he tries to find her another room she says: "Larry, it's no good," but she can't explain what isn't. The conversation peters out. "She didn't answer, as if even the effort of explaining wasn't worth making."

Later, when they are making their inert, climaxless love, she says: "Do you enjoy it?"

"What?"

"Things," she said. "Life?"

It was a question he didn't ask himself. "Sometimes for a short time. Do you?"

"Me? I can't remember what it's like. I expect I've thought about it too much."

But they cannot ask each other why they are unhappy. That would be preposterous. In a curious aquarium gloom, in which all sensory perception is muted, they transmit some little consolation to each other. Eventually they lose each other.

Once, in a pub with Tiger the pilot, Larry momentarily grasps some cohesion, coherence. "People like me," Larry said. "We're parasites. We don't produce anything. There'd be too much if we did. We're tolerated because people who haven't time or inclination to wonder if there's any point in life are glad to know there are some people who think so."

But much later, when Betty has returned, recovered, and has left him again, and his search for the photograph has ended in Sasha's midden room, he is walking in the deserted park with only two other humans in sight moving a long way off under the trees on the lamp-lit paths. "If only he could decide what to do. If only he could feel hopeful that even when he had decided it would not turn out wrong."

Happy As Larry ends on a faint lap upward of hope, but the future is not frightfully convincing. Certainly he is no closer to dignity and consistency, although there is the implication that perhaps now he does not dismiss them as valueless. Condensed as it is above a distorted picture of hyperbolic despair emerges. The despair is not thereby being over-emphasised by me, but again Hinde's writing is meticulous, calm and reserved. The awfulness of the life that he observes, like someone flickering a torch in the Kensington fog, is never anything but natural and true. I think *Happy As Larry* is the nearest expression of Beckett feeling that we have in English, not so totally out of life, for the Beckett creatures have stepped off the edge, but Larry and Sasha and those of the eight millions they have brushed against are wandering along the brink. They are the furthest from the original conception of dissentience we discussed, for these are the extreme delinks. They are paralysed people who have not so much rejected society or protested against society as been capsized by it. Comparatively Wain's heroes, and certainly Amis's, are living on the sunny side of the street.

There are three other books published during the past year which I want briefly to consider in this context, chiefly as examples of the worst aspect of this cult of the confused Outsider hero. Whereas Hinde's exceptional talent and, I believe, genuine intention to communicate a state of mind he knows about made *Happy As Larry* at least a perfect clinic bedside book, I doubt the whole sincerity of two of these I am coming to. *The Ginger Man* by J. P. Donleavy, *Summer In Retreat* by Edmund Ward and *Prospects Of Love* by William Camp were all published within a few months of each other.

The Ginger Man was clearly intended as a tour-de-force and almost was. Donleavy, Brooklyn-born, son of a New York civil servant, attended Trinity College, Dublin, under the GI Bill of Rights, now lives in London. Denying any political outlook whatever, he has told me that he feels dissociated from this present time except in the personal sense that when he first came over he was very much emotionally star-struck with the idea (a Gatsby attitude) of himself and his friends living a lavish life at European institutions of learning. "We all felt," he said, "that things were going to be great, richer, wilder than ever before, and would get better as we got older. Most of us have been somewhat disappointed."

The Ginger Man concerns Sebastian Balfe Dangerfield, an American law student at Trinity College, Dublin, living with his English wife and child in pigsty digs. He hates Ireland, "shrunken teat on the chest of the cold Atlantic". Dangerfield is an educated bum, a sponger, wife-beater and boozer. During the action of the book (for it is too unstrung and cascading to be called a plot) he writes begging letters, has several ruttish adventures and copulates with a pick-up in a coalshed, kicks in the water closet so that his wife downstairs is drenched, drinks immoderately all over Dublin, bellows much Dublin purple talk with his fellow roaring boys, swindles grocers, breaks up bars and snaps a man's fingers, insults and vilifies anyone who obstructs his zigzag course and finally ends up in—where else?—Earls Court with his Irish servant girl.

Whereas Lumley in *Hurry On Down* was presented as being driven into the outer darkness by a fundamental seriousness of purpose, and Larry by his loss of skill at the inner circle rules, Dangerfield is a rogue maladjust. At the second whisky his destructiveness flowers, and, almost as a reflex action, he begins throwing stout bottles, smacking women round the face, beating up cabbies and taking an axe to the furniture. It is an extraordinary picture of a demonic personality drawn with huge, sloshing but cunningly deliberate brushstrokes. The wild ginger man is quite different from any of the dissentients we have so far examined, because he is on the nihilist lunatic fringe. Yet, and this is the interesting point, even he has his stultified longings for respectability, dignity and quiet orderliness of conduct. These pathetic hangover dreams of good citizenship, like a murderer on the run yearning for both boyhood innocence and the Old Bailey drama, always explode in another reeling riot of drink, violence and fornication. Dangerfield's wife is a pink, willowy Englishwoman and arouses the old American envy, the ambivalent desire for and hatred of the gentility and refinement of such Old World symbols as Marion. Although his nationality is different, his social attitude is very similar to Osborne's Jimmy Porter's towards Alison. Dangerfield does not taunt and torture Marion, and goad her about her Admiral father and milksop upbringing, quite so relentlessly as Jimmy Porter does Alison, but the same festering class resentments are there, the same atmosphere of the 1917 Red troops making the aristocrats scrub out lavatories before shooting them in the back of the skull.

Dangerfield's saga continues in a rush of word-torrents, written under the heavy shadow of James Joyce and Henry Miller, inchoate, splurging, tumescent with dialogue and diatribe, bawdy and dirty (". . . rumbustious energy, like that of some gritty and ruthless Restoration comedy," was the blurb's phrase), and often brutally funny.

Yet there is a distinct horror about this book, which is Dangerfield's frantic flight from anything that might mean continuity or responsibility. There is nothing wrong with Donleavy's character delineation: Dangerfield is as consistent and relevant as an epileptic's fit. In a way he is no more extreme in his behaviour than Jim Dixon—he only has a more savage candour. Nor is he further off centre than Larry. But the unbridgeable difference is that Lucky Jim stayed in the circle, Larry wanted to sneak back in, but Dangerfield is the irreclaimable outlaw. When he says near the end of the book "And this is the main thing, I've kept the dignity", it can only dismay as being words of real madness.

Despite its battering-ram force and virtuoso writing *The Ginger Man* is less a genuine cry of dissentience than a bit of swank—a contribution, you suspect, to a cult. Similarly with Edmund Ward whose artist hero Eames in *Summer in Retreat* is seen returning to his hometown in the provinces after five years gallivanting around Europe. Eames is the odd man out, the familiar tough poker-faced artistic wide boy who can never put a foot right and is proud of it. The fact that no one ever addresses him by his Christian name (has he got one?) is supposed, I expect, to indicate that he is that much out of contact with his fellow humans. Before finally quitting the town in a revival of disenchantment, Eames undergoes a series of calamities. There is a good deal of pervasive influence here from both Amis and Wain—the often comical near-slapstick unmistakably recalling Lucky Jim and the attempts at a sort of demonic farce obviously stemming from Wain, with a similar brand of cinerama exaggeration—e.g. he is confronted by a dog in the hall. It bays at him. "Eames . . . picked up a bentwood hall chair as he had seen lion tamers do. The dog pulled off one of the chair-legs contemptuously and spat splinters before baying again."

The style is staccato and clipped, but among the welter of wisecracks and fast writing is a real creative talent. Eames's final

83

remark in the book, when he is hitch-hiking out of town for ever in a lorry, is in answer to the driver's question where he wants to go. "Anywhere but backwards. I'm not paying for the petrol" — the final swagger, the delinquent's cocky snarl at authority. Before that, however, he says with the first trace of sincerity that he doesn't count the six months back in the town wasted. "Six months to find out I was mistaken? I don't think that's bad. I could have taken forty years and ended up with a gold watch and my name on the roll. Lots of people do."

That will seem to many people an honest and realistic point of view. The trouble is that here on the last page Eames is speaking with an entirely different voice from the one he has been using throughout, and the one he switches back to with the last sentence. Eames seems altogether too much of a put-up job, a sort of James Dean myth run off on a roneo machine. He is one-dimensional, a contemporary cut-out of the man who can't fit in, but with no convincing cause for staying on the outside. There is nowhere a sense of dilemma.

There certainly is in *Prospects of Love,* a bare, low-key exercise in writing. Reviewing it in *The Spectator* in May 1957 John Bayley remarked that it belonged to "the type of novel which — in contrast to that spirited recent piece entitled *A High-Pitched Buzz* — I have heard referred to generically as *A Low-Pitched Moan."* That was less than fair but neatly on target. Actually I think *Prospects of Love* was a novel with more skill than it generally rated, although lack of recognition of that was Camp's own fault. The detachment with which he treats the story looks, by logical paradox, almost like sympathetic identification with Mark Andrews, the central character, so uncritical is he of his character's faults, his egomania, his lechery, his hard sentimentality. If, as I think he does, Camp intends Mark to personify the deadly apathetic neutrality present in modern life, there should be some implicit criticism; as it is, many readers must have resisted what they thought were attempts to solicit compassion for the shallow, shilly-shallying defeatist who sparks only at the lures of money and bed.

Camp himself, a thirty-two-year-old economist, is of the middle-class administrator class. He is the son of a Colonial civil servant, went to a public school, then to Oxford. He served in the Coldstream Guards. Later he read for the bar at Gray's Inn, but is now assistant secretary to the Consumer Advisory Council of the British Standards Institute. Politically Camp is left and active. He has been a member of the Labour Party since 1946, was chairman of the Oxford University Labour Club 1949, is a former socialist member of Southwark Borough Council, and he contested Solihull in the 1950 General Election, and he writes in *Tribune*, Michael Foot's socialist weekly. He summed up his hopes for the future for me as: "A world with less pain, less selfishness, less materialism, less American way-of-life, less Beaverbrook philosophy."

Mark, his hero, is the embodiment of most of the above aspects of present-day society, and it may be for his own satisfaction that Camp showed him as being such an unsuccessful operator. In one of his frequent immersions in narcissism Mark reflects that he belongs to the "Young man, administrative experience (but not senior enough); university degree (but nothing like good enough); car driver (but not owner); unwilling go anywhere or do anything, but congenial, remunerative job wanted" class. It also occurs to him that it must be a very numerous class.

What is of particular significance about Mark—although this is never explicit referred to—is that he is the very person who has been knocked out of action by Jim Dixon, or even more specifically by Joe Lampton, the mill town hustler of *Room At The Top*. "The world of Mark's childhood, where people with salaries (as opposed to wages) had had such a good time would never return," and elsewhere he admits to himself that the middle class "simply didn't care about defending their own interests."

Here he is, an amateur prospector in the post-war Death Valley, badly equipped, compass broken, lethargically doing a bit of panning in the Pools, his only hope ("there were no other ways of making money") of escaping from the parched greyness of a marriage and a job that bore him, and a life that is almost melodramatic in its flat emptiness.

For Mark is at the delink brink. He is an unwilling dissentient, a natural conformist who in other times would have lived his life without thought or question in the cosy womb of a white-collar suburb, fulfilled with the *Daily Telegraph*, amateur dramatics and the rugger club dances. As it is, he is in the wrong age and he has been aborted out into a class no-man's-land. What almost— but not quite—arouses your pity in Mark's situation is his utter helplessness. He has no politics, no friends, no books, no opinions, and is engaged only by absorbing acts of self-interest, which proceed with the blind compulsive jaw-rotation of a maggot hollowing an apple. Occasionally he draws back and squints distastefully at himself—"He might as well face it: emotionally and spiritually he was existing from hand to mouth on a diet that consisted mainly of temptation and remorse, in which there was no nourishment. . . . He might as well admit that his principal recreation, consolation, delectation, pre-occupation, and a lot of other words ending in -ation, including no doubt eventually damnation, was sex. Sex wasn't just the poor man's piano. It was his whole orchestra."

During his affair with Juliet, the wife of a friend, he feels to be "seething with energy, ideas, ambition and all those other jolly ingredients that are essential to success". By the time he has lost his job, his wife is having a baby against his express wish and has refused to get rid of it, and, when he is about to leave her, has tried to gas herself, the jolly ingredients have evaporated. It ends, with similar discordance to *Happy As Larry*, on the up-beat: he has abandoned his mistress and returned to his wife in a rhapsody of atonement.

Prospects of Love is not an excitingly written book—it is too monotoned and monochromed—yet it is done with care and honesty. Mark is highly real. "It's a bloody world, isn't it?" is the plaintive comment that is most of the time in his innards if not on his lips. It is this listless acceptance that marks him down as a particular contemporary young man—the precise opposite number of Joe Lampton who has shouldered him out of the way. Joe's eyes are fixed on the place there is for him at the top and he isn't wasting his breath bemoaning life.

John Braine was given a great launching, even in the serious Sundays, and *Room At The Top* sold 35,000 copies in the first year. It was accorded top-of-the-page treatment in *The Evening Standard* and Richard Lister announced that Braine herewith stepped "right up beside Kingsley Amis and John Osborne as a leading member of the new school of young writers". He ended: "If you want to know the sort of way in which the young products of the Welfare State are feeling and reacting, it will tell you." John Davenport in *The Observer* declared it to be "remarkably good", and it was greeted with similar delight in *The New Statesman, The Times Literary Supplement, The Listener,* and other criteria of quality. The *Sunday Times* gave it a column to itself, headed it "A First Novel Success", and took the—for them—unusual step of printing the author's photograph. John Metcalfe began, like a *Daily Express* editorial: "Remember the name: John Braine. You'll be hearing quite a lot about him." He went on to make the accurate prediction: "Joe will set a new fashion in heroes: brash, innocent, cynical—wide and wide-eyed—imitations of him will be bothering us for quite a while," but ended with a curious boner: "It's a long time since we heard the hunger of youth really snarling; and it's a good sound to hear again."

If there's one thing Joe is always careful not to do it is snarl. He always smiles, a little soapily, for Joe's motives and methods are primitively simple. He is a quick-minded twenty-five-year old North Country working-class boy on the make. When he arrives in Warley to take up an accountancy job in the Town Hall he is wearing a fourteen guinea pale grey suit, a tie held by a chromium dagger, and a trilby stained with brilliantine. He rapidly perceives that all these are not quite Warley. His new territory is still Yorkshire but light-industry, clean and suburban—up at the Top are the big managerial-bracket villas, with *Homes and Gardens* furnishing, and sprawled in the gravel drives Bentley Continentals, which are driven out for double Scotches in roadhouses and golf club bars. Joe, with shot-silk dressing gown in case and eyes trailing like tentacles over possibilities, moves into his lodgings. The bathroom is green-tiled; there is a white bearskin rug on the parquet floor— ". . . strictly Metro-Goldwyn-Mayer," he supposes in this first person narrative, "but it fitted in,

87

added a necessary touch of frivolity, even a faint sexiness like scented cachous."

Joe is not one of these mixed-up drifters. He knows precisely what he wants, and he wants with a fierce longing "an Aston-Martin, three-guinea linen shirts, a girl with a Riviera suntan". He wastes no time in manoeuvring within range of these things, and his ladder has rungs of women, whom he privately grades one to ten according to their financial and social rating.

In the local amateur dramatic society he begins to flex his brash, beefy sexual prowess. There he meets the two women through whom he accomplishes what he wants. Alice is in her thirties, married, a bit raddled, generous and warm, and they begin an affair which ends with them falling in love with each other.

The go-getter in Joe overcomes this lapse into softness. He knows that with Alice there can be only scandal and trouble, whereas he sees in teenage Susan, the finishing-schooled plum-smooth daughter of the town's richest industrialist, the doorway to Aston-Martin land, his escape from his under-privileged grimy origins. When she asks him how much he loves her, he replies: "A hundred thousand pounds' worth." He takes the escape route. In consequence Alice, loaded with gin, kills herself in a car accident. Joe has Susan and a job in her father's firm—and also the knowledge that he has sold-out beyond the point of return. "She'd have ruined your whole life," says a friend, consoling him about the death of Alice. "Nobody blames you." "Oh, my God," cries Joe in his last repentance, "that's the trouble."

Room At The Top has its faults. There is an implausible manufacturer father, a prop-cupboard blunt, crude money-maker who respects blunt, crude money-makers, and who, when he finds Joe has got Susan with child, 'tests' his character and then ushers him into the opulent world of the Top. Susan, I personally find not so much implausible as unbearable. Perhaps such a portrait of a shallow, arch, spoilt little sugar mouse is accurate. Yet I find it difficult to believe that even Joe, with his steel-tipped ambition, but who is neither stupid nor illiterate, could stomach a girl who chirps like a sexy tom-tit: "Oo, *wicked!* Susan tingle. Susan tingle up and down. Do it again." There are occasions, too, when the writing side-slips into woman's magazine serialese—"The pillow smelled faintly of lavender; it reminded me of something. It was her scent, cool as clean linen, friendly as beer"—and evocative and fresh though much of his description is, it is tinged with a copywriter's gushy cleverness. The book's most distinctive flavour, both its strength and weakness, is its sensuality, a voluptuous sensitivity to colours, shapes, textures—and price-tabs. (Bernard Wall did a witty parody in *The Twentieth Century* of a young man checking on his mistress's social status by doing a quick mental inventory of the value of her bedroom contents). Momentarily this slithers into a rather curious new kind of romantic slushiness; but most of the time his eye maintains a cool accuracy and, rather in the manner of the short stories in the *New Yorker*, Braine knows precisely how to pinpoint a particular salary level by the use of the correct brand-name (Coty, Riley Pathfinder, Earl Grey, Gold Rolex Oyster), a trick not much employed by British writers. *Room At The Top* is not a novel adventure story, for Joe Lamptons have been purposefully bed-hopping to success ever since society arranged itself in layers. But few books have revealed so explicitly the actual shape and shimmer of the fantasy life longings of a Joe Lampton, and certainly no one until John Braine had described the exact kind of urges operating within the post-war specimen. Looking back at Jim Dixon you realise that, in this respect, you know nothing of his inner life, that the Wain men are personifications of a set of circumstances, and Jimmy Porter of course hates and rejects the very things that Joe so obsessively wants.

"You're the most un-neurotic person I know," Alice tells him, and it is true that he has a single-mindedness, a beautifully brutal simplicity of purpose, that is not a characteristic of the heroes of other contemporary novels. Yet even Joe retains a small buried kernel of dissentience. Although he feels a complacent contempt for the young men of the class he has deserted (he watches one boarding a bus: ". . . navy-blue overcoat, gloves and scarf . . . solid mass of brilliantined hair and mass-produced face, bony, awkward, mousy, the face behind the request on Forces Favourites, the face enjoying itself at Blackpool with an open-necked shirt

89

spread out over its jacket, the face which Wilfred Pickles might love but which depressed me intensely—Len or Sid or Cliff or Ron. . . .") he has not entirely lost his conscience about them. He explains: "I'm like a brand-new Cadillac in a poor industrial area, insulated by steel and glass and air-conditioning from the people outside, from the rain and the cold and the shivering ailing bodies. I don't wish to be like the people outside, I don't even wish that I had some weakness, some foolishness to immobilise me among the envious coolie faces, to let in the rain and the smell of defeat. *But I sometimes wish that I wished it.*" (My italics.)

Despite his ruthlessness, his vulgarity and his calculated lechery (although he remarks "I may be obsessed by sex but there are worse things to be obsessed by", he isn't really obsessed by it—he uses it) Joe is not an unsympathetic character. He is human, and warm impulses flicker like summer lightning through his success campaign. And the part of him that he has deliberately stifled is still sufficiently alive for him to acknowledge to himself, in the shock of Alice's death, that he is a cheapskate and that what he wants is comparatively not worth a farthing.

John Braine once told me what set the plot of *Room At The Top* in motion. "I saw a man sitting in a big shiny car. He'd driven up to the edge of some waste ground, near some houses and factories, and was just sitting there looking across at them. It seemed to me there must have been a lot that led up to that moment."

He has made about £12,000 from the book, which is being filmed, and which was (shredded and de-sexed) serialised in the *Daily Express,* probably irresistibly drawn towards a book whose title so neatly summarises its own philosophy. He is now a full-time writer. He looks back upon a patchy life. He was born in Bradford in 1922, the son of a corporation sewage works supervisor, who worked half-time in the wool mills as a child. His mother, who was killed in a street accident in 1951, was a librarian before her marriage.

Braine won a scholarship to St. Bede's Grammar School, Bradford, where he spent most of the time "in a mental fog—not the school's fault but mine, and left without taking the School Certificate". (He got it at twenty-two, and became a librarian at twenty-seven after failing the examination three times.) Prior to that he worked in a furniture shop, a bookshop, a laboratory, a piston-ring factory, and, in uniform, as a Naval telegraphist. In 1951 he decided to abandon feeding books out to other people and try to live by writing them himself.

"London was a wonderful and bewitching city for me," he told me. "On odd visits earlier I'd just sat in pubs, certain that any moment something marvellous would happen that would change my whole life. When I told my parents I was leaving Bradford to write in London they thought I'd gone out of my head.

"I had £150 saved up and I took a room in Kensington. It was very frightening when I closed the door and realised that there was nothing I wanted to write about."

During the next eight lean months he sold a few articles to the *New Statesman* and other magazines, and did a BBC broadcast, but thin as he spread the money, meal-bills became a problem. At the end of 1951 he fell ill, was told he had TB and was installed in hospital for the next eighteen months, and it was there that he began *Room At The Top*.

Married now, and with a small son, Braine has finally resigned from the library service and is living in a big Victorian house at Bingley, Yorkshire. He has no intention of re-invading the London literary world, even, as it would be now, on the plane of recognition and security. Like Amis and others, who stay out of London partly out of caution, partly because their sources are the provinces, partly because they have no taste for the alleged 'glitter' of literary high life. (Dylan Thomas felt similarly about the London intelligentsia. ". . . its glamour smells of goat," he wrote to Vernon Watkins; "there's no difference between good and bad."). Braine says:

"I sometimes feel that I have no business to call myself a writer at all, particularly since I have no gift whatever for thinking in the abstract. But writing is my vocation, and whether I follow it well or badly I shall follow it until the day I die.

"Joe Lampton isn't meant especially to be of this period and certainly isn't autobiographical. He's just a distinct type of human

91

being. In the Welfare State the young man on the make has to be a bit tougher and learn how to fiddle more cleverly. My job in writing about Joe Lampton was to look at him clearly. It's not the job of a novelist to pass moral judgments.

"Looking at British writing generally, from about 1949 to now I sensed a certain deadness of feeling among writers. Now things seem to be moving. Angry Young Man is a misused and over-used label, but it does have some significance if only that it means that the young writer is rejecting literary formulas. I personally haven't recently espoused any causes, simply because of lack of time, but now that conditions have changed for me and I have the time I shall throw my weight in for anything in which I believe. I shan't achieve much by so doing but if I don't protest—I who, as far as anyone ever can be, am a free man—who will?

"I've been a member of the Labour Party and will be again. I'm not starry-eyed about it, but certain things in which I believe can only be achieved by the Labour Party . . . Put it this way— although I'd like to be in the proper sense of the word an idiot and not bother about Suez and the rest of it, it is my duty to be concerned to do what little I can—let's be really old-fashioned— to make the world a better place. Or, more important, to make sure that there *is* a habitable world, not a radio-active desert."

Braine was brought up a Catholic (his mother was Irish) and continues to be one—"though no doubt not a good one. If you don't believe in God then you'll find yourself believing in Marx or Mammon. Religion is necessary because there must be a firm authority for morality—you must, for instance, love your fellow-men because it's your duty to do so, not because you happen to feel like it. After all, how often does one feel like it?"

Braine defines the novelist's responsibility as being "to show his age as it really is. And the writer has a responsibility to behave well. I'm not thinking of his personal morals, or assigning any particular political beliefs to him. But a writer must be a civilised and tolerant human being, possessing, above all, intellectual integrity. It's not possible, for instance, for any writer to advocate anti-Semitism or the colour bar. The writer doesn't have to inhabit a rarefied moral or intellectual plane, but he must always be, no matter how imperfectly, the conscience of society. . . . I'd like to see the world run by civilised human beings—yes, by eggheads— all of whom could use words to convey meaning, not as a smoke-

screen. I want a world where politicians don't become so fascinated with the technique of government that they forget the purpose of government. Indeed, I want a world in which government
is thought of only as a convenience—I reject all this nonsense of
Black Rods and Woolsacks and Chiltern Hundreds and Who
Goes Home."

He is now nearing the end of his next novel, called *The Vodi*—
"an imaginary organisation dedicated to the furtherance of injustice. It represents the essential unfairness of life. I'm going to
explore the ways of fighting the Vodi—that's all I can say."

Braine states flatly that he didn't write *Room At The Top* with
any conscious propaganda intention of criticising modern society,
or specifically doing an exposé of the rich wool merchant community. Personally I don't see why that should have been supposed, because it is, with more clarity than possessed by most
novels, the story of an adventurer, a man travelling from envy to
callousness. Yet what drew so much instant attention to the book
was the true feeling of living in the present, or at least the just-
past Forties—the £5,000-a-year background of fat expense-account
indulgence contrasting with rationing and a coal crisis at the first
frost—but also the sense of moral perspective that the book has.
Although it is told in the first person, it is not subjective and self-
absorbed like *Prospects of Love* and *The Ginger Man;* Joe
Lampton is a lout and a lecher, a money-grabber ready to knock-
up a virgin as a necessary detail of his master-plan, yet you feel
that Lampton, seeing his own history in retrospect, has the correct
measure of himself.

Again—'contemporariness' isn't enough. Roger Longrigg published *A High-Pitched Buzz* in 1956 and *Switchboard* last year.
These are rather the British equivalent of American advertising
novels, such as *The Hucksters* and *The Build-Up Boys*, flagellation displays that bleed all over you with a mixture of remorse
and pride, full of exurbanites in 'sincere' black silk knitted ties,
who love-hate their advertising sponsors. *A High-Pitched Buzz* and
Switchboard have, superficially, a much more civilised patina. Now
that the advertising agency, along with Lloyds, the Bar, and the
Stock Exchange, is regarded as one of those marginal but just

permissible commercial enterprises at which a youngish gentleman may earn his £3,000 a year, it has become the setting for the post-war 'light' smart novel in the Waugh-Mitford line of country.

Longrigg's world is that of Tony Armstrong Jones, Julian Slade and Sandy Wilson, the shoddy-chic jungle between Belgravia and Cheyne Walk, where the young men in bowlers chatter with debs training as Constance Spry flower-arrangers or reporting for the *Evening Standard's* "In London Last Night" column. The setting is mews houses with tubbed bay trees and carriage lamps. The heroes are Henry and Jeremy and Jonathan, they knew each other at Oxford and were in the same regiment, and they work in elegant offices at slogans and lay-outs.

It is not, to say it again, the function of the novelist to express opinions, to lay down the law, or to hawk around solutions for the riddles and insanities of human life that he examines in his work. About ten years ago in *Les Temps Modernes* Sartre had a piece called "Writing For One's Age", which carries some valuable reflections on the position which a writer may have to take up in the post-war world, and they are worth giving at some length.

"A book has its absolute truth with the age," Sartre says. "It is *lived* like an outbreak, like a famine . . . a living bond of rage, hatred or love among those who produce it and those who receive it. If it succeeds in commanding attention, thousands of people reject it and deny it: as everybody knows, to read a book is to re-write it. *At the time* it is at first a panic or an evasion or a courageous assertion; at the time it is a good or bad *action*. Later on, when the age is done with, it will enter into the relative, it will become a message. But the judgments of posterity will not invalidate those that were passed on it in its lifetime . . . Books that are handed down from age to age are dead fruit. They had, in another time another taste, tart and tangy. . . .

"Thus, one must write for one's age. . . . But that does not mean that one has to lock oneself up in it. To write for one's age is not to reflect it passively; it is to want to maintain it or change it, thus to go beyond it towards the future."

There is stated the defect in the Longrigg sort of 'contemporary' writing, and I do not sort him out as a scapegoat but because his writing is talented and shrewd, not just flashing cleverness and charm—a serious writer, I would say. Yet there is that "locked-in" feeling that Sartre rejects, the passive reflection. The flamenco coffee bars, the Eton ties and British warms, the Milroy at 2.30 a.m., the Pyramid parties, the Magdalen Commemoration Ball and the double-double brandy account executives—it is all an exact and, already, nostalgically 'period' evocation of the early Fifties. But it is about as 'disengaged', adjusted and self-satisfied as novel-writing can be short of rubbish; it is certainly the utter obverse of not so much *Happy As Larry* but *Mr. Nicholas,* which is the same stratum at about the same time seen through the spectrum of a different personality.

For that reason it is worth hearing something of Longrigg's own views. He is twenty-nine ("Eternally twenty-nine," wrote Richard Lister in the *New Statesman* about Lucky Nigel, in a review of *Switchboard*), was at Bryanston, was a Demy of Magdalen, was an officer in the 60th Rifles between school and university, and is now in advertising making television commercials, which he considers "an interesting and fairly well-paid job". He is a member of the Conservative Party.

That appears to be a portrait, done in pastels, of almost any David, Jeremy or Peter in the debs' delight circle of fashionable London, where the prevalent stupidity is given an almost elegiac ring by the arrogance with which it is performed. Yet they are, after all, the indestructible hard core who bobbed, champagne-cork-like, to the surface again when the Labour Government had retired breathing hard; they are the British version of the man in the grey flannel suit, the tough-smooth Right whom the public schools are now geared to producing, whom Osborne would destroy and Amis thinks are just funny.

This is their outlook, interpreted by Longrigg:

"The reason I began writing was partly a feeling that the literary portrait of my generation was all being painted by provincials: by envious, chip-on-the-shoulder people who didn't do or know about the things I and my friends enjoyed. Critics have described me, with more or less contempt, as an un-angry young man, as one of the smooth-faced men who is doing well out of the peace, and

95

as an Insider. Exactly. *Preferring* to be angry or rough-faced is either perversely silly, or a literary pose, or the expression of resentful envy. We last see Jim Dixon on the highroad to smooth-faced unangriness. That this is taken to be a good thing for him is one of the true and sensible things about that remarkable book. Of course it is a good thing for him! We all hope he will make a lot of money and live in a nice mews house. If I have an opinion I want to air it is this: nothing is so conducive to happiness, sense of proportion, the perception of universals, and good writing as absence of grudge. . . .

"The private griefs, ambitions and insecurities of an individual can be as wholly contemporary and as obsessively involving as the agony of Hungary or the class war viewed from the ironing-board. . . . I absolutely disagree that a writer has a 'responsibility' to society—his *only* responsibility is to be honest, and this is an artistic responsibility and in no sense a social responsibility."

The Longrigg kind of writing is certainly "tart and tangy" with the taste of our times, but really it is fundamentally delinked from them.

"I poured myself out a half tumbler of gin, and sat down and laughed very considerably. After that I began to feel hungry. It was after two o'clock. I went into the kitchen and made myself a long luxurious meal, consisting of *paté de foie gras,* salmon, jellied chicken and tinned asparagus, raspberries, Roquefort and orange juice. I decide that, in spite of the enormity of Sadie's crime, I would not drink her wine. I found some brandy in one of the cupboards and sat a long time over it, regretting only that Sadie didn't smoke cigars . . . At last I heard Finn coming bounding up the fire escape. He had found a beautiful hairpin and it didn't take him more than half a minute to deal with the lock."

That Lucky Jimmish situation, familiar in its tone of moral brigandry, is from one of the early chapters of *Under The Net* by Iris Murdoch, which came out in 1954—about a year after *Lucky Jim* and Wain's first novel. *Under The Net* and *The Flight From The Enchanter,* Miss Murdoch's second novel published in 1956, now—looking back only these two years—have a powerful period redolence: they look like firework set-pieces, designed to commemorate with peacock fancy a particular occasion.

Under The Net concerns an episode in the rootless, restless life of James Donaghue, known as Jake, a talented but lazy hack writer who lives mostly by translating near-pornographic French books for an English publisher. Cadging, scrounging, pinching and sleeping around (on friend's camp beds or on the Victoria Embankment benches), Jake's existence is instantly recognisable in the context of the novels of the early Nineteen-Fifties. It isn't that you weren't aware of the existence of this kind of literary hobo. Indeed, anyone in the writing trade has either gone through a period of it himself, or at least known some of these nomads, usually charming, interesting but finally ferociously harmful for their conscienceless methods of self-promotion—while you, vulnerable with your feeble theoretical attachment to the standards of good-citizenship, practice the Queensberry Rules, they from the first moment use every effective trick of all-in-fighting, but quite objectively, without any personal vindictiveness. Gold-bricking of this dedicated sort almost amounts to a Soho light industry, an ancient local craft. But it is only in recent novels that the modern practitioners have been 'featured', seen in action and in their private moments.

Jake in *Under The Net* is a remarkably attractive fellow, with the sort of honest dishonesty that is irresistible. He knows his own character with clear shrewdness—"anything rather than original work". He says: "I have shattered nerves" (the story is told in the first person) which necessitate a formidable intake of spirits. He sees himself as a "professional Unauthorised Person; I am sure I have been turned out of more places than any other member of the English intelligentsia." He has that wonderful taxi-driver knowledge of Inner London that such bums usually do possess: he could sketch a route between any two points, linking them by a chain of pubs—and not just any pubs: the ones worth drinking in. He has that practical back alley know-how indispensable to one of those shadowy men of letters. He knows what time the parks open and shut; he has "a psychic capacity for finding drink at all hours"; he can lead you to the best all-night coffee stalls; and he knows that "one doesn't have to walk far in the streets of London before coming on a hairpin", the only implement he needs for picking a lock. Yet Jake is not actually a criminal and is basically indifferent to money, which he regards in a Brechtian way as being so intrinsically immoral that he would always prefer to get it by a mild swindle than to receive it in exchange for doing a job. In the midst of apparent destitution he feels "like a fish which swims calmly in deep water", all about him "the secure supporting pressure of my own life. Ragged, inglorious and apparently purposeless, but my own."

That is an understandable and even sympathetic point of view. However this human and good-humoured man is precipitated by Miss Murdoch into what was not quite so much in 1954 but is now certainly an extremely hackneyed environment—that of the hallucinatory quest through a palpitation of half-lit and only half-understood events, with the lower-half of the London scene flickering like a magic-lantern in the hands of an excited idiot child. In *Happy As Larry* the Holy Grail, the Golden Fleece, the lodestar, the up-to-date idea of Id or Self, or whatever it is that is being stumbingly sought, is a blue photograph; this is also the case in *The Flight From The Enchanter;* in *Under The Net* the spiritual carrot is a lost *rapport* with a rich, ruminative eccentric named Hugo and a book entitled *The Silencer* in which their younger selves have been locked. This quest, and Jake's attempt to return again into a relationship with a kind of elderly Juliette Greco cafe-singer, careers through a tumult of abortive experiences—literary *Lauras,* half-identifiable faces seen in a passing train, allegorical figures lost in the crowd just as contact seems possible, symbolic puzzles almost solved the moment before being washed out of reach and comprehension by a new dissembling tide.

The Flight From The Enchanter is an even taller story. We are again in the half-submerged circle of London shabby intellectualism, and this novel is a fantasia about how power poisons and dominates the lives of many who would appear to be impervious to it. The hub of the book's meaning is a mysterious and malignant person named Mischa Fox, one of the international financier caste whom I presume to be the enchanter, or Devil, of the title. There is no interlocking of relationships; in a thin dreamy way the characters impinge upon each other only because of their casual chance encounters in the orbit of Mischa Fox, which is certainly 'life', but which is also a distortion of life because despite their momentary dependence upon each other (they are constantly flitting from one to another, like vampire bats feeding on each other's blood) there is no sight of any one of them living independently of the others, as, after all, people do: even a person's most intimate and important relationship with another occupies at any given time only one aspect of his personality—they are like geometrical figures in alignment at only one angle of their surfaces, while catching a myriad of different reflections unknown to the other. *The Flight From The Enchanter* has a curious febrile brilliance, unreal, over-charged and at one or two of its bad moments as tritely mystical as *The Passing of the Third Floor Back*. There is in *The Flight From The Enchanter* an increase in incoherence—where *Under The Net* veered now and then into an ironical reverie, in which self-disgust came uppermost in Jake's mind, Miss Murdoch's second novel is wilfully anarchic. The shifting of mood and tempo have here leaped into a violent disorder, and most chapters end on a mysterious hint. She has exchanged the examination of motives which occupied her attention in the first, to philosophical conjuring in the second.

The above are, in my view, the things that are displeasing about her first two novels. What I have not so far remarked upon is their rich comedy, their mature sense of pity, and, despite the magnification which she imposes upon every scene in order to ridicule or emphasise, the sure grasp of atmospheric detail in an extraordinary range of situations, *milieus* and characters. Further, having made all the above criticisms, there is one huge distinguishing characteristic, and that is the excellence of her writing. As became additionally clear in her third novel *The Sandcastle* (which I shall return to later), she is, in a universal sense a *good* writer. All her books give one the satisfying pleasure that only good writing can— the really authoritative use of words, the felicity of phrase, the meticulous style which does not at the same time mean a nervous limitation of ideas. This fundamental solid ability as a writer has been strangely little remarked upon. Her novels so far have been praised, but usually for their 'brilliance', 'wit', 'asperity', 'farce', 'gusto', 'originality', and so on. I do not remember seeing much attention paid to their accomplished *professionalism*. Although *Mr. Nicholas* is a better single novel—for its blade-straight intensity and the certainty with which every word slots exact as a brick into the structure—and although *Cards of Identity** is more devastating in its intellectual power, Miss Murdoch may prove to have the greatest potential of any of the post-war writers.

In none of these books is there any particular protest—not the assault upon literary conventions that is present in so many of the other first novels of the Fifties. From the start Miss Murdoch possessed urbanity, an assurance, and an already developed originality. Her professionalism may partly be due to the fact that when she published *Under The Net* she was thirty-five—which makes her not only a little older than most of the other first novelists of the Fifties, but, much more important, it puts one of her feet in a pre-war world that most of the others did not know as adults, or even as adolescents. It has given her much wider terms of reference. One reviewer of *The Flight From The Enchanter*—it was, if I remember correctly, Maurice Richardson in the *New Statesman*—complained that she was suffering from affectations caused by modern European influences and attitudes "which do not travel across the Channel". That seems to me to be unacceptable for two reasons. It takes the almost Kiplingesque view that behind the moat of the Channel our island race lives inviolate, immune from the neuroses and contingencies that panic the foreigners of those distant shores, an outlook that is in accord with neither NATO nor the fashion-market. Second, it admonishes one of the few newish writers who have a broader field of experience, and in consequence a more trustworthy scale of sensibility, because she puts it to use. Of course Iris Murdoch does display signs of having read Dostoievsky and Kafka (she has on a separate occasion been accused exactly of this). It is of interest that she alone of all the post-war writers I have talked to and corresponded with includes Sartre and Proust among her influences.

She was born in Dublin in 1919, daughter of Protestant Anglo-

*See page 139 *et. seq.*

Irish parents. Her father came of farming stock and was himself a Civil Servant. Miss Murdoch went from Badminton School, Bristol, to read classical Greats at Somerville College, Oxford. From 1942-44 she worked at the Treasury and then for UNRRA in London and abroad. In 1947 she returned to university, to Newnham College, Cambridge, on a philosophical studentship, and since 1948 has been a tutor and fellow of St. Anne's College, Oxford. Marie Scott-James in a review of one of her books remarked that there was a touch of "the detective-story writing don", and that is perhaps justified; but it can be seen that Miss Murdoch, who is now married to John Bayley, a don at New College, and also a novelist, has been outside the cloisters. She was a member of the Communist Party when a student and has since been "sporadically active" in the Labour Party.

This wider experience is evident especially in *Under The Net*. Although Jake appears superficially to conform to the post-war dissentient hero, the shiftless Earls Court prospector, he is altogether a profounder character. To begin with, he is in his mid-thirties. He is actually acquainted with *Murphy* and *Pierrot Mon Ami*, and does not, as Jim Dixon would, give an embarrassed howl of derision at the name of Beckett, or, at the thought not only of going abroad, but of actually lending an ear to European intellectual voices. His political outlook is flaccidly Labour—"English socialism is perfectly worthy, but it's not socialism. It's welfare capitalism." Lefty Todd, the Michael Footish aberrant left-winger hammers at him: "You call yourself a socialist, but you were brought up on Britannia rules the waves like the rest of them. You want to belong to a big show. That's why you're sorry you can't be a communist. But you can't be—and neither have you enough imagination to pull out of the other thing. So you feel hopeless. What you need is flexibility, flexibility!" And later: "What you need is to become involved."

That is the last thing Jake wants. He is "a connoisseur of solitude": he has always "travelled light" and he will not allow even easy money to encumber him too much. He has come to the point where he no longer expects to know a human being, except, with luck, "after one has realised the impossibility of knowledge and

101

renounced the desire for it and finally ceased to feel even the need of it. But then what one achieves is no longer knowledge, it is simply a kind of co-existence; and this too is one of the guises of love." Jake is the essentially true man that he is because he has seen through intellectual shams—"such intellectual work as I have ever accomplished has always left me with a sense of having achieved nothing . . . If one no longer feels in living contact with whatever thought the work contains, the thing seems at best dry and at worst stinking; and if one does still feel this contact the work is infected through it with the shifting emptiness of present thought." Yet the immense chasm that there is between him and the more typically Fiftyish Lucky Jim dissentient is that it never occurs to Jake that he is anything other than an intellectual—he quite naturally and instinctively takes the intellectual's stance on any problem, personal or universal—whereas his younger counterpart is so terrified of being identified as an intellectual that, like a stick insect, he tries his hardest to look like any of the dead wood he is at present attached to, with just his secret spitting and mockery.

Quite obviously Miss Murdoch read the criticisms of her second novel attentively, those warnings against wildness and metaphysical gymnastics, and in *The Sandcastle* she became circumspect and controlled. The fantasy is filleted, leaving just the occasional and effective sudden stab of symbolism. There is nothing obtrusively 'contemporary' about *The Sandcastle*—indeed, it is an almost historical pattern: the obsessive love of a middle-aged man for a young girl, and, for a very different reason, the girl's reciprocation. It is a plain, discerning account of the catastrophe of love, in this case the way in which it destroys the boring, mechanistic 'unhappiness' of the routine-ridden life of Bill Mor, the school teacher, his waspish, cold wife and his two teenage children, from whom he is as remote as a radar signal. In with the 'happiness' that seems to be invested in the person of a young girl painter come disruption, chaos and suffering. It is that not unprecedented scene—the domestic hell, home sweet home with the lid off. Again, although in this category I personally put *Mr. Nicholas* higher, *The Sandcastle* is unfolded with skill and integrity. Here, you feel, is one of the first of the post-war writers to be approaching an understanding and recognition of her own talent and resources, and—fortunate in having a wider perspective, something of that European outlook that most of her contemporaries have not—is able to write naturally, perceptively, of her own world without grafting on a few 'contemporary' fixtures and fittings. There is no deliberate rebellion, no 'anger', no crying havoc for the sake of having her voice heard, in the case of Miss Murdoch—she is of her time, receptive to its colours, smells and temperature, simply in the sense in which someone of distinct talent and sound reading should be sensitive to her surroundings, the 'instrument' of his age that any true writer must be. Miss Murdoch is one of the few of the new generation of writers whose work is integrated with the Fifties without being deliberately adjusted or copyist.

For, of course, originality of mind and inventive skill do not have perversely to oppose existing intellectual standards. There is another traditional pattern to be followed, the revolution from within, the extension of established literary values into the new territory that present-day moral and social pressures are opening up. Displaying a sharper sense of the artist's responsibility—and the very area in which his work lies—than many whose emotions are shriller but whose imagination is duller, Miss Murdoch seems to have reached a decision about how to tackle her job of writing novels, to have come to a state of *wholeheartedness* that is rare in this country at this time.

"If the books didn't sell I think I'd be a bear trainer," Ernest Hemingway remarked in an interview a few years back. "I like to wrestle with the bears." You do not have to be a romantic to the Hemingway degree to feel that there are too few of the British post-war writers we have so far looked at who are willing to wrestle with bears, that with a few exceptions there is a general flinching away from wrestling with any of the *real* problems, because of either an inability to recognise them for what they are in a world connotation, or because of a failure of spirit, a preference for non-participation.

103

John Osborne is tall and slender with wavy hair and a feminine, delicately horsey face (although Cecil Beaton in *The Face of the World* saw him as "a good-looking camel") which is given a satanic edge by an amused, malicious mouth. He dresses in a somewhat démodé foppish manner (hound's-tooth check 'sports' jackets and paisley scarf in open neck white shirt) which suggests the pink clean-limbed character who strides on at the start of British drama and cries: "Who's for tennis?"—an appearance that may indeed have been influenced by having spent eight years on the provincial rep stage portraying such chaps.

How does it come about that Osborne is not still playing these parts in Hull, Harrogate and points north? The events of 1956 are fairly well known. Until the evening of May 8 the name of John Osborne had no significance except to himself and presumably his family and friends. After that night, in his twenty-eighth year, it was a name that mattered and one that was to be increasingly inescapable in the coming months. Fame came of course as a result of *Look Back In Anger*, put on by the talent-fostering English Stage Company, and which had an instant kindling effect that for once justified that overworked newspaper jargon word bombshell.

The play was not unanimously liked by the critics but it went like electric treatment through their occupational curvature of the spine: they jerked upright in their seats and paid keen attention.

The *Times* kept its head. Like a housemaster the morning after the school Christmas production jotting down some comments designed to encourage the boys while at the same time keeping them in their place, it took the line of unmoved, faint interest.

"This first play," ran the notice, "has passages of good violent writing, but its total gesture is altogether inadequate. . . . The piece consists largely of angry tirades. The hero regards himself, and clearly is regarded by the author, as the spokesman for the younger post-war generation which looks round at the world and finds nothing right with it . . . it is easy to understand that his restless disgruntlement, expressed in set speeches of great length and ferocity, must sooner or later make the place too uncomfortable for his companions." It is interesting to note, incidentally, that in March last year, when the by then famous play returned to the Royal Court, the *Times* had warmed towards it. This time their nameless reviewer wrote: "Widely acclaimed as the most exciting play of last year, Mr. John Osborne's *Look Back In Anger* appears in revival very like *The Vortex*, which established Mr. Coward as the sympathetic voice of another post-war generation. It has the same air of desperate sincerity. The heroes of both plays are neurotics, but they suffer, and when an author can convey that suffering on the stage is genuine it matters not how thin-spirited the sufferer. We are moved."

Most papers and magazines were moved more than the *Times*. Tynan in the *Observer* cried: "It is a minor miracle . . . the best young play of its decade." Cecil Wilson of the *Daily Mail* did not greatly care for the play and was left "gasping for spiritual breath" by the "monologue of self-pity and unrighteous indignation", but he continued: "We can perceive what a brilliant play this young man will write when he has got this one out of his system and let a little sunshine into his soul."

T. C. Worsley in the *New Statesman* found it an imperfect play but "a most exciting one, abounding with life and vitality, and the life it deals with is life as it is lived at this very moment—not a common enough subject in the English theatre." He described

Osborne's mistakes of construction as "howling" and complained about the "cheat" of the "phoney reconciliation" at the end, but ended: "All the same, don't miss this play."

This was something of a send-off. But more important was the word-of-mouth *cachet* it collected—'all London' (meaning certain squares, streets and mews scattered between Ludgate Circus and the Old Brompton Road where reputations are given dry runs and then either rejected or promulgated) was talking about it, just as three weeks later *The Outsider* was the latest okay ploy for the gamesman. 'Everyone' was going to see *Look Back In Anger*.

Nor was this a mere passing fashion, quickly to be deserted. A year later, when it was revived, it was even more seriously assessed, and in the meantime it had been seen by a rush of audiences—long after the smart pacemakers had been and gone—all of which seemed to react violently, either in pshawing detestation of the bolshy young rotter who behaved so abominably to his wife, the colonel's daughter, or with a dizzy exaltation at all the lovely hate flying about. When it went on in New York last October a page and a bit was cleared in *Time* magazine (which does not lightly apportion that amount of space to one story) which, while issuing reproofs in its customary dental surgeon manner, did also employ such words as "brilliant", "dynamic", "witty" and "eloquent".

Almost precisely a year after *Look Back In Anger's* opening, Osborne's second play *The Entertainer,* with Sir Laurence Olivier in the leading part, was presented by the Royal Court Theatre on May 10, 1957. Although Cecil Wilson must have been disappointed that Osborne had not heeded his advice and admitted sunshine into his soul, the *Times,* ever attentive to prestige, allotted it ninety-eight lines (*Look Back In Anger* got forty-two). In the meantime Osborne's name had been drumming from all directions on the public ear, either as the subject of news stories and gossip paragraphs, or labelling articles which with great frequency he wrote, overcoming his repugnance for the Press, for a variety of publications. More often than not in these newspaper articles he let it be known that he loathed newspapers. His earnings from all sources (including newspapers) for that year have been estimated at £20,000.

It is a fairly lissom leap, from the National Assistance Board to money of that size. There is presumably some reason why in the Fifties a section of the British public heard Osborne's thrombotic, vituperative dialogue as a sort of battle-cry from the espresso barricades and paid him twice the nation's rate for the prime minister for voicing it. Let us then, look at what he has to say and decide exactly what manner of dissentience this is.

Osborne is romantic and sentimental about the Ordinary People. When you close in on that phrase and try to specify who exactly of the population of Great Britain have the standards of decency and honesty which Osborne finds sickeningly lacking in the sections of society he has thrashed so often, difficulties arise.

Certainly, to start with, Ordinary People are not the main interest in his plays, although the Huggett-like family in *Epitaph For George Dillon* is presumably an attempt at portraying the kind of working-class circle in which a nomadic theatrical finds himself temporarily billeted. But Jimmy Porter and Archie Rice could hardly be represented as a couple of typical post-war Britons, one a sadistic sweet-stall proprietor with university training, the other a boozy music-hall comedian with a public school background. Are Ordinary People, then, those whom he attracts to his plays? It seems not, for he has stated that his audiences are mostly "fashionable turnip-heads" who laugh in the wrong places and snigger when a character says "something particularly outspoken". He does not seem confident of being able, by mathematical analysis, to assemble a good muster of Ordinary People from the public at large, for while writing in defence of neurotic stage characters in the course of reviewing some Tennessee Williams plays in *The Observer* (January 1957), he remarked: ". . . one person in twenty in this country will at some time in his or her life enter a mental institution (and what are the other nineteen doing? Going to see *Salad Days*, I suppose). . . ." Nor is he moved by the virtues of kind-heartedness, grit and cheery industry which Ordinary People are supposed to possess in such generous proportions.

In the *News Chronicle* (February 27, 1957) Christopher Chat-

107

away wrote an anti-AYM article, in which he presented himself as A Very Satisfied Young Man and attacked the cult of passive despair. "A week ago," wrote Chataway, "I met a young man . . . distressed by the number of road accidents, he works as a voluntary male nurse in a hospital for ten hours every week. He is presumably in Jimmy Porter's eyes one of the 'wet'." In reply to this, two days later, Osborne said: "You end up like this: 'I know a young man, father of four children (*anybody who has four children must be decent. Everyone knows intellectuals are childless*). He isn't angry (*Good lad.*) He works as a male nurse for the criminally insane. He doesn't moan and whine.' Even if it is only nuts and bolts the ordinary I'm-Not-Angry-Young-Men are producing, their furious, ordinary activity makes them remarkable. *They* aren't complaining, *they* aren't making a fuss, *they* are pulling with the rest of us—and thank heavens, because it all helps to sell mass circulation newspapers." When in August last year I saw and talked to Osborne in Moscow where he was presenting *Look Back In Anger,* I did not get the impression that the sanctified 'ordinariness' of the Soviet system appealed much to him, either. In a *Daily Express* article in October 1956 he expressed his contempt for everyone who likes sport and gardening—"These two occupations add up to what is everything English, dull, puritan and useless." His phrase for the working population in an article he wrote in the *London Magazine* (April 1957) about the techniques of getting culture across, was "the monster in the ash can". He even distrusts any critic who has not lived in a street with outside lavatories, this inevitably being the source of "simple, unacknowledged ignorance" (*Declaration*), whatever that means.

Since Osborne seems to have sprayed most corners with his flitgun of scorn, where then is that gigantic amorphous mass of decency with which he witheringly compares all other attitudes and activities?

Despite his emotional attachment to a state of mind and heart that begins just round the next corner—to all those people who presumably have not seen, read or even heard of any of his plays—Osborne clearly has a genuine sense of affinity with working people, a sincere faith in the huge majority population who have no idea which is the smart pub to use, whose name they ought to be dropping at any particular moment, or what is currently endorsed table talk—the population who always use the usual local, who draw strength from family loyalties, and who have abiding, if rather rigidly limited, standards. That this is so comes through his *Declaration* contribution, "They Call It Cricket".

Nineteen of the twenty-two pages shrill and shake with overstated and, you begin to suspect, simulated indignation about snobbery, Royalty, etc., but for three pages near the end he switches to a personal note and talks about his own family and childhood. The difference is arresting and fascinating. After the rather boring pyrotechnics, a sort of neon-lit nag, there is the interlude of real writing, of true, warm recollection, with blood flowing through it, and love instead of spleen. It is worth quoting fairly fully. After mentioning that he and his mother lived on 22s 6d a week at one time, he continues:

"My mother's parents were publicans—to be accurate, they managed a succession of pubs in London—until my grandfather 'lost it all'. My mother has worked behind the bar most of her life. She still does because she likes to 'be with other people'. Her own mother, who is now eighty-four, retired a few years ago on a small pension from Woolworths . . . She is a tough, sly old Cockney, with a harsh, often cruel wit, who knows how to beat the bailiffs and the money-lenders which my grandfather managed to bring on to her. Almost every working day of her life, she has got up at five o'clock to go out to work, to walk down what has always seemed to me to be the most hideous and coldest street in London. Sometimes when I have walked with her, all young bones and shiver, she has grinned at me, her face blue with what I thought was cold. 'I never mind the cold—I like the wind in my face.' She'd put her head down, hold on to her hat and *push*.

"The whole family pushed, and whenever they got together for some celebration, there would be plenty to drink, however hard things were. That alone is something middle-class people find difficult to understand or forgive. As a small boy I would be given 'a little drop of port', and sit apprehensively always, while my grandfather told me about *The Bells* and bawled bits of the Bible at me. . . . I would sit flushed with port and embarrassment while he told me that he would live to see the day when I would be Prime Minister of England.

"During all this the rest of the family would be yelling news to each other. A lot of it would be about some illness or other. My grandmother would come in and out of the kitchen, usually picking the wrong moments to interrupt my grandfather. . . . Often if I could escape I would follow her into the scullery and get a slice of the 'dinner', some winks, and possibly some story about how my grandfather had spent a weekend with some famous music-hall artist at Brighton. . . .

"By dinner-time—which meant about two o'clock in the afternoon—the emotional temperature would be quite high. There would be baffling shrieks of laughter, yelling, ignoring, bawling, everyone trying to get his piece in. A big celebration would be the worst, like Christmas, when there was invariably a row. Sometimes there would be a really large gathering, and we would all go over to Tottenham, which was the family headquarters.

"Setting out from South London, it was an exciting journey. One never knew what might happen. There would be two or three dozen of us—somebody's brother would have a pint too many at the pub and perhaps hit his wife; carnation button-holes would be crumpled; there would be tears and lots and lots of noise. . . . They 'talked about their troubles' in a way that would embarrass my middle-class observer. I've no doubt that they were often boring, but life still had meaning for them. Even if they did get drunk and fight, they were responding; they were not defeated."

That reference to 'talking about their troubles' seems to me to have especial significance and to explain a great deal of the voluble candour, the characters tearing strips of skin from their chests, the firework emoting, that audiences fed on reticent mutterings through stiffened upper lips found 'indelicate' and embarrassing. It is further illuminating to learn of the class conflict that Osborne sensed from boyhood. He goes on to talk about how his mother's relations baffled his father's family. They came from South Wales, were middle-class, calm and quiet. Whatever arguments occurred were nearly always about income, and were characterised by gravity and long silences. They also had struck hard times, and Osborne's father had been used to wearing his cousin's cast-off Eton suits. But the point here is that it was an Eton suit world on that side of the family, and, although there had not been a cook or maid in the house since the first world war, assessments were made in the terms of Eton suits and houses with domestic staff.

"They were kind charming people," Osborne continues, "and I was deeply fond of them . . . they had a sense of fun which was as much a part of their assumption about life as their simple expectation that they should be waited on, that their children should go to public schools, that there should always be 'income'."

Osborne was born in Fulham in unsmart south-west London (but only a bus stop or two from the Royal Court Theatre in smart Sloane Square where his name exploded in star-shells) in 1930. His father was a commercial artist who died of tuberculosis when Osborne, an only child, was eleven. It was a childhood of furnished rooms in shabby side-streets and local LCC schools. His father's family stepped in, sent him to Belmont College, a boarding school, from which he was expelled at the age of sixteen for slapping the headmaster round the face, tit for tat.

*　　*　　*　　*

His formal education over, he decided to become a journalist and got a job on *The Gas World* for £2 5s a week, a mistake he quickly rectified by switching to acting and taking a child's rôle in a touring version of *No Room At The Inn*. The next ten years were a monotonous alternation of the dole and twice-nightly rep at about £2 a week, upon which he married (an actress named Pamela Lane, from whom he is now divorced; he married Mary Ure, who played Alison in *Look Back In Anger*, last autumn) in 1951. During this time he wrote five plays. His first, *The Devil Inside*, was produced at Huddersfield when he was nineteen, but no copy appears now to be extant. When success came in March 1956 it could not have been more total and such an extreme swing in situation.

111

Did *Look Back In Anger* and *The Entertainer* really arise out of a particular view of life—or directly out of old, deeply introspective, personal resentments? Were they really a diagnosis of a sick society and a recommendation for treatment—or one man's class confusions thrown open to the public like the trippers' weekend at a peer's stately home? And let me hasten to add that neither of those questions imply any criticism of the plays on that ground—they are put only to suggest that perhaps the reputation that the plays, and so Osborne, have gained—that of a one-man insurrection against the Establishment—may be based on a giant misconception. The look back in anger may be entirely a personal splurge of nostalgia which has enough application to enough people to have become thought of as a terrorist plot for de-stratifying classbound old Britain.

This may be the best place for going through both plays. The three acts of *Look Back In Anger* all take place in the Porters' flat in a big Midland town. It is a sleazy setting: hotchpotch, beat-up furniture in a cramped attic room. A skylight stares out on to emptiness. Jimmy Porter is described in the printed script as "a tall, thin young man of about twenty-five . . . He is a disconcerting mixture of sincerity and cheerful malice, of tenderness and freebooting cruelty, restless, importunate, full of pride, a combination which alienates the sensitive and insensitive alike. Blistering honesty, or apparent honesty, like his, makes few friends. To many he may seem sensitive to the point of vulgarity. To others, he is simply a loudmouth." And Osborne adds, with a fierce shot of insight: "To be as vehement as he is is to be almost noncommittal."

Despite Osborne's potted interpretation of Porter's personality, by his own words and acts the tenderness and cheerfulness are practically invisible: it is a consuming rancour which lights him up like a Christmas tree and which will probably give him a span of theatrical 'immortality'.

As the curtain rises Porter and his prole friend Cliff are sprawled in arm chairs reading the 'posh' Sunday papers. There is silence but for the dull thump of Alison's iron. Dressed in an elegant hobohemian fashion, hair cascading in languorous disorder, she drudges—that is the impression intended—at the ironing board. She is, we soon learn, better bred than he—she is turned in "a key of well-bred malaise", and we soon catch sight of her sickly abasement before her scorpion husband's poisonous tongue.

It is quickly obvious that the silence in the flat as the play opens is as unnatural as the quiet on the Western Front. Jimmy slings the paper aside and the creeping barrage of vituperation begins. First the papers, then Christianity, the English Sunday, the American Age, the upper classes, and his wife, are raked over with rapid fire.

In the course of the play we learn that Alison is a colonel's daughter, that Jimmy carried her off from her outraged parents on a metaphorical off-white charger, and that she has never been able to bring herself "to believe in him". Jimmy is out of what can now be seen to be a recognisable social cocktail shaker: his father, we gather, was a militant but rather ineffectual working-class left-wing idealist who got himself wounded in the Spanish Civil War, came home and died when Jimmy was ten. His mother is slightly 'better' socially, a snob and a climber. He went to a provincial university, played trumpet in and led a New Orleans jazz group after leaving (you don't 'come down' from Jimmy's university), tried journalism, advertising and (out of date symbol) selling vacuum cleaners, and is at present running a market sweet stall with Cliff, the good-humoured stooge and feed-man who almost (but not quite in the full sexual sense) makes up a *ménage à trois*. Jimmy at one point in his raging announces to Cliff, Alison and her actress friend Helena that he "may write a book about us all". Up to then and for the rest of the play there is never a hint of any creative impulse, for all we have seen is a destructive lamprey personality, siphoning up vitality from anyone within reach he can stun with his tongue and wrap his suckers around. However, tangentially he threatens them with a book. "It's all here," he says, slapping his forehead. "Written in flames a mile high."

So much for Porter's biography. On that mouldering Sunday afternoon Jimmy tries to inject a little kick into the general lethargy by shifting gear from generalised abuse to particular

113

venom about Alison's family in an endeavour to wrench a reaction from her—for it is her quiescence that drives him to an almost insane pitch of frustrated loathing.

"Nobody can be bothered. No one can raise themselves out of their delicious sloth," he says, half-seriously. ". . . Oh, heavens, how I long for a little ordinary enthusiasm. I want to hear a warm, thrilling voice cry out 'Hallelujah, I'm alive'. I've an idea. Why don't we have a little game? Let's pretend that we're human beings, and that we're actually alive . . . Nobody thinks, nobody cares. No beliefs, no convictions and no enthusiasm. Just another Sunday evening."

Cliff continues smoking and reading the papers. Alison continues ironing, Jimmy continues talking, veering from a eulogy about an ex-mistress named Madeline to taking Alison and her family to small pieces. Her brother Nigel is "the straight-backed chinless wonder from Sandhurst", "the platitude from outer space", who despite his vagueness is aware that "he and his pals have been plundering and fooling everybody for generations". Nor should anyone be fooled by the Marquess of Queensberry manners of Mummy and Daddy, he points out, for "they'll kick you in the groin while you're handing your hat to the maid". As for Alison, "this monument to non-attachment", she is scyophantic, phlegmatic and pusillanimous; he describes to Cliff what "a refined sort of butcher" she is at her dressing table at night, like "some dirty old Arab sticking his fingers into some mess of lamb fat and gristle"; in love-making she has the passion of a python—"she just devours me whole every time, as if I were some over-large rabbit. That's me. That bulge around her navel . . . Me, buried alive down there, and going mad, smothered in that peaceful looking coil. . . . You'd think that this indigestible mess would stir up some kind of tremor in those distended, overfed tripes—but not her! She'll go on sleeping and devouring until there's nothing left of me."

It can be seen that when Cliff tells Helena: "This has always been a battlefield . . . simply a very narrow strip of plain hell," he is not, within this context of melodrama. being melodramatic.

Alison also talks to Helena, her school friend, now a chic, tough actress, who comes to stay in the house while she is playing at the local Hippodrome, and for whom Jimmy professes an implacable enmity. Alison tells Helena how she came to marry Jimmy—he turned up at a party with bicycle oil over his dinner jacket, looking "young and frail". They married with no money, no jobs and no home. He took her to live in a friend's flat "over a warehouse in Poplar". The friend, Hugh, is an even more predatory class-hater than Jimmy, and says that England is finished—"all the old gang was back—Dame Alison's Mob, as he used to call it". Using Alison as the 'in', they spent their weekends raiding the enemy in W.1, S.W.1, S.W.3 and W.8—gatecrashing cocktail and house parties, plundering the privileged of their food, drink and dignity.

Osborne devotes some time at this juncture trying to whip up a sympathetic picture of Alison the bruised, genteel hostage, yet despite what sort of opinion you have by now formed of Jimmy, there is immediate *rapport* with him when later on he says, almost quietly for him: "I rage and shout my head off, and everyone thinks 'poor chap' or 'what an objectionable young man'. But that girl there can twist your arm off with her silence. I've sat in this chair in the dark for hours. And, although she knows I'm feeling as I feel now, she's turned over and gone to sleep."

There are other isolated places where Jimmy's hopeless unhappiness becomes clear and bleak, with the lather of hyperbolic torment wiped off, where he recalls sitting as a boy at the bedside of his dying father, and says: "You see, I learnt at an early age what it was to be angry—angry and helpless. And I can never forget it," where he says half-humorously: "There aren't any good, brave causes left. If the big bang does come, and we all get killed off, it won't be in aid of the old-fashioned, grand design. It'll just be for the Brave New-nothing-very-much thank-you. About as pointless and inglorious as stepping in front of a bus. No, there's nothing left for it, me boy, but to let yourself be butchered by the women."

He makes sure that any residue of sympathy from such momentary sincerities is drained off by snarling when he learns that Alison, "that cruel, stupid girl", is going to have a baby: "I don't care if it has two heads." The note Alison has left to say she is leaving him but will "always have a deep, loving need" of him makes him "puke": "Deep loving need! I never thought she was capable of being as phoney as that!"

Cliff also walks out on him. While Alison is away from the torture-chamber, Helena fills in as partner—it is a startingly effective start to Act III where Helena the seasoned doll is meekly domesticated at the ironing board, at exactly Alison's stance. But finally Alison returns, abased and wrecked, as he always wanted to see her, by a miscarriage, and Helena has a rush of conscience and takes off. There is a final scene where Alison is screaming her abjectness: "I want to be corrupt and futile! . . . Don't you see! I'm in the mud at last! I'm grovelling! I'm crawling!"

They are at last on the same wave-length. His sensitive set (Very High Frequency) picks up her vibrations and he opens up his fantasy to her. There have been earlier demonstrations of their private bed-whimsy: he is her bear ("Wheeeeeeeee! A really soooooooooooper, marvellous bear"); she is his squirrel ("Hoarding, nut-munching squirrel. With highly polished, gleaming fur, and an ostrich feather of a tail"). Now the bear hugs his squirrel and, regarding her with "a kind of mocking, tender irony", says that from now on they'll live on honey and nuts and lie in the sun, but they must look after each other: ". . . . we've got to be careful. There are cruel steel traps lying about everywhere, just waiting for rather mad, slightly satanic, and very timid little animals."

One major aspect of Jimmy's character I have not yet referred to—his atavism. He may rant: "Reason and Progress, the old firm, is selling out! . . . Those forgotten shares you had in the old traditions, the old beliefs are going up . . . There's going to be a change over. A new Board of Directors, who are going to see that the dividends are always attractive, and that they go to the right people," yet it gradually becomes apparent that Helena is being soberly accurate when she tells Alison almost at the end: "Do you know—I have discovered what is wrong with Jimmy? It's very simple really. He was born out of his time . . . There's no place for people like that any longer—in sex, or politics, or anything. That's why he's so futile . . . he thinks he's still in the middle of the French Revolution."

You already know that, because some of Jimmy's rare relaxations into tenderness, in a repining nostalgic way, have occurred when he has been alluding to the world he never knew—the Edwardian 'golden era' I talked about in Part One. Telling Cliff about Alison's father, Colonel Redfern, he struggles to sustain his contempt, but fails when he admits: "I think I can understand how her Daddy must have felt when he came back from India, after all those years away. The old Edwardian brigade do make their brief little world look pretty tempting. All home-made cakes and croquet, bright ideas, bright uniforms. . . ." He picks up his scourge again and adds: "What a romantic picture. Phoney, too, of course. It must have rained sometimes."

When I came to read the play I saw why Jimmy could hate Alison so intensely—because she was so consistently and fundamentally wrong about him that she could say, in innocence, to her father: "You're hurt because everything is changed. Jimmy is hurt because everything is the same."

That is flatly not the case with Jimmy. Jimmy is very mixed-up indeed on this point, because Jimmy's secret regret is that everything *isn't* the same, and his secret hero is Colonel Redfern and all the self-discipline, certainty and courteous gentleness that he despises *forte*, and, *pianissimo*, yearns for. Here is the curious paradox of Osborne's success. Apart from his spatchcock brilliance, as a playwright, he was instantly seized upon as the voice of the Dean-agers—Jimmy Porter was talked about as the personification of the thwarted threshings of a three-quarters educated post-war Briton who has seen a social revolution half take place and his own opportunities economically cut to about a quarter of what he hoped for. Jimmy Porter uses pungent present-day language, packed tight as a cartridge with explosive charge and no room for grace and concessions and fine meanings, yet for all his idiomatic jazz-cellar raciness he is much less of a modern man than Jim Dixon, or C. P. Snow's administrators, or even the real-life Colin Wilson. Covertly Jimmy Porter longs for the cultivation and the simple self-assurance of an obsolete class at which he must, because of his background and his training, overtly jeer.

He is, in fact, an anachronism not out of envy but out of regret

117

for a warmth that has gone from these chilly technological times, and is no more typical of this particular age than any other neurotic at any other time. Nor has John Osborne, as far as I know, ever said that he is supposed to be. I suspect that Jimmy's popularity as a folk-hero arose less from recognition of a widespread *social* plight, than from delight at encountering at last in the English theatre such vitriolic articulateness about fairly ageless states of mind. For essentially Jimmy Porter's neurosis is a sexual one which wraps itself up in class clothing, exactly the same love-hate conflict, the warring of desire against resentment that a woman, by apparently lying submissively on her back, can so humble and exhaust a man, that has been dealt with by such a broad range of minds that includes Strindberg, D. H. Lawrence and Thurber.

It is amazing in retrospect to see the wild shots that were loosed off during the period when everyone was theorising about Jimmy's predicament. He was variously described as an anarchist, a romantic, a defeatist, a rebel, a dreamer, a Hamlet, a schizophrenic, a Disorganisation Man, a moralist, an egotist, and, most unexpected of all, as a physical contortionist of exotic ingenuity (Mr. Graham T. Ackroyd wrote in an exulting letter to the *New Statesman:* "He eats. He defecates. He fornicates. It's all simultaneous.").

I would have said that there was far too much dredging around for meanings, for explanations, for the larger significance. I would have said that Osborne's intention was to put on the stage a portrait of a maladjust, a man who in the conditions of the times finds it impossible intellectually to work on more than one cylinder, and whose sexual energy is bottled up and festering within him.

What, I think, has never been emphatically enough remarked upon is what a louse Jimmy Porter is. I don't believe I am adopting any archaic inapplicable standards of bygone chivalry when I remark upon this: he seems to me, by all the patterns of agreement by which people associate with each other, to be unspeakable. I am not quarrelling with the contention that such people exist. Indeed they do, and we all probably know one or two, and there is every good argument for putting one, well-rounded and no pretences made, on the stage. But Osborne should not be hurt if this creation is identified and labelled for what he is.

I do not find myself perturbed by Jimmy's irreverence for the *status quo*, but I do abhor his unscrupulous use of principles he does not believe in, and world problems that don't touch him, to exploit his highly personalised gripes. I am not moved to indignation by the fact that it is a colonel's daughter he is torturing, but I do find his treatment of the human being she also happens to be offensive and obscene. I don't object to his railing against so much that is ridiculous in present-day Britain, the keeping-up-with-the-Thirties ritual, but I find boring his obsessional conviction that it is all arranged to spite him. I find it credible that two women should fall in love with this emotional lamprey because women do monotonously fall in love with such characters. I don't find it credible that Cliff, simple, affectionate oaf though he is supposed to be, would dedicate his devotion to him. For the Jimmy Porters destroy women but not usually men—men shy back from the fly-papers they dangle but upon which women so readily gum themselves up. When you detachedly list Jimmy Porter's cardinal characteristics, sadism, self-righteousness, hysteria, sentimentality, viciousness, immaturity and coldness, they sound like a quick summary of the type of character who would have found instant employment in Belsen.

Then why was there such a gasp of half-shocked, half-delighted acclaim when the play struck London? Because a great many of us incorporate the above characteristics, and occasionally we behave with all of them at the controls, and it was a great conscience-spree to see them acted out before our eyes in the most tearaway fashion imaginable—it was almost like an Oxford Group public confessional, with Jimmy Porter up there on the stage saying and doing it all for us, and we all came away feeling winged-ankled, purged of a great ballast of guilt.

I don't know what Osborne *intended* to do, but I doubt if it was entirely this. His character sketch at the beginning of the play containing words like "tenderness", "pride", "blistering honesty" and which are never—or for only the briefest divergence—supported in the event, indicates that perhaps Jimmy was originally foreseen in rather different proportions, perhaps as a person far more responsively adjustable to his surroundings and to events than one who drains the life-juices out of people to fuel his anger.

The overstatement that was an integral part of the play's excitement also blurred Osborne's judgment of what he was doing—and the audiences' critical faculty. I don't want to spend a lot of time discussing the play's construction, metabolism, etc., yet some of its more glaring oddities should be pointed out. Osborne has tetchily hit back at criticisms of the class incongruities and improbabilities in *Look Back In Anger*. "If I put a detail like that into a play," he said in "They Call It Cricket", referring to his grandmother being on a pension from Woolworths, "some bright social observer would be certain to wave me aside: 'One of its strange weaknesses is the apparent wrongness of its sociological facts. For example, one often found oneself wondering if the old woman wasn't merely an intellectual idea sketchily worked out rather than felt—that pension, surely we all know . . .' "

Osborne really cannot get away with that. He should know, and if he doesn't he has a long road ahead of him before he begins to understand the writer's job, that a play, or any imaginative work of art which is attempting to illuminate some area of life, must be far more circumspect and conservative about grotesque inconsistencies of detail than life itself, which is preposterously far-fetched. In other words, you might not be especially surprised to read of a real life Bishop whose mother still scrubs floors in Somerstown, who got to Eton on a scholarship, who temporarily left the church to fly as a non-commissioned tail gunner in a Wellington 1940-2, and whose agitator father was shot to death escaping from a Georgia chain-gang during the Depression. But if you were foolhardly enough to try to put that unusual character across in a play or a novel you would have to do the most elaborately subtle suggestion and groundwork before daring to introduce him.

Yet the Porter set-up is almost as extravagantly implausible. What are Jimmy and Alison doing in this Midland industrial town, since neither appears to belong there? Why is Jimmy running a sweet-stall, of all things? Why should Mummy have set detectives on him, just because she didn't think he was suitable for Alison? Why should Alison be slaving at an ironing-board like a Clifford Odets tenement woman?—I think it was J. B. Priestley who pointed out that a childless young woman, not out at work herself, need hardly occupy her weekends in this way.

These all seem to me to be melodramatic fudge, motiveless and arbitrary, which were impulsively brought in to compensate for the lack of tension in the play (for it is mostly a one-man spectacular), for the half-expectation of other people arriving which Osborne maintains, I suppose, half accidentally since their non-appearance certainly has no point in itself, and for his strictly disallowable end where, on no basis whatever, bear and squirrel plan their honeyed future.

There are gaping flaws in social sense, such as when Alison describes their pillaging of the rich, which is suspiciously like the country-house pirate raids carried out by Esmond Romilly, Churchill's Communist nephew, and his wife Decca, Lord Redesdale's daughter, from their Rotherhithe house, which Philip Toynbee recalled in *Friends Apart*. Apart from the fact that hardly anyone nowadays has house parties of the Thirties kind and that anyway the Porters would not have social access to them (an Indian Army background wouldn't carry much weight with a resuscitated Cliveden Set), this is entirely out of character. Jimmy Porter is no Esmond Romilly, politically or temperamentally, and he would not deliberately expose himself to a situation in which he might not be master.

Yet in a curious way Jimmy Porter's dissentience, his disgust and protest, are rooted in that Esmond Romilly period: sitting in his post-war left-bankish attic he snarls and sneers about conditions that were fundamentally blown-up in the Blitz and longs for a society that drowned in the mud at Ypres. It is all most odd, and when we are considering Osborne's present *enfant terrible* reputation as the younger generation's Wyatt Earp, always ready to fire from the hip, this subjectiveness in his characters must be examined—and we must take into account how similar is *The*

121

Entertainer in its redolences, in its backward-looking and in its sadness about vanished vigours.

The Entertainer was first presented at the Royal Court Theatre in April 1957 for a limited run, and then transferred to the Palace in September, with Laurence Olivier in the role of Archie Rice, returning there in January of this year.

Archie is a music-hall comedian, third-rate gagman in a ramshackle rock 'n' roll nude show, with a desperate mechanical line of patter that seems just a gasp short of a scream. "I 'ave a go, lady, don't I? I do 'ave a go." He is fiftyish, greying, jaunty, flash, randy, leering, hat on side of head, grin like the gash left by a tin-opener, bright dead eyes, always quick with the quip that can deflect any suspicion of seriousness of responsibility into another smutty cackle. As this is an Osborne play, however, it should not astonish to learn that he is no ordinary old pro. He has been to a public school—which may be the excuse for Sir Laurence's uneasy slithering between slangy Mayfair and what sounded like a Cockney trying to speak proper.

Immediately glaring at you is a similar bristling set of social incongruities and *non-sequiturs* similar to those of *Look Back In Anger,* and apparently shoved in just for the hell of it. Both the deadbeat loud-mouthed failure Archie and his courtly, rotund old bore of a father, both of whom have all the trappings of the pier-head troupers, old and new versions, are supposed to be products of a London public school. Archie jibes: "It produced one Field Marshal with strong Fascist tendencies, one Catholic poet who went bonkers and Archie Rice." But his father is intensely proud, both of spending "thousands of pounds" on Archie's education, and the fact that he himself "was educated at one of the finest schools in England".

Archie's brother is a rich barrister, his wife is a blowsy dull-wit who left school at twelve and who works (note this) at Woolworths on the electrical counter, his daughter is an art-teacher engaged to a bourgeois businessman and a bit of a progressive, his younger son is a tough womanising young sergeant who is murdered in the Canal Zone, his other son is a cocky, gabby conchie who stokes hospital boilers and sings 'cheeky' songs at the family booze-ups they like to have in the parlour. Their house is in the grubby outback of a seaside town, the other side of the shunting yards, where the trolley buses run and next to a gasometer and a fish and chip shop.

It is all perfectly possible, just as that Bishop is, and all a puzzlingly muddled premise from which to start commenting upon an entertainer and his family. The assumption is that Osborne means this microscosmically, that they are not just a bunch of seedy theatricals but an image of a society in putrescence.

The construction of the play is sketchy and whirrs along like a demented magic lantern, dropping the slides at uneven speeds, as a family scene is chopped up by Archie out there on the boards in the midst of his gruesome blue patter, which is a brilliant recreation of the bitter, hostile impudence that marks the music-hall bum.

But what is the 'story'? It clearly grew with real tenderness from Osborne's own knowledge and down-at-heel experience of the submerged stage (the dedication in *The Entertainer* is: "To A.C. who remembers what it was like, and will not forget it; who, I hope, will never let me forget it—not while there is still a Paradise Street and a Claypit Lane to go back to."). Osborne wanted to distil a bit of Paradise Street's thick and spicy essence (which you could probably bottle and sell like H.P. sauce) and make more widely known that curious rootless life of catching Sunday morning trains in the Potteries and smoking away corpse-coloured winter afternoons lying on beds in little cold rooms while the trams clank and screech over the cross-roads. Something else superimposed itself. When he was writing about Archie Rice Suez happened, and the closest post-war approximation to Munich pain, shame and fury swept Britain.

John Raymond in the *New Statesman* shrewdly pointed out that the violent emotion sparked off by *The Entertainer*, and its bitter image of selfishness and decadence gone cancerous, was the sight of audiences jeering cruelly at themselves—for despite the Trafalgar Square rallies and the good deal of individual disgust, the national feeling was as Raymond pointed out, of impotent rage that "the Wogs hadn't been smashed up". Upon the perennial hapless seediness of the touring pro, Osborne grafted the furious political atmosphere at the moment of Suez. And—more by luck than judgment again, you felt, or that might be an unfair interpretation of a natural dramatist's intuition—he struck exactly the right surly, sour defeatism with which the mid-Fifties Britain seethed, but this could not conceal the intrinsic bittiness and shapelessness of the play, with its spasmodic ravings, retchings of frustration, cynical self-seeking and, finally, the sudden exhaustion of whipped-up emotion.

It was a lack of cohesion, even a lack of sense, that I personally could not accept at the time. *Look Back In Anger* excited me on the evening, and it was later, when the branding iron's mark had cooled off, that I began to look back in criticism. *The Entertainer* did not have even that immediate collision upon my emotions. Despite a pyrotechnic piece of capering by Sir Laurence Olivier (but not the brilliantly flawless performance that some critics gasped about) it was altogether too bizarre a mixture of good and bad to be digested whole. It is recklessly original in its form, and through the mess of imbalanced snippets and lopsided development of characters, the nostalgia, bitterness, conflict and ecstasies of despair of the three generations of one washed-up British family comes an intense and vivid atmosphere. An atmosphere of what?

In the early scene there is old Billy, the derelict Edwardian, exactly voicing the sentiments which were at that time ringing plangently through hundreds of thousands of semi-detached sitting rooms: "What d'you make of all this business out in the Middle East?" he says to his grand-daughter Jean, not expecting or awaiting an answer. "People seem to be able to do what they like to us. Just what they like. I don't understand it. I really don't."

Genuine and germaine. But a few minutes later it becomes clear that Osborne intends Jean to represent youth in protest, militant Young England, for when Billy is ranting on about "people nowadays"—you can't tell which are women and which are men, not from the back—she remarks with startling irrelevancy: "Like the Government and the Opposition."

Billy, although violently abhorring those which, one begins to suspect, are Jean's political hopes, "the Left", nevertheless has great faith in her. "You'll *be* somebody"—she won't waste her life away. That exchange across the wide arid plains of age ends with the now increasingly familiar Osborne anguished cry for lost values. Rambling on through his gossipy good-old-daysing, Billy ends, softly: "I feel sorry for you people. You don't know what it's really like. You haven't lived, most of you. You've never known what it was like, you're all miserable really. You don't know what life can be like."

We are cut in here to Archie flogging away at his grubby act to, presumably, the holidaymaking "monster in the ash-can". He is singing a song, which, like most of his material, is a paean to self-preservation. Archie makes the old sentiment "F— you, Jack. I'm all right" sound like Hallelujah. This particular song begins:

> Why should I care?
> Why should I let it touch me!
> Why shouldn't I, sit down and try
> To let it pass over me?

Back to the Rice residence, where, joined by Phoebe, Archie's wife, Jean and Billy are tippling the gin Jean has brought. It is at this point that Jean's unhappiness is clarified—she has quarrelled with her fiancé and broken off her engagement. The reason?

"I went to the Rally in Trafalgar Square last Sunday . . . Because, Granddad, somehow—with a whole lot of other people, strange as it may seem—I managed to get myself steamed up about the way things were going."

Billy remarks: "Well, I should think you want your bloody head read!"

That, it appears, was Graham's (the fiancé) feeling, too. A bit gin-sozzled after a long emotional session about young Mick in the Army in Egypt and young Frank who refused to go, Jean concludes with this declamation: "We're all right, all of us. Nothing to worry about. *We're* all right. God save the Queen!"

Another interlude of Archie, grinding and nudging and rattling away, with another Hallelujah song which goes:

We're all out for good old number one,
Number one's the only one for me!
Good old England, you're my cup of tea,
But I don't want no drab equality.
A Union Jack unfurls behind him—
Those bits of red still on the map
We won't give up without a scrap. . . .
Number one's the only one for me.

We are returned to the sitting room, where Billy is back on the old wistful tack: "They were graceful, they had mystery and dignity then." Archie comes in from the theatre with a carrier bag of beer bottles, quoting Sterne and pretending he doesn't remember whether it was by him or George Robey (see Garnett Bowen in Amis's *I Like It Here* gulping with embarrassment when he inadvertently blurts out a quotation from *Childe Harold*). Like someone gyrating his arms to stop falling off the cliff-edge, Archie jokes and clowns frantically, even when he is told that Jean went to the Rally (which has begun to assume the significant overtones of the Reichstag fire). His death-defying act doesn't stop Phoebe interposing: "Oh, Christ, I wish I knew what was going to happen to us!"

She finds out next morning. Mick her son has been taken prisoner after shooting down a lot of wogs. During the next day when they are trying to find the courage to celebrate the assumption that Mick will be released and flown home, we learn a lot more about the private life of the Rice's—of Archie's systematic one-night stand affairs with the Nude Show girls, about Phoebe's stubborn clinging to her few rotten threads of happiness, about their individual guilts and purposelessness. Archie sums them up: "We're dead beat and down and outs," he says, with a savage complacency. "Why, we have problems that nobody's ever heard of, we're characters out of something that nobody believes in. We're something that people make jokes about, because we're so remote from the rest of ordinary everyday, human experience."

Certainly Osborne hammers home this feeling of being excluded from ordinary citizenship. "We'll try to be a little normal just for once, and pretend we're a happy, respectable decent family," says Archie; at the start of *Look Back In Anger* Jimmy Porter screams: "Why don't we have a little game? Let's pretend that we're human beings, and that we're actually alive."

In Act Two there is a febrile little boozy party, with Billy reminiscing about old variety digs and the singing of mock Kiplingesque patriotic songs, and Phoebe is given her sentimental moment of tremulous linnet-song. Archie remembers a coloured blues-singer in an American honkytonk and says with a fervour that doesn't communicate to me: ". . . to see that old black whore singing her heart out to the whole world, you knew somehow in your heart that it didn't matter how much you kick people, the real people, how much you despise them, if they can stand up and make a pure, just natural noise like that, there's nothing wrong with them, only with everybody else . . . Better than all your getting on with the job without making a fuss and all that, or doing something constructive and all that, all your rallies in Trafalgar Square!" Then he goes on to tell Jean that it's no good her being a sentimentalist—"you'll have to sit on your hands like everyone else". He gets drunker and more garrulous. "I don't feel a thing, and neither do they" (the apathetic monsters who pay to see his collapsing show). "We're just as dead as each other. . . . Nothing really touches me."

Then in comes Frank to say that the Egyptians have killed his brother. Earlier, in the middle of the celebration party, he had broken off into an odd trembling tirade: "Can you think of any good reason for staying in this cosy little corner of Europe? . . . You'd better start thinking about number one, Jeannie, because nobody else is going to do it for you . . . They're all so busy, speeding down the middle of the road together, not giving a damn where they're going, as long as they're in the middle. *The rotten bastards!*" Now, it all seems to have become doubly true for Frank, and perhaps for them all.

The last act begins with a song that was deleted from the play when it was transferred to the West End. According to Tanfield's Diary in the *Daily Mail* the lines were booed, as well as cheered, when it first went on at the Royal Court Theatre, and upon hearing that it was to be cut out Osborne said: "Cuts cannot be made without my approval and I resisted. I was forced to give in. I don't understand the objections."

Nor do I, really. It is a lament sung by Frank for the dead Mick, and goes:

> Bring back his body and bury it in England . . .
> Those playing fields of Eton
> Have really got us beaten
> But it ain't no use a-grievin'
> 'Cos it's Britain we believe in . . .

Which does not seem to be especially treasonable or seditious, only rather vapid.

The family are gathered for the funeral, edgy, masochistically forlorn and with all hopes and standards relinquished. Jean turns on her father—he's "two pennorth of nothing", and Archie agrees: "Yes, I should say that sums me up pretty well."

Then Jean, standing looking upward like Joan of Arc on the bonfire: "You don't need to look at me! I've lost a brother too. Why do people like us sit here, and just lap it all up, why do boys die, or stoke boilers, why do we pick up these things, what are we hoping to get out of it, what's it all in aid of—is it really just for the sake of a gloved hand waving at you from a golden coach?"

And when she learns that Archie is preparing to shove his aged father back on to the boards to shore up his show and save himself from bankruptcy and jail, she is horrified: "Are you going to destroy that too? He's the only one of us who has any dignity or respect for himself . . . and you're going to murder him."

In next to no time Billy is dead, and on the stage is a coffin draped with a Union Jack. Jean is trying to explain to Graham, her ex-fiancé who has just panted into the play in the last five minutes to try to win her back, why there is a vast incompatibility between them. "Have you ever got on a railway train here, got on a train from Birmingham to West Hartlepool?" she asks him. "Or gone from Manchester to Warrington or Widnes? And you get out, you go down the street, and on one side maybe is a chemical works, and on the other side is the railway goods yard.

Some kids are playing in the street, and you walk up to some woman standing on her doorstep. It isn't a doorstep really because you can walk straight from the street into her front room. What can you say to her? What real piece of information, what message can you give to her? Do you say: 'Madam, d'you know that Jesus died on the Cross for you?'."

That has a frightful stench of phoniness about it, just words trying to inflate themselves into significant Statements, yet I can't somehow entirely blame Osborne. Of course he invented this mawkish hot-making girl, yet on the other hand you feel that he's rather saddled with her and with a sort of desperate piece of bravura like a V.C. infantryman stubbornly advancing under thick crossfire of banalities, he finishes Jean off with this: "Here we are, we're alone in the universe, there's no God, it just seems that it all began by something as simple as sunlight striking on a piece of rock. And here we are. We've only got ourselves. Somehow, we've just got to make a go of it. *We've only ourselves.*"

There, in the end, is Archie, nobbled at last by the income-tax man, turning down his rich brother's offer of a ticket to Canada although he knows the alternative is prison, pumping out his last act. The Britannia tableau is behind him. "What about *her*, eh— Madam with the helmet on? I reckon she's sagging a bit, if you ask me. She needs some beef putting into her—the roast beef of old England."

Voice cracked and tired, face like lard, his valediction is: "Life's funny though, isn't it? It is—life's funny. It's like sucking a sweet with the wrapper on," for the one thing you can say about Archie Rice, one of the hollow men though he is, is that he is never quite defeated.

The total upshot of *The Entertainer* is Frank's shrill, incoherent shout of rage against authority: *"The rotten bastards!"* You have to take it step by step in the above way to see the full range of its self-bafflement. It is a network of alarm bells shrilling throughout an empty building, all connected to the same circuit but none within earshot of the other. It is full of theatrical jabs to the ribs, biting dialogue and moments of splendid hostility suddenly towering which show Osborne's erratic but occasionally profound

E

understanding of the human heart—such as the scene where an absurd row flares up over Billy eating the cake that Phoebe was keeping for Mick's return.

Those things are real and recognisable, yet they are nuggets in a mishmash of undeveloping tritenesses, a display of emotional flagellation with Osborne indiscriminately heaping in his social prejudices regardless of whether they fit the characters or not. Intrinsically, like *Look Back In Anger*, *The Entertainer* has no statement to make—only the intention that he has made plainly known, to make people feel.

In a variety of places he has advertised his socialist politics and his emotion-rousing purpose. In a *Sunday Times* profile Siriol Hugh Jones quoted him: "Tory is still the rudest four-letter word I know." In the midst of an *Observer* book review he declared his loathing of "the milk-in-first and phlegm boys", the disengaged playgoers who believe "that suffering is some form of inferiority . . . that protest is vulgar, and to be articulate is to be sorry for oneself". In a talk at the Arts Theatre Club he said: "I don't like the kind of society in this country in which I am living." In a *News Chronicle* article he wrote: "A man who is indifferent to his own pain and sorrow is nearly always indifferent to the pain and sorrow of others. And for a very good reason—he can't feel. This is part of our sickness. We can't feel." In an interview with Jeffrey Blyth, *Daily Mail* New York man, about his chastisement of the Royal family in *Declaration*, he said: "All I set out to do is to say what people are thinking . . . I want to make people feel." And in the *Declaration* piece itself he said: "I want to make people feel, to give them lessons in feeling. *They can think afterwards*. In some countries this could be a dangerous approach, but there seems little danger of people feeling too much—at least not in England as I am writing." (My italics.)

As he was writing, or at least just a few months later, the Russians put a dog named Little Lemon into an artificial satellite and despatched it into space. Within a few minutes of the news release in Britain that Little Lemon was whizzing overhead in its test-tube kennel even Osborne must have been satisfied by the eruption of feeling. The Soviet Embassy came under withering fire from telephone callers, a Canine Defence League delegation arrived in person, the R.S.P.C.A. roared into action like a red-eyed Patience Strong, and every newspaper office in the land was bombarded with letters full of anguish, wrath and Russian devilry. Slave-labour, the Russo-German pact double-cross, the general routine murder, inhumanity and lying that is one documented aspect of the Communist regime—all that combined has never aroused a flicker of indignation or distress comparable with the wave of perturbation that swept through our doggy nation. Even that conscientiously crusty *Daily Mirror* columnist Cassandra, the Captain Hook of Fleet Street, burst into angry tears and published a black-edged In Memoriam notice for Little Lemon.

Had the British Government wanted to go to war with the Soviet Union there has never been a more propitious moment when public sentiment would have probably been at the right heat for immediately despatching a squadron of H-bombers to liquidate the nation of dog-haters. (It is instructive, incidentally, that some weeks later a Soviet Embassy official, chatting with a journalist at an Embassy cocktail party, could not believe that it was all a spontaneous upsurge of indignation, but took it for granted that it was a cunning plot organised by Mr. Macmillan.)

I do not wish to disparage a love for animals, merely to suggest that all the above disproportionate distress, first, hardly supports Osborne's charge that the British "can't feel", and, second, seems to me to illustrate the dangerous excesses of absurdity that are the outcome of 'feeling'. That was 'feeling' at its most preposterous, but I can hardly believe that even Osborne was disappointed with the intense emotional reaction to Suez, when the country was cleft in two (and the political parties as well) by a grave moral issue.

Osborne's kind of dissentience is, as he loudly and challengingly declares, all emotive, a truculent foot-stamping. Worst of all, it seems to me to be retrogressive and menacing, a campaign for returning to the impulsive reactions of childhood. When it is more imperative than any other time in history to emphasise and encourage the importance of individual thinking—because there have never been rampaging at large such persuasive mass techniques for obliterating both individualism and private thought— Osborne and his sympathisers begin campaigning for 'feeling'. "Give 'em hell, Mr. Osborne!" cried James Cameron in a *News Chronicle* review of *Declaration*—although he did amplify: "If John Osborne can make his customers feel, good luck to him because if they feel enough it may stimulate their curiosity and when they start investigating the roots of their dilemma they will in all probability be even angrier than he." Cameron took it an important step further than Osborne seems interested in doing, for the essential incongruity in his emoting is that this is done under the banner of socialism—a plea for the aphrodisiac approach, the weathercock swing to the newest stimulant to the senses, precisely the condition of mindless mob response that enabled Hitler to gain power in the Thirties, and why the dictator state has become the most powerful paradox of this century of enlightenment.

This simplified blood-and-soil socialism of the 'Method' leftwingers strikes me as fairly alarming. The fact that Osborne's plays sparked such a violent response shows that there is a considerable hunger for 'inspiration'. There is evidently a group forming up among the anti-intellectual intelligentsia—if *Declaration* can be relied upon, and it sold the astonishing total of twentyfive thousand copies in the first three months.

Among the contributions to that polyglot production are two others that unite with Osborneism. In a piece entitled "Theatre and Living", Tynan writes a modern digest of Robert Blatchford Merrie Englandism in which his customary cutting edge seems to have become blunted by the tough fibrous quality of some of the boloney therein. I do not mean to be rude about his trenchant demand for plays that "affirm candour, valour, grace and sensuality", for enthusiasms, because "fear of ebullience is a great enemy of our culture: it freezes the pipes". Well, yes. But when he goes into emotional overdrive with this: "I ask for a society where people care more for what you have learned than for where you learned it; where people who think and people who work can share common assumptions and discuss them in the same idiom; where art connects instead of separating people; where people feel, as in that new Salinger story ["Zooey", by J. D. Salinger, which appeared in the *New Yorker* last year], that every fat woman on earth is Jesus Christ; and where those who carry the torch of freedom are never asked to run with it into the ammunition dump", you see that you are accidentally overhearing an inter-university debate, for, as I suspect Tynan knows, this is just gaseous phrase-fashioning. Of course that is society as we would like it to be, but, as should be obvious to anyone who has become adult in the post-war world, it is not a society that can be legislated into existence. What is utterly absent from this, and other, cries for liberty, equality and fraternity is the slightest interest in or knowledge of the actual political situations that hem us in today and the actual processes of government by which they must be solved. Far from assisting the cause to which he is pledged, this seems to me to be political filibustering.

Declaration has worse in wait. A few pages on is a hectoring effusion by Lindsay Anderson, a film-maker, and sympathy altogether dries up at this beating of the left breast. This is entitled "Get Out And Push". After a lead in about the way things like nannies and Noel Coward simply make him throw up, he then prances forward and slaps the checks of lots of people he thinks haven't enough contact with the workers, calls Amis a coward, Wain an empty-headed avuncular Tory, and Colin Wilson jejune.

This is a queer but predictable performance—Anderson's voice grinding away like a tumbril, denouncing the Britain that is still rotten with class distinctions, and carefully dropping in (as proof of his inside information, being the most charitable explanation) that he is upper middle class, public school, sired by an Army officer, and so on, after which he proceeds to subpoena George Orwell for evidence against Amis for "conforming to the pattern of snobbishness and pusillanimity".

Anderson makes documentary films and, staunchly uninfluenced by the fact that he also has made *The Adventures of Robin Hood* for Independent Television, here denounces the British cinema industry as commercial and corrupt. He recently

133

did a film about Covent Garden. It was dedicated to "Jim, Bert, Les, Peg and Iris, whose muscles. . . ." or something of that sort. It purported to show the *people*, living-labouring-loving style, who are the weft of a complex bit of industrial machinery for supplying a huge metropolis with its daily fruit and vegetables. The film showed nothing of the sort. It was a 'lyrical' sequence of artfully composed shots of horny hands passing boxes to other horny hands, lingering close-ups of seamed faces, laceworks of spuds and filigrees of artichokes, all interlaced with a cute, jaunty-cockney tune. Nowhere was there the nuance of a hint that this casbah of stalls and barrows and lorries is where four-letter words crackle in the air and strikes happen and where it's filthily blue-nosed cold most of the working hours.

This phoney idealisation, this bogus 'common man' identification done in a corduroy cap and with a private income; is exactly the sort of 'sincerity' Orwell loathed, for it has all the stink of that guilt-ridden period of cocktail party Communists and Mass Observation Balliol men with an uneasy 'pleb' accent. It is conformist play-acting as drearily dated and with about as much application to the present predicament as *East Lynne*.

Here is Anderson talking about the people he got to take part in his Covent Garden film: "Those good and friendly faces deserve a place of pride on the screens of their country; and I will fight for the notion of a community which will give it to them." It is this patronising, sentimental guff, at the same time old-fashioned and pretentious, that turns away many men of goodwill, queasy with disgust, from Labour. It misappropriates enduring ideals and invalidates them by pretending that they are attainable in this hideously complex age by Sankey and Moody fundamentalism. Perhaps Anderson has been infected by his *Robin Hood* scripts, for he shows no understanding of the fact that primitive rob-the-rich-to-help-the-poor policies make no sense, and have no relevant appeal, in the People's Capitalism that the western world is opting for. There have been ominous warnings that Colin Wilson and his associates are preparing a mystical fascism, and I shall be discussing that later. It is such as Anderson and the 'Method' leftists, the romantic reactionaries of radicalism, who bear heavy responsibility for the arrival of the Outsiders. If that turns out to be something to be sorry about, remember who helped to bring it about—the bleeding hearts who wanted everyone to "feel", not think their way out of our troubles.

So, bleeding most profusely of all, yet certainly not an idealogical slummer like Anderson, here is Osborne in his worst piece of writing yet. "They Call It Cricket" is mostly a tirade against the Royal symbol—"the gold filling in a mouthful of decay". This came right in the middle of last year's flurry and fuss, when there was panic in Angela Thirkell circles at what seemed the imminent institution of a republic, when, apart from Malcolm Muggeridge, one peer after another was reneging. There are some powerfully pertinent observations in Osborne's piece, such as: "While the cross symbol represented *values*, the crown simply represents a *substitute* for values"; "Is no one aghast at the thought of a lifetime of reading about the first day at prep school, the measles, the first dance, the wedding, and finally the beauty of *the* ceremonial?"; and "There has never been one outstanding moral issue on which the Church has taken a firm, unequivocal stand for simple, social decency, let alone for the Gospel".

Unfortunately, apart from the final, rather moving, reminiscences of his childhood, recalled with tenderness and amusement (and which I talked about earlier), the above sentences are prised out of a coagulated mass of volcanic lava. This is a personal demonstration of how to 'feel'—strident, flushed, violent and clouded with a sort of blood-mist before the eyes. And out of it all, out of his demolition of the whole Royalty system, is not one constructive proposal. When the *Daily Mail* American correspondent brought up this very point with Osborne—what should take the place of a monarchy?—he replied: "I don't pretend to offer a solution or an alternative. If we create a void something will fill it."

No doubt, and that seems to me about as sensible and honest as the conduct of the Communists in the Spanish Civil War who were devoting their time to internecine back-stabbing the anarchists and liberals, while the Franco forces proceeded to win the war.

135

Let's beat our way out of the froth of the Feel First contingent and bring in their villains for identification parade. The Queen, Sir William Haley, Ephraim Hardcastle, J. Arthur Rank, Wing Commander Douglas Bader, Noel Coward, Lord Hailsham, Cyril Connolly, John Lehmann, Evelyn Waugh, Nancy Mitford, Arthur Koestler and the headmaster of Eton—these are the enemies of the people and we are supposed to take them seriously, to react as Winston Smith and the Ministry of Truth staff had to each morning at the Two Minutes Hate in which Goldstein, the party traitor, was ritualistically execrated. This assembly is presented as the secret Establishment high command that is, with suave and sinister adroitness, conducting Britain to the knacker's yard. Emotionalism can be seen to be not enough: perhaps, after all, a better tenet is to think as well as feel. My personal view is that pleasantly melodramatic though the Feel First policy is, it does not accord with the present day facts of life. I think it was Paul Johnson who wrote somewhere that it is a mistake to suppose that the modern state resembles a prehistoric monster with huge body and tiny brain—for actually it has no brain at all, merely a public opinion poll. That seems to me to be nearer the truth.

Nevertheless the mood that Osborne crystallised continues to exist and he continues to exploit it. This activity extends, incidentally, into rather novel fields of journalism. Quietly confident that the "cheap jacks" and "bribed gossip mongers" of Fleet Street cannot contaminate him, he has in recent months, among other free-lance activities, appeared in *Lilliput* and in *Woman and Beauty*. For *Lilliput* he accepted the invitation extended to "eight headline men to make their Choice of the Season" and chose a Connock and Lockie Norfolk jacket which was bought for him and photographed in the December issue. *Woman and Beauty* put a question to him. "We are women of an era terrifying in many ways for its speed and progress," it stated bafflingly. "How do we compare with women of other, more gracious eras?" In his five-hundred-word reply Osborne kept his emotions under splendid control and did not reiterate the statement made earlier (about the Baby Doll type of American man-eating girl) in a more sophisticated publication that "the female must come toppling down to where she should be—on her back". Instead he displayed a flexible skill at winning ways: "I like today's woman because of her wide-eyed and generally genuine interest in so many things . . . But I don't like a too-knowledgeable woman— I feel it is against her sex . . . Let's finally say I do admire today's woman."

Interest in Osborneism is in the main serious and intense. It was enlightening to study the letters that, week after week, followed the publication of an article by Christopher Hollis entitled "Keeping Up With The Rices" in *The Spectator* last October. Hollis, after combing through *Look Back In Anger* and *The Entertainer,* methodically listed the things the Angry Young Men *aren't* angry about. Upon the verbal evidence of the plays, he pointed out, they are not protesting about war, economic conditions, Communism or anti-Communism, or even the H-bomb, for "the mood is, indeed, that such a destruction would be welcomed rather than the reverse. For it is against the universe that the plays are in revolt." The conclusion Hollis came to was: "Like Harriet Martineau before him, Mr. Osborne must first 'accept the universe'. As Carlyle would have put it, 'Gad, he'd better'."

The correspondence started the following week with a letter from William Donaldson, a Magdalene undergraduate and editor of *Gemini* (Winchester, private income and U-class) pronouncing "Keeping Up With The Rices" as "exceptionally silly", and, after declaring his allegiance to everyone in *Declaration* except the Wilson triumvirate, listed the reasons why young men are angry today: "They are angry because England is still riddled with class-consciousness, because the Establishment still rules, because the English upper and middle classes tend to be ignorant, insensitive philistines, because English films are ghastly, because the English theatre means *The Reluctant Debutante* and *Dry Rot,* because the Conservative Government is ineffectual if not actually dangerous, because the English Elite, who should after all be educated would rather read the *Tatler* than the *Spectator,* and because the attitude of the English towards such venerated traditions as Royalty, the Archbishop of Canterbury, the BBC, etc., is unhealthy and in every way sickening." Donaldson ended by hinting that Oxford and Cambridge are on fire with such feelings.

In the following issue a Cambridge man, Hugh Davidson of Corpus Christi, seemed not to have noticed the blaze and expressed astonishment at Donaldson's claim that the two universities were packed with Angry Young Men, as he "always thought that Oxford and Cambridge were one of the things the Angry Young Men were angry about". Another correspondent remarked that he feared Donaldson's catalogue would reinforce the view that "the discontents of many younger writers are without direction or logic, and that they are only 'harmlessly' 'letting off steam', etc.".

From the Special Forces Club came the next instalment. "Surely no one but a myopic moron can fail to see that there is a sickness in this country," wrote a supporter of Donaldson, "spiritually, morally and aesthetically." He added that how it was to be cured was not yet known, but a diagnosis had been made. Finally there came a letter from the East End, from a grammar school boy with a war-time childhood, affiliating himself with *Declaration* and putting forward a sizable explanation of it all: "Won't a psychologist come forward and attempt to explain the effect on children of growing up with a war?" he asked. "Later in life they become hypersensitive."

The most hypersensitive of them all, and the begetter of the controversy, did not obtrude his opinion. Osborne remained silent after his last brush with the *Spectator* when he was interviewed at home by Robert Hancock. Hancock described him as the Ruby Murray of the British legitimate theatre—"most critics of both artists can tell you how terrible their act is. Few can explain why it so successful and profitable," and pointed out that *Look Back In Anger* had been translated into nearly every European language, been seen by five millions on commercial TV and was then to be filmed in England, produced on Broadway and presented in Moscow.

Osborne wrote to *The Spectator* protesting at Hancock's article, which had contained a description of the possessions of Mary Ure (who was not at that stage his wife) scattered about his flat. "That's the trouble with journalists; you want to tie a label round any-

138

thing," he had rebuked Hancock, and this is one of the minor puzzles about Osborne. He is always hair-triggered in his detestation of journalists and newspapers, which may be partly due to having worked on the *Gas World* as a youth, partly to having had to put up with some galumphing dramatic criticism when he was plodding around the provinces in rep. He advances his especial hatred at the use of the phrase Angry Young Man. It was with interest that I noticed, reading through his contributions to the British press, how regularly he has gratuitously dragged in the phrase himself. He found Angry Young Men in Moscow; he decided that Vladimir Dudintsev, author of the novel *Not By Bread Alone*, was an Angry Young Man when he reviewed it in *Books And Art*; and he never misses a trick in interviews, wherein by abusing journalists for using the phrase he is enabled to employ it. (In the twenty-two pages of "They Call It Cricket" there were thirteen separate jibes at journalists, ranging from "bribed gossip mongers" to "the journalistic stunt of the Angry Young Man business".)

The real injustice that has been committed against Osborne is in attributing too much significance, too many overtones, to what he has done. Excluding his quick-turnover journalism he has had three plays produced, all of which are distinguished for their electrifying language and their trapping of a current sense of apoplectic futility, but none of which pretends to define or solve, or even state, man's dilemma at this particular point in history. I do not think Osborne has so far had the sort of conscious intentions that writers such as Beckett, Brecht, Camus and Sartre have evolved for themselves and by which all their work abides. It is unfair either to criticise his productions by those standards or wring from them meanings they have never possessed. All the same, Osborne must accept the situation in which he finds himself—that he has the ear of a generation and, having stirred up their feelings far more excitingly than he could ever have dreamed he would do, he cannot resign from the job and leave it to others to "fill the void". Or at least, he can—but that is an abnegation of a writer's responsibility, the kind of sly artistic titilation without orgasm that belongs more to the *Silk Stockings* magazine or a strip-tease show than to the legitimate stage. But a deepening in the understanding of the problems and internal lives of real people, not espresso buccaneers or symbolic working-class heroines, an increase in compassion and a disciplining of sentimentality, a better sense of perspective and less involvement in momentary convulsions of frustration, a maturing in his present opinion that accusations do not artistically need implicit recommendations—in fact what can be summed up as a moral attitude—all this may begin to emerge in his next play or the one after.

In the meantime I suspect that we are in for a phase of the more luridly callow aspects of Osborneism. This is going to be dissent in its most simplified, destructive and naïve form. As I write I can almost hear the orchestra of typewriter keys, a symphony of clicking fervour sounding from London to Dublin to Newcastle-on-Tyne, along all the chains of suburban roads and basement flats, as the manuscripts smoking with protest roll off the portables. It has been too soon yet to see much of the new dissentience, but I think the shoulder-shrugging, grimacing, thick-ear provincial novel, which followed on Amis and Wain, is losing popularity.

There have already been minor emotional spasms. One came promptly after the *Look Back In Anger* stir, a play entitled *Don't Destroy Me* by Michael Hastings, which was put on at the New Lindsay Theatre in August 1956. In June last year the English Stage Company, pursuing its new voices policy, produced his second play *Yes—And After*. A few months later he published a novel *The Game*.

The only reason for drawing attention to these works is that Hastings was projected at just about the same time as Tommy Steele and other golden calves of the rock and skiffle underworld, when James Dean had just killed himself in his Porsche and was busily being converted into a legend by the studio publicity boys, and the crazy mixed-up kid cult was at its vibrant pinnacle. Hastings had the vital ingredient: he was a teen-ager. The news that he was an eighteen-year-old East End tailor's cutter invaded even the solemn columns in the journals which would not normally mention that Terence Rattigan is a forty-six-year-old or that

William Shakespeare was a Stratford-upon-Avon butcher's son. Soon after his first production, Hastings was given an Arts Council grant, took off for New York and made William Hickey by taking a millionaire's daughter on the town.

Solely on the merits of his so-far published work it is difficult to see why any of the above events should have taken place. He published some poetry in a review named *Nimbus* when fourteen. *Don't Destroy Me* is dedicated to James Dean and deals with a sixteen-year-old confused boy in a Jewish Brixton boarding house whom I recall rolling his head against a wall while striving to articulate some not over-complicated thought, such as "Do you live upstairs?" to the waif girl who does, and which is in general feeble in emotion and tortuous in execution. *Yes—And After* concerns a South London policeman's thirteen-year-old mentally retarded daughter who has been raped and who recalls the experience in hyperbolic spirals of fear and exultation. *The Game* is told in the first person by a fourteen-year-old epileptic Jamaican living in the wasteland of the inner London suburbs, and is an episodic, formless book, a shallow mixture of flat plodding writing and whirling fits of poetising.

All these writings bottle up the spirit of frustrated, glum adolescence, exactly the lowering leather-jacketed look which Dean raised from the sulks into an art-form. The trouble is that there is no reason in any of them to change one's mind that an adolescent is not necessarily the best interpreter of adolescence. The reason why Raymond Radiguet, Thomas Chatterton and even Françoise Sagan were published is not because they were teen-agers but because despite their youth they had a fulfilled experience to communicate and the mastery of words with which to do it. The reason, one suspects, why Hastings, Jane Gaskell and Berthe Grimault have been published in the past year or two is because in a full-employment economy, with a vast monied juvenile market, youth is cultivated, flattered and pampered, and bestowed with a glamour it has never previously had. Lack of years carries a *cachet* whether you are drumming hell out of a mistuned guitar, writing a novel or just acting the jean-ager behind the bamboo curtain in your local *capuccino* shebeen (the one

141

exception in the pestilence of premature books is Kenneth Martin's *Aubade,* published last November, which despite its imperfections and tiny arena has an intense truthfulness).

That is not necessarily alleging that these ultra-young of the youth brigade cannot write, and in particular Hastings may turn out to have genuine ability beyond his present rather fey flair for presenting incoherence without a coherent understanding of it. What is so regrettable about this fashion of the Fifties for publicising those whose bones are barely set is that it does the writers themselves so much harm. There is nothing unique, not even new, in young people writing. Almost every professional writer has made his first attempts at poetry or a novel or a play, or at least keeping an intimate journal, in his teens. The difference is that the writer—short of the authentic genius—was aware that this was his apprentice stage, that his way to competence and the point at which he would be worth listening to, lay through quite a few years of private work, in which the satisfactions to be found were the act of creation itself and the gradual learning of the craft of making thoughts cohere and meanings emerge. The difference, also, is that not until today have writers going through this necessary stage been indecently encouraged by publishers to display their precocious jottings to the public, a practice which comes near to seduction under the age of consent.

I would not call *The World's Game* by Hugh Thomas a totally mature work, but this was certainly one of the most interesting novels to come out last year. Thomas had reached the comparatively advanced age of twenty-six when he published this, his first.

His father was in the Colonial Service and Thomas was at school at Sherborne, then at Cambridge where he was what he calls "a romantic Conservative". From university he went to the Foreign Office and during the years 1954-56 was secretary to the British delegation to the United Nations Disarmament Sub-Committee. For about nine months, until last autumn, he lectured in political theory at the Royal Military Academy, Camberley. Now he is writing full time. His new novel *Rotten At The Core* is due out shortly, and he is at present working on a history of the Spanish Civil War, a history of the Royal Military Academy, and a study of foreign affairs since 1945.

Thomas is now a member of the Labour Party, and is Labour parliamentary candidate for Ruislip-Northwood. He has expressed his political attitude to me in this way:

"I distrust *emotional* engagement. Writers are concerned with clarification and emotion muddies. But *engagement* is essential. One is concerned to describe, if possible to alter, certain things in a community, not in an individual. The Suez crisis was the cause of the end of my relationship with the Foreign Office. I have for some time felt myself intimately involved with the H-bomb, and I am a passionate opponent of capital punishment, the present homosexuality laws, the Cyprus policy and the public school system. I think, however, that those who spend so much time on these rather glamorous 'causes' would serve their fellow humans better if they thought a little more about pensions, housing, the *details* of the defence budget, controlled global disarmament rather than unilateral, the price of bread as well as of whisky, and the political future of Africa.

"It is now clear to me that organised religion, throughout history as at the present time, is an ally of those fears, prejudices, customs and selfishness that hamper the fight against disease, poverty and hunger. All religions are superstitions and I have yet to find a superstition which has any value. Provided one can eradicate those illogicalities the future for the human race is dazzlingly bright. If not, not—as the old Aragonese oath of allegiance ended. The means exist in the world to abolish misery, to give comfort, leisure and education to all. Bigots oppose us— Catholics and Communists, nationalists and men of class-consciousness, people who willingly choose ignorance and others who distrust pleasure. All our futures are bound up with this drama. The writer's task is to increase, by the use of wit, or compassion, or eloquence, the sum of self-respect in the world. This task is the same in 1958 as in 404 B.C."

I think it is informative to hear first the attitudes and beliefs that Thomas brought to the undertaking of novel-writing, for in this context he is a particularly interesting specimen: he was one of the New Right, one of the young men who went through university in the early Fifties when the Tories, recovering lost confidence, ruled again, when Billy Graham seared through Britain and the Catholics came back into fashion. This was the period when conservatism and neutralistic conformism began taking control of the mental atmosphere of the universities—the time when, as Amis wrote in his Fabian pamphlet, no undergraduate who wanted to be in the swim could afford to skip church. Thomas went through all this and, as it were, came out the other side.

The World's Game (the title is taken from Domenico Trevisiano, Venetian Ambassador to Rome, in 1510: "The Pope is determined to be lord and master of the world's game") is about the interior of the Foreign Office. Seen through the eyes of Simon Smith, the young Third Secretary, it is an airless, ritualistic world of complacency, compromise, triviality and cynicism. Diplomatic posts are assessed by the quality of the fashionable life of this or that capital ("One dies in Jarkata, literally dies. There are no restaurants, nobody to talk to. . . ." "But Jedda is much worse, even alcohol is banned.") and there is a pervading sense of good minds lethargically decaying like oxygen-starved goldfish in a tiny bowl. Simon's colleagues—Giles, Miles, Jocelyn and Dickie—are exactly the same circle as Roger Longrigg's, and no doubt they were at school and university together, and now encounter each other fairly regularly at Chester Square and Hans Place parties. Nor, really, does their regard for their jobs differ much. Longrigg's young men, in their British warms and bowlers, walk through Grosvenor Square to their advertising agencies; Thomas's, also in bowlers but more likely in blue meltons, converge by way of St. James's Square, Pall Mall and Horse Guards Parade. Whereas the Longrigg men work in 'tasteful' offices, with Klees on the wall and cigarettes in silver boxes, the Whitehall three-ply pens of the Thomas men are ill-lit and dusty, full of brown cupboards, wire trays, dirty cups, chipped inkwells and out of date maps. Yet the approach they make to their respective writing tasks—concocting deodorant slogans, drafting minutes and replies to parliamentary questions—have the same urbane, detached disesteem, not exactly dishonesty for that presupposes ethical standards to be flouted and these men seem oblivious of any purpose or consequence of what they do.

In many ways *The World's Game* is an odd product, a melange of many styles and moods, and it contains some rather notable bloated Disraeliesque writing (on one page we are steered through a quicksand of frivolity and a wasteland of cynicism, and almost washed under by, in fast succession, waterways, a current, a tide, an ocean and a whirlpool) and the characters tend to make not conversation but litanical lorgnette-twirling peroration. Nevertheless it is original and bold in its return to an elegant asperity of manner which was thrown out with the bath-water by the anti-decadent knuckleduster novelists. The outmoded formality of *The World's Game* not only well suits the deliberate rococoness of the people it deals with, but is an admirably ironical way of off-handedly exposing the terrifying internal insensitivity of brinkmanship—for hydrogen warfare is what these Lancaster House triflers are indolently playing with between ordering flowers for the hostess of the weekend and making off, hotfoot, for the evening's first sherry.

Simon, in fact, in the course of the book, is seen moving from doubt to decision—he becomes convinced that "this junkshop of out-of-date architecture and furnishings was indeed really responsible for the British folly in Cyprus, defeat in the Middle East, ignominy in Africa. The junkshop, on the one hand, and pride, on the other . . . were the main reasons for the decay of the nation." Observing his department's tea-drinkers standing around talking to each other of the restaurants, theatres and parties for which they are bound that night, he realises that "those were the things which really concerned them"; there is "something about the whole structure of the Foreign Service which encouraged this superficiality; constantly to be dealing with matters of supreme triviality . . . with the same grave respect as the most important."

Simon suddenly recognises that he is in love "with action, truth, integrity". He is also in love with Laura, wife of his chief. He feels lost in "the champagne jungle", because although momentarily he believes that the disarmament conference upon which he is engaged has achieved success—the Russians consent to inspection—to his dismay and consternation the Western diplomats, preferring that their elaborate ritual of conference and ambiguity should proceed with customary inconclusiveness, ignore this and drone on implacably towards mass self-destruction. When it is too late to believe any longer in the sincerity of this department of the Establishment, and also too late to preserve his idealised passion for Laura, Simon rather leaps out of fastidious and tepid character and goes off to Israel, when war with Egypt is imminent, in a one-man demonstration against the non-intervention policy of Britain in general and "the cowardice, snobbishness and anti-semitism of the British upper classes" in particular.

Thomas catches with great skill and subtlety the ennui and un-reality of this looking-glass world of government: ". . . the Private Secretary, still busy dictating notes for a speech which surely no one would ever deliver . . .", the polite impervious officials devising "with a complete absence of emotional engagement, plans for a Disarmament Conference which, it appeared no one believed would have any success . . .", the pomp and ceremony of the Conference at Lancaster House, "a gilded mockery; the parade of interpreters and verbatim record-takers give the impression of being mere irrelevant, supporting members of a cast in an old-fashioned comedy."

Set against Osborne's dervish dance of rage, *The Word's Game* is a pavan, stately, graceful and a little pompous, and deservedly it has not startled and excited in the way that *Look Back In Anger* has. Osborne's work has fire and dash, all the skyrockets and mines of serpents going off at once. Thomas's book has a constrained feeling about it, is often stilted and overcooked on the 'reflection' side while underdone on characterisation, and its wit is concealed in Chinese boxes. Yet, wholly, this novel is artistically better and socially far more important than *Look Back In Anger* (I do not see that *The Entertainer* qualifies at all for mention in this context). When Thomas told me: "I distrust *emotional* engagement," I think he may have been expressing caution about a tendency he recognises in himself, for of course *The World's Game* is highly emotional in its temper and Simon Smith is as emotional in his impulses as Jimmy Porter in his. The huge and vital difference is that while Jimmy Porter's anger is static and in-turned, Simon Smith progresses towards a point of dissentience through a developing set of circumstances, and finally he *decides upon a course of action*—quixotic, emotional, it may be, but Smith examines, analyses and takes action.

It may, of course, be partly because that is so untypical of our times, and because Jimmy Porter's sullen sort of griping is, that one has attracted so much more attention than the other; certainly Jimmy's personality and *milieu* are far more recognisable than the remote timeless upper-class pattern of Simon's career. Yet it is impossible not to prefer disgust that generates idealism to disgust that festers defeated within itself. It is impossible, too, not to feel that here was a protest worth making, a rebellion worth celebrating—a blow against the gossipy, lazy, narcissistic machine which, while excluding the nation rather as the villagers were excluded from the hunt ball, performs in the name of the nation policies so successfully blurred of definition and filleted of resolution that Britain drifts, wallowing, ever nearer to the rocks. Osborne says: "I want to make people feel . . . I shall simply fling down a few statements—you can take your pick. They will be what are often called 'sweeping statements', but I believe we are living at a time when a few 'sweeping statements' may be valuable. It is too late for caution." Thomas says: "Writers are concerned with clarification and emotion muddies. But *engagement* is essential."

Osborne in one of his more logical tirades against "the trained traducers" of the Press (this time it was in the *News Chronicle*) pointed out that so meaningless was the label Angry Young Men that it had even been attached to Nigel Dennis, "the most charming, kindest and mildest of men, who is over forty and the father of teenage children".

Dennis is forty-six, works for the London bureau of *Time-Life Inc.*, and in fact contributed some on-the-spot research into one of the earliest examinations of the 'movement'—a not very accurate (e.g. Amis, Wain, Osborne, Hinde, Braine and Peter Towry were lumped together as "a group" of "moral and political neutralists") digest in *Time* last May headlined LUCKY JIM AND HIS PALS. Dennis himself, however, was sucked into the 'movement's' vortex because his play *Cards of Identity* was produced at the Royal Court in July of 1956, just after *Look Back In Anger*, and

147

it became known that he was a friend of Osborne's—therefore the label Angry Young Man was smacked on his forehead.

In fact, although Dennis himself is not in any sense "angry", either in temperament (he is a diffident and shy man who strenuously avoids Press interviews) or in his work, what he has written is intensely involved in the cultural revolt of the post-war years, and his vision of life is sardonic and troubled. More than most of the writers I have so far discussed, and certainly more than Osborne, Dennis is deeply preoccupied with the problems and dangers of modern society. Especially is he preoccupied with that central problem that seems so much clearer and nearer to European and American writers than it does to British, the diminishing of the personality of man—not so much the loss of identity as the individual's voluntary acquiescent surrender of it, like giving up your passport to the hotel security cell when you arrive in the Soviet Union.

Dennis's first novel, *Boys and Girls Come Out To Play* was published in 1949 (when it won the Anglo-American Novel Contest). The book *Cards of Identity* came out January 1955 and, as I have said, was staged eighteen months later. In June last year a new play, *The Making of Moo*, was put on at the Royal Court.

Cards of Identity is a remarkable book, one of those rare pieces of virtuoso work about which one can say, all at once, brilliant, boring, undisciplined, hilarious, astonishingly inventive, bathetic, repetitive and excitingly original—and finally its failings do not matter because it has real importance. Its subject, which is satirised on an uncompromisingly high intellectual plane, is the feeble hold that the individual has on his individuality in this rootless age. Dennis's fantasy is set in Hyde's Mortimer, a rambling and ramshackle house of the old school, built for people with expensive tastes and cheap labour, which is taken over by the Identity Club.

The Identity Club's purpose is to manufacture identities, to themselves become adept at sliding into any skin more appropriate and convenient to pertaining conditions. When three of the organisation staff, middle-aged man, middle-aged woman and young man, arrive at the musty, unoccupied house to prepare it for the Club congress, they instantly assume the guise of squire, wife and scion, and they swiftly give the treatment to the seedy Henry Paradise and his wife, to a local doctor and nurse, and to a village woman, transforming them respectively to butler, house-keeper, gardener, Land Girl and maid, all equipped with new pasts which they 'remember' with the mixture of mournful guilt and self-satisfaction with which we all remember our pasts.

The diagnosis of these separate cases is extremely witty and perceptive. The frenetic GP whom they transmogrify into a taci-turn ponderous gardener has "the insanity of the phlegmatic Britain-can-take-it type. He has gone on taking it for so long that he no longer knows exactly what it is he is taking." Henry Para-dise, now Jellicoe, the masochistic forelock-tugging butler with a rum-soddened history, says as a butler should say: "The word 'security' only makes my heart flutter. It's not a natural word, sir. We must struggle on like animals, sir, and those of us who fail must crawl under a bush and die." To the re-labelled Mrs. Chirk, the village woman, Captain Mallet, the new lord of the manor, explains the situation in which human beings the world over now are placed: "You must try and understand that the old days are over," he lectures her, "the old days when you could take your identity for granted. Nowadays, all the old means of self-recogni-tion have been swept away, leaving even the best people in a state of personal dubiety. . . . Very wisely, governments all over the world have sought to stop this rot before the entire human population has been reduced to anonymous grains. They give you cards, on which they inscribe in capital letters the name which your fading memory supplies before it is too late. It is their hope that by continually reading and re-reading your *name*, you will be able to keep your hold on a past that no longer exists, and thus bring an illusion of self into the present."

Captain Mallet is touched by the thought that each of these people now enjoys "a full and passionate identity which each regards as the great human axle round which the turning world has been built". But it is the President of the Identity Club who puts Hyde's Mortimer and its staff into perspective in the Britain that is itself tottering about trying to find an identity in the

149

cruelly changed post-war world. To the gathering of members he says: "This sort of house was once a heart and centre of the national identity. A whole world lived in relation to it. Millions knew who they were by reference to it. Hundreds of thousands look back to it, and not only grieve for its passing but still depend on it, non-existent though it is, to tell them who they are. Thousands who never knew it are taught every day to cherish its memory and to believe that without it no man will be able to tell his whereabouts again. It hangs on men's necks like a millstone of memory. . . . How right that we should assemble in one of the last relics of an age of established identities. Today, when it is rare to find any man who can be said to know his self, it is clubs such as ours which tell these sufferers who they are. . . . We can make all sorts of identities, from Freudian and Teddy Boy to Marxist and Christian." And he points out the boon they have been to the newly-enrolled domestic staff: "We have returned them to their favourite era of injustice and drudgery."

During one of the cases-histories which are presented to the conference, a dispossessed upper-classer sums up what has gone wrong with dear old England: "All the initials have gone from inside the bowler hats. All the value's gone out of the currency. There's no meaning in the church bells, no punch left in the hyphens of surnames. I don't like it at all."

The conference is told of an attempt to re-assert the *spirit* of Old England by elaborating the ritual of Easing the Badger. This is such accurate satire that it reads exactly like the sort of advertisement for British tourism that you see in the *New Yorker,* with coloured pictures of Beefeaters, kilted caber-tossers and a carefully angled shot of a Stratford-upon-Avon curio shop (leaving out the sodium lamps and TV aerials). The Co-Wardens of the Badgeries take part in the parade through London with the Coffiners, the Datcheries, the Portators, the Body of Threshers, the Royal Key Holders and the Cushion Fashioners, and the stuffed token boar-badger is inserted into a symbolic den and then eased out with the Co-Warden's official emblem, a symbolical gold spade. "I hope," remarks one of the officials, "you will never wake up to find that the life has departed from beneath these symbols like peas

150

from under thimbles. . . . Once you go on to charging that spiritual symbol with a material significance, you get into deep water. So I urge you to hang on to the abstract aspects of the Badgeries."

When the parade takes place the populace stare admiringly at the "unreeling of so much obsolescence".

Cards of Identity gathers a giddy momentum as it proceeds, making wild whirling bombardments with flour bags upon the Law, Religion, Homosexuality and most other institutions, with a final jibe at the almost-extinct *belles lettres* savant. To foil an investigating policeman, the Identity Club conference is quickly converted into a duke showing bob-a-nob visitors around the stately home, and they enter the library where a man with high and furrowed brow and twitching face is sitting at a writing-table.

"Here is one of the family at work," explains the duke. "He will not be in contemporary society very much longer . . . but, without him and his predecessors we should not have any culture at all. Throughout the centuries, ever since the dissolution of the monastries, he has written modest commentaries on theology, Greek legend, Stonehenge and water-divining—none of which is of much interest nowadays and, indeed, never was. He has been to literature what the rock-gardener has been to horticulture. He was never what is called a creative type, but he was always sensitive and tolerant, decently dressed, and came to meals punctually. A dim figure, you may say, but it is precisely dim nonentities which constitute the past for which we yearn."

If the traditional 'writer' is to literature what the rock-gardener has been to horticulture, Dennis might be said to be one of those do-it-yourself flame-throwing kits advertised in gardening journals for swiftly disposing of weeds and underbrush. His second play, *The Making of Moo*, is equally extravagant and ruthless in its dissentience. Its theme is the great religion swindle, and its setting is somewhere behind God's back in the Colonial wilds. A British engineer is faced with a grave problem. His new dam, he learns, has unseated the river god and it is necessary speedily to supply the local tribe with a substitute deity and focus for their attention.

This the engineer proceeds to do by rewriting the Highway Code as a ready-reckoner Sermon on the Mount, introducing tomato juice and toast for the ceremony of worship, electing the coloured servant as Pope, and turning the bungalow into a temple where two visiting lawyers are sacrificed. The new god is Moo, named after the familiar call of cows.

The Times reviewed *The Making of Moo* with a wrinkled nose, which is a healthy sign: ". . . a somewhat tasteless undergraduate lark," "vulgar without being funny" were two of its objections, although it did also remark upon its wit and liveliness. The play was considered sufficiently outrageous to give *The Star* an excuse for running a front-page protest by Robert Wraight with the banner heading *A Shocking Play* (the next night Joan Plowright, in the part of the Prophetess of Moo, went on stage carrying a copy of the paper). There were other sharp cries of reproof from the newspapers about the offensiveness of "mocking religion". A stern rebuke was sent by wire to *The Star* by Wolf Mankowitz, who said: "What incredible idiocy it is to cry bad taste to the only effective satire on the dangers of religion to be staged in years."

The more serious criticism that can be made of Dennis's work is its flooding over into what Peter Zadek, the theatrical producer, neatly identified in the case of *Cards of Identity* as "intellectual tomfoolery", although he added that it was the only play produced by the English Stage Company that had tried "imaginatively to find new form for new content". Zadek's phrase is perfectly just—Dennis has such a rich glandular excretion of indignation, such an exuberance of glittering insight, that too much foams out, and the result is, too often to be ignored, a boring waggishness.

Yet the point that I cannot over-emphasise is the size of Dennis's talent, the acuteness of his eye and the sting that is contained in his good humour. He is valuable precisely because he is rare. How direly has the British theatre and the British novel been in need of the 'bad taste' Dennis so uproariously sloshes about, that Amis— stopping short of *I Like It Here*—so militantly propagated, that Hugh Thomas, in a milder and modulated way, displayed by lifting the lid off that inner temple of the Establishment, the

Foreign Office, the 'bad taste' Osborne so passionately believes in ("Some men let themselves wallow in their feeling and get strength in them from the wallowing they have in loving" wrote Gertrude Stein). Yet now the distinction can be seen between passion and purpose, the strategical way in which Dennis deploys his ridicule in accordance with a premeditated, hard-headed plan, compared with Osborne's blind threshing about.

What comes through all Dennis's work with a clear sharp light is his contempt for dead in-turned symbolism. He sees society today as a sinking ship, with too many survivors clinging tenaciously to wreckage of old privilege, instead of striking out and swimming hard for a new shore. Worse, within that ship are most of the passenger-list, complacently sitting on their bottoms in the overheated lounge, too set and complacent to open their ears to the sirens.

J. B. Priestley is one of the most under-estimated men now writing. Because he rather overdid the gruff-uncle now-let-me-tell-you-lad act he has for the past ten years been discredited. Yet in fact, beneath the grousing, rather sourpuss manner, he has been writing in the *New Statesman* a series of essays entitled *Thoughts In The Wilderness* which contain some of the most perceptive and lucid observations on our present way of life put on paper. "There is now a vast crowd that is a permanent audience waiting to be amused," he says in one of them, "cash customers screaming for their money's worth, all fixed in a consumer's attitude. They look on at more and more, and join in less and less."

Priestley's contention might be summarised as the huge illusion, created by the admass manipulators, that we are all experiencing expanding new freedoms whereas actually everything that really matters is shrinking or being censored out of existence. That is also the contention of Dennis, and, really, of Osborne too if you do a good deal of the interpretation for him, because Jimmy Porter is the rogue-hero of the times, the man who hates being forced into rebellion when all he really wants is to move into the position of authority that could be available to him, yet who can't, when it comes to it, stomach the renunciation, oath-taking and selling-out that entails.

153

When I was beginning to become aware of writers outside the school curriculum in the late Thirties, one of my major discoveries was Franz Kafka. At the present Kafka is in eclipse, and he is no longer the intellectual's touchstone and point of reference that he then was. He seems to me to be a strange omission from the reading of contemporary philosophy-devourers, for in an unexpected and elliptical way Kafka's analyses are more applicable today than they were when he was writing (how startling it is to realise that he died in 1923—rather like Picasso being considered a 'modern' painter, when his most influential work was done before the First World War). Of course Kafka was incessantly and almost morbidly aware of his Jewishness, and it was that that was the basis for his exploration of the *separation* of a human being from his community. Kafka wrote about loneliness—the scrabbling of a man against the transparent membrane of his own personality, unable to penetrate through to the people he sees—the prisoner-within-the-skin idea which Wain clumsily and superficially experimented with in *Hurry On Down*. Yet now the Kafka predicament has taken a paradoxical further twist. It is rather like Rimbaud seeing good as the obverse of evil—so has this separation-situation become almost one to be sought for. It is no longer a problem of loneliness—it has become an obligation to retain your identity outside the admass, not to be sucked under. What Kafka saw as a terrible affliction ("to be alone brings nothing but punishment") has become something to hang on to, because that may be the only fresh starting point. The threat today is that social integration may be the beginning of personal disintegration.

Camus's Outsider finally realises as he faces his execution that what had seemed to be numbness had been happiness, and that the only thing necessary for him to feel less lonely is that around the guillotine there should be "a huge crowd of spectators and that they should greet me with howls of execration". As we have seen, that sort of courage, the ability calmly to gaze upon the extreme consequences of being out-of-step is essentially a European state of mind. Yet with the exception of a few present-day writers such as Dennis and Hinde, the younger British dissentients' worry is how to adapt without losing too much face or paring down his personality *too* much—but, in the last analysis, he is prepared to adapt. What he really wants is an offer of conciliation from the other side, a sort of intellectual Summit Conference. And that is a natural, inevitable outcome of the lack here of the bigger sense of life, the ability (or courage) to draw back and face that bigger and ominous perspective. Between Lucky Jim's eagerness to keep his job while he is also trying to keep his self-respect and compensating for his cowardice by muttering blistering imprecations of his superiors, or Jim Porter's ritual flagellation, and the Camus Outsider's calm contemplation of "the benign indifference of the universe" there is an immense hiatus. In one case the personality—the 'identity'—is fussed over with a kind of cold-hearted selfishness, and yet is debased by self-mutilation; in the other it is rejected as being of no importance whatever.

Is that all there is? No. Another attitude has emerged in Britain in the Fifties, one which professes to see a religious solution but which, unlike the anti-clericalism of Dennis and Osborne, ignores the irritating detail of official Christianity, the Established Church that is one of the pillars of the Establishment, and the faintly degenerate vogue for Catholicism. This, of course, is the attitude held by those who have been variously named The Crowd, the Wilson Wanderers, the Outsiders, and the Nietzche Boys—that is Colin Wilson and a few like minded new writers.

At the pinnacle of his notoriety last year such was the richness of sensation and sexy scandal Colin Wilson provided, of exactly the right palate for the popular Press, that for a time it was difficult to pick up a publication—high or low in brow—that did not contain some story on him or reference to his book *The Outsider.* This was the period of such hit films celebrating overnight stardom as *The Tommy Steele Story* and those featuring Elvis ("The Pelvis") Presley and Bill Haley, who, when rock 'n' roll finally floundered, sank out of sight imploring, through his last movie title, "Don't Knock the Rock", a plea that was not heeded but which has a certain plangent immortality. It was during this phase that a critic in one of the weekend reviews predicted that any moment an enterprising picture company would be cashing in with *The Colin Wilson Story.*

That was intended as a tart remark, but it was too possible to be funny. Personally I regret that no sharp-eyed Wardour Street ideas man did seize the opportunity, for although the history of the film industry is paved with the biographies of Great Composers and the discoverers of the bubonic plague, it would I think have been unique for an author to be given the treatment. It is difficult to see why a screen-play of Wilson's golden year wasn't quickly knocked out, for there was all the material for what in B-picture circles is known as a "cliff-hanger". Wilson's parabola,

1956-7, was spectacular: from out of nowhere (or, to be precise, from out of a sleeping bag on Hampstead Heath) up through a dizzying arc of fame and fortune, with a steep nose-dive into disfavour.

That should not be taken to imply that Wilson is finished and gone. At the time of writing he has wisely fled from the headlines quietly to work and write, and it may be that henceforth, now that the fumes of success have cleared from his head, we shall see a rather different Wilson. But the First Wilson Phase is worth recording in detail for two reasons—because it is an intrinsically fascinating story of a *blitzkreig* upon the literary Establishment which ostensibly failed but which is going to have far-reaching effects, and also because the circumstances were so typical and symptomatic of the Fifties.

When *The Outsider* was published in Spring 1956 Wilson was just short of his twenty-fifth year, a fact that was heavily under-lined by Gollancz—the 137-line blurb ended arrestingly: "The author of this remarkable book is only 24." Upon that Sunday in May, the 27th, he was acclaimed by two of the most eminent critics on the two most serious Sunday newspapers. Said Philip Toynbee in *The Observer*: ". . . an exhaustive and luminously intelligent study of a representative theme of our time . . . truly astounding . . . a real contribution to an understanding of our deepest predicament." As is fairly widely known, Toynbee revised his opinion of Wilson's luminous intelligence with startling abruptness when his second book *Religion and the Rebel* appeared eighteen months later, during which time Wilson's had become a lurid name, like that of a literary Diana Dors, and this desertion of an apparently sinking ship is one of the interesting aspects of the Wilson saga that will be discussed more fully later. But on this first smiling Sunday morn there was not even a hint of this future estrangement. Chiming with Toynbee's rave notice in *The Observer* came Cyril Connolly's vibrant baritone in *The Sunday Times*: ". . . this extraordinary book . . . one of the most remarkable first books I have read for a long time . . . quick dry intelligence," and Connolly urged all who were living dull lives

157

at low pressure "to keep an eye on Mr. Wilson, and hope his sanity, vitality and typewriter are spared."

The excitement and the paeans swelled larger. In *The Listener* the anonymous reviewer (actually, I believe, Kenneth Walker, whose book *Venture With Ideas* Wilson had declared "absorbing") stated without any reservations: "The most remarkable book upon which the reviewer has ever had to pass judgment." There was not unanimous approval but the edition sold out in a day and another two impressions were printed during May. In the first six months it sold more than 20,000 copies—although in the trade it was reckoned that a large proportion were 'furniture sales', copies bought for casual, conspicuous display in the current gamesmanship stakes. In the same dramatic terms as Osborne's overnight reputation, with the same manifest certainty of a rocket bursting through the earth's atmosphere into outer space that distinguishes the real dazzle of success from the more customary plod up a slight incline, Wilson was famous. Suddenly he was a target for all the tuft-hunters in London, someone to claim acquaintance with, a big game bag to have drinking your cocktails or eating your dinner, and there were even those who discussed the ideas in his book seriously. He was photographed and written up in *William Hickey* and *Tanfield's* and most other gossip columns; he was thrust before the television cameras and put upon platforms; he was sculpted by Laurence Bradshaw; *Life* reconstructed his rocket to fame, even posing him in sleeping-bag on Hampstead Heath, and headlining the feature FUSS OVER ENGLISH EGG-HEAD; he was blazoned upon the cover of the American *Saturday Review of Literature;* most wonderful of all for a writer, he was an editor's white-haired boy, and had access to editorial space anywhere. (*The Sunday Times* even made a formal announcement a week after publication day that he would be reviewing "a series of books" for them—a project that died young.) Straight off, he bought £300 worth of books and ended his public library apprenticeship.

And this difficult diagnostic book *The Outsider,* about as unlikely a best-seller as you can think up, went on selling and selling, and Wilson the unknown poor boy became the possessor of thousands of pounds and the belief that he was an established thinker.

I have sketched in the circumstances of those first weeks of renown so that the contrast with all of his preceding twenty-five years may be understood. This is what Wilson has told me about himself:

"I was born in Leicester, June 26, 1931. My father has worked in the boot and shoe trade most of his adult life. Both parents were Leicester born; both came from large families. My mother's family were 'theatre'—my grandfather was an 'Irish' comedian. My parents weren't at all well off; myself and my brother came pretty quickly after they were married (my brother Barry is eighteen months my junior). There was a great deal of 'short time' in the boots in the Thirties, so I think we had a considerable struggle. Times didn't really improve until during the war, when my father could earn between £10 and £15 a week as a storekeeper. Another brother was born in 1942, and a sister in 1947.

"My brother and I had a pretty free time of it in our childhood; mum and dad weren't at all strict. Dad tended to be short-tempered and rather a menace, but was okay so long as we kept out of his way. Mum treated us with exceptional freedom (she is only nineteen years older than me)—telling me all the 'facts of life' before I was six—including all the juicier bits of family scandal, and treating me generally as a confidant. I think she had a hard time of it. She hadn't many friends—hardly any close ones—and read a lot. I used to read all the *True Romances* and *True Detective* magazines after she had finished with them, and most of her library books. (She had a terrific admiration for D. H. Lawrence—one I never shared, even when most under her influence.)

"I hadn't a particularly distinguished school record. I got a scholarship to a secondary school at eleven, The Gateway Secondary Technical School, Leicester. Came bottom of the class in my first year there, but began to rise slowly through a sudden passion for chemistry that developed through a chemistry set I had for Christmas when I was eleven. Decided then on a scientific career. Wrote my first book—an attempt to summarise all the scientific knowledge of the world in six small volumes—at thirteen, in the long August holiday. A girl friend had chucked me, and I needed something to take my mind off the humiliation.

"Took engineering, hosiery (Leicester's other main industry) and boots and shoes at school. Detested all three. Left school at sixteen, having got school cert., with four credits, but only a pass

159

in maths., which I had to take again to get matric. (and so forward my scientific career!). I have always detested work so much that I never stuck a job for long. Before I went into the RAF at eighteen, I had a job in a warehouse, then returned to the Gateway as a lab.-assistant (with matric.). But I had lost interest in science in the meantime, and had started writing plays and short stories (the plays much influenced by Shaw). They chucked me out after less than a year. Then I went into the civil service for a year—taxes—until the RAF, and became an established civil servant.

"Out of the RAF—resigned from the civil service (I was thrown out of the RAF after six months, but the story is unprintable). Did several odd jobs—worked on a fairground as a barker, then on three farms as a farming student, then went off to France.

"On return from France, got a job in an engineering works. Lasted through the winter of 1950. Did several navvying jobs, and a job in a chemical factory (I had already done two navvying jobs on leaving the RAF—none for longer than a fortnight). Then married in June 1951, and came to London. Worked as builder's labourer, repairing bomb damage at St. Etheldreda's, Ely Place. Then got a job in a plastic factory (Frazer & Glass) North Finchley, which I held for eighteen months. During that time, I moved around a great deal from home to home—a baby arrived in due course, and landladies tended to get nasty about his crying. Had six homes in eighteen months (furnished rooms). This was the major cause of my separation from my wife—she went back to Leicester after the sixth ejection to wait while I found another home; but we never lived together again.

"I worked in another plastic factory, then was on the dole for a month, then got a job as a hospital porter, which lasted through most of 1953, until I went to Paris again. Met Bill Hopkins about this time, and we were in Paris together, and talking a great deal about the literature we intended to create, etc. Bill began his first novel in Paris, and I outlined many of the ideas of *The Outsider* to him there. I think we had an immense effect of stimulation on one another.

"Back in England at Christmas, I worked in a big store in Leicester, then, after being sacked, in a shoe factory (my only one!). Returned to London (plus Joy!) and did a succession of jobs—laundry, two office jobs (sacked from both), plastic factory (started sleeping outdoors at this time), dairy, Lyons, another laundry, evening work in Coffee House, Haymarket. This covers 1954. In late 1954 I had stopped sleeping on the Heath, and gone indoors at New Cross. Wrote *The Outsider* in 1955, working at the Coffee House. Gave up work in September 1955, after Gollancz gave me a small advance (£25, followed by another £50—I had £125 in all before the book came out the following May).

"I began to write seriously when I left school at sixteen. Reason? Because I hadn't the faintest doubt of my genius, and could see no good reason why I shouldn't become either the greatest writer or greatest scientist the world has ever known. Sometimes a feeling of my talent so overwhelmed me that it gave me a headache! I know it isn't 'good form' to admit things like this, but I think you know that my belief in myself is a sort of local patriotism, not to be confused with immodesty!

"This age seems, like all ages, dull and lacking in direction. I hope to alter this. I feel that I have thrown a great deal of my colouring into the age, and will throw a million times more before I'm done. But the decade seems to me a blank canvas, to be filled in, not a ready-made picture.

"I admire Eliot more than any living writer, and feel that he has influenced my outlook more than any other. A great writer is made by a single deep, overwhelming 'conviction', a craving for unity. In Sophocles (as in Hemingway) this unity is supplied by the emotion of tragedy (or heroism). In Eliot (as in me) by a horror at the stupidy and confusion of the world, and a craving for the unity of God. This is real conviction—not Auden's half-baked communism, or Spender's apotheosis of pity. (Incidentally, this is why I consider that Sartre is not great—his work is a faithful mirror of the chaos of our age, its rootlessness and anarchy, but has no binding craving for unity, no great tragic or religious emotion.)

"I have never espoused any political cause. In my teens, I felt complete contempt for the espouser of causes; now I am more charitable, but no nearer to participation than before. I am a socialist because Shaw was, but socialism is not very deeply engrained in me. I had a period as a Hyde Park orator (on anarchism), but this was only to follow Shaw's example, and try to destroy my terror of audiences. The only kind of movement I can feel much sympathy with is a religious one, like Newman's Oxford movement or Fox's Quakerism. I have very little 'love of humanity' in the sense that Victor Gollancz has; I detest cruelty and injustice, but feel I have far more important work to do than leading crusades against them.

"Religious belief is the $64,000 question. I was brought up vaguely as an Anglican, but detested churches and Sunday schools, and still do. If today were the Sixteenth Century, I would be in the Catholic Church like a jack rabbit. But today isn't. We are in a disintegrating civilisation and the church is a wrecked thing

F

that provides no shelter, no matter how deep one's religious needs are. We need a new religion to unite us and give us purpose.

"One day, I believe, man will have a sixth sense—a sense of the purpose of life, quite direct and un-inferred. But until that superman appears, man needs a church to tell him that man is essentially a creature, an imperfect thing, whose highest purpose is to become a saint. I think the Outsider is a sort of missing link between man and this man of the future with a direct sense of life's purpose. I think I am a man with religious impulses as strong as those of Gotama, Plotinus or St. John of the Cross, born in an irreligious age, an age preceding the breakdown. My deepest interest is religion. My deepest need—to create my own.

"A writer's first responsibility, like that of all men, is to God, the life-force or whatever you prefer to call it. If he serves that, he serves his fellow men; if he doesn't, he doesn't serve his fellow men. I repudiate the Soviet type of responsibility to the state. First and foremost comes integrity. He must have a real sense of purpose, not an ersatz one supplied by patriotism or political alliance.

"As a writer I am interested in making men change, not in changing their social conditions or curing their immediate ills. A man who sets out to 'influence society' is a scoundrel, for his real aim is power; his real driving force, the most puerile kind of ambition. The really influential man must be the psychologist (and I mean a real psychologist, like Nietzsche or Pascal or Dostoevsky or Gurdjieff—not a congenital idiot like Freud). He must be the educator, not the scout-master. (All politicians are glorified scout-masters.)

"My hopes for the future are, as a writer, to leave a mark as deep as that left by Plato or Goethe, and, as a member of the human race, for a higher type of man."

Wilson dealt much more lengthily and analytically with this period in his Autobiographical Introduction to *Religion and the Rebel*, an 18,000-word account of the spiritual development that had anticipated *The Outsider*. In the *Daily Mail* of February 26, 1957, I wrote a rather exasperated article suggesting that it was time he put forth more evidence of his writing ability, as *The Outsider*, with its sporadic slices of original writing between the extensive quotes, provided insufficient basis for accepting his own claims of genius. The Autobiographical Introduction does at least show that he is a writer of fluency with a plain, telling style. Without, I hope, overlapping on the above history too much I

162

think it is worth quoting here fairly fully from that Introduction where he amplifies certain key experiences in his life, taking "one's own experience apart under a microscope", as he describes it.

He begins by re-defining what is for him "the heroic figure of our time", the Outsider, and I will return to that when we come to consider the book in more detail. He dates his "sudden mental awakening" at the age of twelve—it was then that he came upon Sir James Jeans's remark in *The Mysterious Universe:* "The eternal silence of these infinite spaces terrifies me," and this produced in Wilson "a sense of mystery that was so intolerable" that he wrote a twenty-page letter to Sir Arthur Eddington asking him please to explain to him what the universe was all about.

At a single sitting one night in 1944 he wrote an "Essay on Superiority", and it seemed "that I had penetrated deeper into unbelief than any other human being; that by questioning too deeply I had cut myself off from the rest of the human race. My brother came to bed in that same room while I wrote. Towards three o'clock in the morning I turned off the light and climbed into bed beside him, feeling at the same time an awful fear that God would strike me dead in the night. I felt that I had destroyed in myself a certain necessary basis of illusion that makes life bearable for human beings. I had done this in the name of 'truth'; and now I felt no elation, only a sort of fatigue of the brain that would not let me sleep. Truth, it seemed, had no power of intensifying life; only of destroying the illusions that make life tolerable"—a not unfamiliar viewpoint and one which London has recently seen electrifyingly expressed in two American plays, Eugene O'Neill's *The Iceman Cometh* and Tennessee Williams's *Cat On A Hot Tin Roof*, but not a realisation common in teenage working-class boys.

This was for him the beginning of a long period of futility, the "worst and most depressing period", in which he wrote as an antidote to misery or boredom. He was obsessed with the idea of futility and purposeless repetition, examining everyone he met to see how close they were to seeing the world as he saw it. "I was already beginning to enjoy that first terror of feeling myself completely alone."

By the time he was sixteen the periods of depression came oftener and lasted longer. Every evening he filled pages of his journal with his boredom and frustration, and "diatribes against the people I dsliked". He wrote his journal with the idea of ultimate publication as "I had no doubt that every word I had ever written would one day be of interest to students".

During Easter 1948 he had spent the day reading Janko Lavrin's book on Russian literature. He continues: "I went into the kitchen to switch on the stove to make tea, and had a black-out. It was a strange sensation. I stood there, fully conscious, clutching the stove to keep upright, and yet conscious of nothing but blackness. There was an electric-like sensation in my brain, so that I could readily have believed that I had been given an electric shock. It was as if something were flowing through me, and I had an insight of what lay on the other side of consciousness. It looked like an eternity of pain. When my vision cleared, I switched on the kettle and went into the other room. I could not be certain what I had seen, but I was afraid of it. It seemed as if I were the bed of a river, and the current was all pain. I thought I had seen the final truth *that life does not lead to anything; it is an escape from something,* and the 'something' is a horror that lies on the other side of consciousness. . . . All the metaphysical doubts of years seemed to gather to a point, in one realisation: What *use* is such truth?"

Shortly after he asked the English master what the word 'nihilism' meant. "Belief in nothing" he said. Wilson continues: "At once I thought I had found a name for my own state of mind. It was not just *lack* of belief in *anything*—it was active *belief in Nothing.*" His nihilism received a check—on the day that, after writing for an hour in his journal, he thought: "This must cease immediately; *I will not go on living like this.* I was all too familiar with these revivals of strength that was sucked away again the next day. Then I saw the answer: Kill myself. It cheered me immensely." In his chemistry class he took from the shelf a bottle of hydro-cyanic acid. "As I took it down my mind made a leap, and for an instant I was living in the future, with a burning in my throat and in the pit of my stomach. In that moment I was suddenly supremely aware that what I wanted was not less life, but more."

After leaving school came the succession of hated jobs, but Wilson was not a natural drifter, scared of responsibility and roots. "Wandering entailed too much 'thought for the morrow'; it made life a perpetual anxiety . . . life without security is dreary and demoralising."

Earlier in his shorter notes Wilson refers to going off to France after his discharge from the RAF. In the Introduction there is an amusing and interesting sketch of this period. "In September 1950 I decided to go to France. It was not that I wanted to write in a garret on the Left Bank, or seek Murger's *vie de bohème* off the Rue du Bac. My desire to write had almost died out, and I felt that intellect was a disease keeping me away from life." In Paris he silted up in the 'Akademia' of Raymond Ducan, brother of the dancer Isadora, "a naïvely egotistic old American" who wore toga, sandals and a band fastening his long grey hair, and who printed his own Whitmanesque poems on a printing press with only capital letters. He preached a philosophy he had called 'action-alism'. Wilson was enrolled as a 'disciple', given three vegetarian meals a day and a couch to sleep on. "But he soon found me out— that the three meals a day meant more to me than the lectures. . . He gave me a stiff dressing-down, in which he told me that I was an adventurer and an impostor, and gave me twenty-four hours to find new lodgings. I was not resentful."

He returned to Leicester, then came down to London. The following section, in which he describes his endeavour to win the freedom of time and mind to write his novel about Jack the Ripper, and yet get the money to keep himself alive, is told dispassionately and simply, and is an oddly moving insight into a personality obsessionally determined to force through to what he must do. At first to save a grub-stake he cut out paying rent by pitching a tent beside the Whetstone plastic factory where he was working. When he had saved enough to last him a few months at the rate of £2 a week, he quit the factory. He then bought a sleeping bag and a rucksack for his belongings, and after writing during the day in the British Museum, slept out on Hampstead Heath all that summer and autumn.

"But sleeping out was a nerve-racking business." The police patrolled the Heath, and he dared not go on until after midnight. He breakfasted in a busman's cafe on Haverstock Hill on a slice of bread and dripping and a cup of tea for 2½d. The evenings were difficult. At eight o'clock the libraries closed. "There was nowhere one could spend a few hours in warmth and quiet until midnight. . . . I always felt exhausted and ill at ease as I cycled around London with my sleeping-bags rolled up on the back; it was a strange sensation, having nowhere to go, nowhere to retire to at night, nowhere to spend the evening reading."

When cash ran out he washed up in coffee bars. The first part of the novel was finished and he gave it to Angus Wilson, who was then an assistant superintendent at the British Museum Reading Room and who had offered to read it. At this time he was seeing a great deal of Stuart Holroyd who showed him the opening chapters of his *Emergence From Chaos*. "Suddenly I made a decision. I too would write a critical book—a credo. I would dash it off quickly, and then get back to the novel. In half an hour, one morning, I sketched out the plan." This was *The Outsider*. By now he had another job, sitting at a desk answering a telephone, and he took in his typewriter and worked on his credo book. He finished it in three months, received an advance from Gollancz and for the first time in his life was able to give up work and do nothing but write. But when the proofs arrived he was "terribly dissatisfied with it: I hadn't managed to put in half as many things as I wanted, or to pursue half as many lines of thought."

The final part of the Introduction rings with true reporting—a retrospective sizing up by a man who has just been through the wind-tunnel of sudden fame. "The success of the book winded me, and made me more certain than ever that it should have been twice as long and far more carefully planned. I had believed passionately in the book and had never doubted its importance as I wrote it. But it was intended as essentially a preliminary step towards a far bigger statement. After the delight of the first good reviews, and the knowledge that new impressions were being called for, I became aware of what had happened to the book itself. I was congratulated by critics on having started a craze, on inventing a new parlour game to replace Nancy Mitford's 'U and Non-U', called 'Outsider or Insider?' The whirl and publicity went on for months, and soon I realised that I had become a stranger to my own book. The people in it, who for years had seemed to live with me, had suddenly become alien; a painting by Van Gogh no longer moved me; Nijinsky's *Diary* stayed on my shelf unread. It was interesting to hear people discussing me—as when a child falls into a doze at a party and hears the grown-ups talking about him—but only because it was like seeing myself in distorting mirrors. Besides, after a while, people began attacking the book, and declaring that it had all been a mistake, and that I was not a 'promising young writer' after all."

At the beginning of the Introduction he recalls how the book's success sucked him into the process of becoming an Insider; one of the "highly efficient pigs" which modern men are reduced to in a civilisation "that always makes a noise like a dynamo". He candidly owns that *The Outsider* received more attention than he or Gollancz had expected. "Quite suddenly I became involved in all kinds of activities. For many months after it was published I had almost no time alone, caught up as I was in a round of interviews by reporters, lectures, broadcasts, reading and answering letters, invitations to dinner, and so on. The result was exactly what I had been afraid of: I found myself losing the preoccupations that had led me to write *The Outsider*. Strangers who claimed to be Outsiders wrote me long letters explaining their symptoms and asking for advice, until I began to suspect parody. In this whirl I discovered that I ceased to be aware of the states of consciousness that lie beyond my ordinary two or three notes. . . .

"I find that being regarded as a 'promising young writer' or attacked as a charlatan or a woolly-minded freak, tend to destroy my certainty of purpose. The prospect of spending my life trying to make myself worthy of a few pages in *The Cambridge History of English Literature* seems to me a particularly dreary kind of treadmill." And he adds: "I see now that I must try to escape the subtle falsifications of my aims that the success of *The Out-*

sider caused. I must retrace my steps to the period before it was published, and begin working again from there."

I have spent a good deal of time on the detail of Wilson's background and life because it is important evidence in the context of this portrait of the changing culture of our time. Wilson is certainly not typical of the post-war generation: obviously the consistent bass note in the fugue of his formative years was his 'difference', his separateness, the vision that was intelligible to no other human being he knew and to himself only through his reading of the agony of mystics. In this instance, it is his own conviction of uniqueness that is significant—because of the tortuous path he had to hack out for himself towards expression of that uniqueness through the jungle of post-war Britain, the boring dullness of his State education, his overwhelming sense of futility in the provincial town, National Service, the unskilled factory work, washing-up in espressos and Corner Houses, and finally the preposterous fulsomeness of his lionisation, which could not have happened to that degree in any previous period.

Wilson is unperturbed by denouncements of him as being a paranoiac—probably because his own attitude is that "the difference between the lunatic and the sane person is only that the sane person prefers to get other people to co-operate in maintaining his delusions," and again: "Only in the dead, I felt, was there no emotional prejudice; consequently, only the dead may be called sane." He has also said that there is little to choose in spiritual health between the workman who has spent forty years in the same factory and is spiritually warped and stunted, and the novelist who writes the same kind of novels for forty years and has a house on the Riviera. Normality means, *per se*, low tensions, sluggish sensibility and lack of spirit, and whatever faults you wish to pick in Wilson and his arguments, none of the above can be numbered among them.

It is, I think, this single-minded drive that has brought him a lot of the trouble he has recently seen. In the summer of 1956 he, his friend Joy Stewart and I went down with Daniel Farson to stay with Negley and Eve Farson at their North Devon house. I was driving and Wilson sat beside me, and for all the journey we talked about Outsiderism—except for one brief divergence. I saw a rabbit and exclaimed with surprise, for this was at the peak of the myxomatosis plague and the countryside had been wiped clean of them. Wilson did not understand my surprise, which doubled when I discovered that he had never heard of myxomatosis. The reason was simple; he never read a newspaper, because he would not sacrifice from his work the amount of time that required. His thinking is formidable in his own chosen routes; like a river which has scoured into limestone until it runs densely in the depths of a ravine, yet there are vast areas it has never encountered.

On another occasion, when I was in Birmingham with him on a television programme, he mentioned lunching with Sir Oswald Mosley whom he thought "rather a decent chap". As the opponents of the Wilson group have accused them of neo-Fascism, of an admiration for the dictator principle in general and the German Nazis in particular, and as the Wilson group have recently been going to some considerable trouble to deny this and demonstrate that their anti-humanistic exalting of the Will does not mean that they necessarily desire the return of jackboots and the concentration camp, this seemed an injudicious remark. A journalist present acidly took him up on his meeting with Mosley, and in the conversation that followed it emerged that Wilson had no knowledge *whatever* of the history of Mosley and the British Union of Fascists, and, even more amazing, nothing but the vaguest notion of the big political issues of the Thirties and Forties. On either side of Wilson's self-acquired education, his omniverous and discerning exploration through fairly remote territory, are vast virgin forests of naïvete. I think it has often been his genuinely innocent ignorance of the complex, dangerous forces of publicity he has blunderingly stirred up which has been mistaken for arrogance and impudence.

As in the Autobiographical Introduction to *Religion and the Rebel*—the ingenuous honesty with which he blows the gaff on the processes of writing. He explains how he, accidently almost, came to "dash off" *The Outsider;* how he "jotted down a list of the type of men" he would bring in; how he cast around for a starting

169

point, and how he decided Barbusse's *L'Enfer* would do, and how, near closing time in the library, he noticed a sentence that he thought would make a good, striking start and copied it down. That is almost unethical disclosure of professional secrets. It is worse than a conjurer explaining his mysteries. It is mostly that mixture of honesty and naïvete in Wilson that brought about the train of events of the following eighteen months. On another occasion at a literary lunch he airily referred to *The Outsider* as "a fraud, dished up to look like an impersonal appraisal of our time when really it expressed a completely personal vision". Elsewhere he has described *The Outsider* as just a "filtering off" of his journals and referred to "the gimmicky element" in it. *The Daily Express* carried a report of his luncheon talk headed WILSON ADMITS HE IS A FRAUD, a story that was milked by American and Continental papers. In *Declaration* Wilson comments upon these events with characteristic child-like amazement: "I was forced to write several dozen letters to the various papers explaining that I had not meant that I had written *The Outsider* as a hoax. . . . The whole episode revealed to me that the writer in our age is confronted with a quite unique problem; it is no longer simply a question of making himself heard; but of making sure that he not heard too well.' '

From the start there were those who agreed that he was being heard too well, and antagonism bristled. In June 1956 a Brian Porter, who "with due apologies to the Gollancz cover-blurb writer" announced that he was *only* twenty-one, wrote a letter to the *Times Literary Supplement* which asked: "I wonder if your reviewer would agree with me that, no matter how many books Colin Wilson has read, there is still plenty of scope for his wholly delightful and penetrating kind of literary clap-trap?" and went on to suggest that in his next book Wilson should weld together into a panegyric on Bernard Shaw: "The place of Julian of Norwich in the soul of François Mauriac; Regine Olsen and the existentialism of Bishop Butler; the possibility that Kingsley Amis has (secretly) been incorporating the doctrines of Rozanov into his novels; should Simone de Beauvoir start a Sartre fan-club?; Aeschylus, Sophocles, and Euripides—a Lesbian trilogy?; the

170

significance of the *Duino Elegies* in Professor Ayer's thought; did Nietzsche kiss Lou Salome? Would Wittgenstein and Camus have liked each other? Plato's *Symposium* and modern birth-rate; did John Clare really love Cosima Wagner? Or was Dionysus in love with Fanny Brawne? The inter-subjectivity of Gabriel Marcel and teddy-boy gangs; Berdyaev's influence on modern gas-turbine design; Walt Whitman—an ironsider; or a Karamazov? or just a man?" By the autumn he had been satirized in *The Spectator*, parodied in *Punch*, and been made the subject of the *New Statesman* competition.

A little after, following some slighting remarks Wilson made about Shakespeare, "a great poet with the mentality of a female novelist", John Carswell, the critic, wrote to the *Times Literary Supplement:* "Mr. Colin Wilson's recent reference to the extraordinary quotability of that second-rate fellow Shakespeare has sent me to *The Outsider*. . . ." He had examined the quarter of the book that consists of quotations, his suspicion having first been aroused by a misquotation from Keats. Using the editions Wilson states he used, Carswell checked forty-six quotations taken from seven authors, totalling 249 lines. He found eighty-two major errors (words or punctuation distorted so as to affect sense or scansion) and 203 minor errors (commas supplied or omitted, capitals introduced or disregarded, words misspelt or spelt otherwise than they are by the author, etc.). That, he estimated, worked out an average of over one error per line quoted, and he ended his reprimand: "What does matter is that such a gallimaufry of misquotation and the standards it implies should have been passed into edition after edition (I used the fourth) by a reputable publisher, and greeted with enthusiasm by many (you, Sir, were not among them) whose business it is to guide the public taste."

By this time, too, Wilson had had a bad evening at the Royal Court Theatre, where he had taken part in a debate with Arthur Miller and Wolf Mankowitz, and had been badly savaged by Mankowitz ("arrant, inexperienced nonsense"), not the most delicate of dialogists, who repeated the act on a television programme where he again displayed his growling antipathy to Wilson's ideas and his methods of expressing them (one was a further assault

171

upon Shakespeare, who had now slumped in his estimation to "a second-rate writer who wrote quotations suitable to be printed on calendars").

Undismayed, Wilson continued in a state of evident euphoria to propagate those ideas and recklessly to scorn those he believed deserved it. For example, in a lecture he gave to the Society of Young Publishers, after a sideswipe at a contemporary type of "rather funny humorist" (identifiable as Kingsley Amis) who was writing nothing "useful to the needs of the time", he declared: "So far I'm thoroughly contented with me. I've made a lot of money, a large reputation, and I intend to finish as the greatest writer European civilisation has produced." Declining to join the Shaw Society, he declared: "I shall leave a clause in my Will ordering instant extermination of anyone who dares to set up Wilson Societies."

The reputation which Wilson was rapidly acquiring was for self-important bombast, one increased by an article in *Books and Art,* a transcription from a tape-recorder interview done by Daniel Farson, but which Wilson later claimed had been edited and compressed to the point of altering the meaning. Nevertheless in the question and answer form in which it appeared it contained such exchanges as: "You have said you want to be an atomic bomb on the minds of our time. What is your philosophy?"

"You can only define a philosophy in relation to the climate of thought in its own time. Now, as far as I'm concerned, our civilisation is an appalling stinking thing, materialistic, drifting, second-rate. I feel that television and the newspapers give the second-rate an infinitely bigger chance than ever before to express themselves."

"Yet you are always glad to appear on television, and you've made the front-page often enough."

"Any real man of genius must be prepared to take on the most difficult forms of self-expression."

"You think of yourself as a genius?"

"Oh, of course. . . . It may prove untrue but I've got to work on that assumption."

As the interview proceeded Wilson added that what he was in

revolt against was an age in which people did not make that assumption of genius. He nominated two people alive with the rare quality of genius: himself and Bill Hopkins (who at that time had not been published: this was what is known as a softening-up plug). He then explained his attitude to publicity—the first step in getting your ideas accepted was to make yourself a household name.

"Scott Fitzgerald said that a writer never achieves the same fame as a film star," he said, "I think that can be disproved and then, deliberately using that, hurl one's ideas in like bombs. I believe the age makes the men in it. Florence was ready when Savonarola came along, Germany was ready when Hitler came along, Italy was ready when Mussolini came along." And he concluded by answering the question if he thought of himself as the leader of the whole age: "It's not that I think of myself as such a leader, but simply that, seeing things the way I do, the whole burden of it is on my shoulders. I may be the only man to bring things back to consciousness in the present age."

It has often struck me as quaintly incongruous that this unsophisticated public-library missionary, who has steeped himself in Arnold Toynbee and Wittgenstein, should have been so fascinated by that gin-sling writer Scott Fitzgerald. Wilson constantly refers to him. He has been, I think, deeply attracted by the way Fitzgerald became an emblem and a hero figure to his own generation, by the dazzling idea of being an outrider of his period. Wilson returns to that subject in *Declaration:* "Once," he says, "I had an intense suspicion of the word *Zeitgeist,* because I did not see how the 'age' could have a spirit. Yet Scott Fitzgerald wrote of his own period; it bore him up, flattered him, and gave him more money than he had dreamed of, simply for telling people that he felt as they did. The same thing seems to be happening to a number of young writers today—myself among them—so perhaps, after all, there is such a thing as a 'spirit of the age'. So I have come to accept that 'the age' might possibly feel the same needs I feel myself, and have dismissed the fear that I may be seeing only a distorted reflection of my own face." Again: "The basic human craving for a sense of purpose reasserts itself as a desire to re-

173

create the heroic: to re-create it indiscriminately in the heroes of Everest and Kon-Tiki, in the film star or popular crooner, the 'rebel without a cause' (in its original meaning, the juvenile criminal). My Outsider fitted neatly into the pattern of obsession; consequently, like Scott Fitzgerald, I have found the age 'bearing me up and flattering me' for providing it with a catchword, a symbol, such as James Dean has provided in the Fifties, or Rudolph Valentino in the Twenties. I have no basic objection to this: for I have also believed that the Outsider is the heroic figure of our time."

It can be seen that this is the point in Wilson's nature where a sharp commercial sense has been grafted on to the innocence. With the bright image of Fitzgerald, the pied piper of Young America, before his eyes, and self-inculcated with not only the ideas of George Bernard Shaw but also with his technique at publicity-by-outrage and self-advertisement, Wilson pressed home his advantages. Not finally, so skilfully as his guiding stars, but at the start with astonishingly blatant results. With an ease that must have been the envy of all the copywriters in the country, he established what is called in the trade 'high brand-remembrance'. Overnight he stamped upon the British public the insignia of himself: that beanpole doppelgänger with the curiously periscopic neck thrusting stiffly up from the funnel of the speckled fisherman's jersey, the hood of hair, the heavy goggle-glasses, and the trademark stuck. Perhaps too well.

He was given a full page plate in Cecil Beaton's lush album of photographs *The Face of the World*, looking strangely sinister. Flattened against the wallpaper, with a shaft of light slanting across his face and making his eyes black sockets and his mouth a razor scar, Wilson seemed there to hold the promise that his enemies allege: Orwell's prediction of the boot forever stamping in the human face. He was seen in a different, more frivolous light by the cartoonists who found him a natural, and they soon had plenty of excuse for guying him.

At this time Wilson was living in a house in Notting Hill which had the appearance of a Displaced Persons' camp. With his girlfriend, Wilson occupied a two-room flat of fairly startling squalor

and disorder: a big square oilcloth-covered table crammed with
the remnants of meals, typewriter, papers, empty wine bottles and
books; a camp bed and an inflatable mattress; a broken chair; an
Einstein formula writ large upon the door; a portrait of Nietzsche; a bicycle; and a shelf of books including volumes of forensic
medicine containing some lurid coloured pictures of cadavers.

It was into this nest that Joy Stewart's father, John Stewart, a
Bedford accountant, burst on the evening of February 19 last
year, brandishing a horsewhip and shouting: "Aha, Wilson! The
game is up! We know what's in your filthy diary." Wilson was
eating artichokes at the time. Mrs. Stewart belaboured him over
the head with her umbrella, while her father, sister and brother
tried to drag Joy from the room. She declined to be dragged.

The Stewarts' decision to attempt the removal of their daughter was the finding of one of Wilson's journals by Joy's young
sister. When reporters and cameramen panted on to the scene in
response to a telephone call from Mr. Gerald Hamilton (the
alleged original of Christopher Isherwood's "Mr. Norris"), who
happened to be visiting Wilson at the time, Stewart produced the
diary to demonstrate that Wilson was "no genius—just plain
mad", and cried indignantly: "He thinks he's God." The arrival
of the police brought a tense calm.

The story was splashed by the morning papers, and to forestall
further family clashes Wilson and Joy ducked out of London and
down to Devon. Wilson, however, was co-operative with the news-
papermen despatched to find him and granted interviews which
kept the story alive. In his Barnstaple hide-out Wilson explained
to Rufus Endle of *The Daily Mail* that he and Joy had temporarily
separated until the hunt died down.

"I have hidden her because I cannot risk another kidnapping
attempt by her family," he said. "As soon as all this furore has
died down we shall be together again, and as soon as my wife will
divorce me we shall marry."

About the diary discovered by Joy's sister he said: "Some of the
notes related to the Dusseldorf murders and the actions of sex
maniacs. That is because I am writing a novel dealing with a
sadistic murderer of the Jack the Ripper type. I came across a long

175

report of the Dusseldorf murders which seemed to provide such a parallel that I wrote copious notes about it, but that doesn't mean that I myself am a sadistic murderer.

"It is true that I have written rather freely on sexual problems and there is a lot of self-exploration of my own sex problems. But it is not pornographic. It is just a psychological study."

In the meantime the newsmen had dug out the address of Mrs. Betty Wilson and a six-by-eight picture was printed of her in her Plumstead flat with five-year-old Roderick on her knee. Wilson issued a statement to correct "a bad impression that had been given". He said: "I am not neglecting my wife. I receive £100 a month from my publisher and of that I give my wife £25."

The papers were also after that diary. Wilson turned down a sizable cash offer from the *Daily Express* but—with characteristic generosity—gave permission to one of his hard-up friends to do a deal for himself with the *Daily Mail*. On February 23 the centre page was devoted to this, with a huge cartoon by Emmwood showing the pullovered figure in flight with diaries bouncing from his skull and the caption FAME IS THE SPUR. The entries in this dog-eared closely-written notebook are so revealing that they are worth reprinting fairly fully.

"The answer to *The Outsider's* central problem is, of course, work. Boredom chokes all fires."

"I can overcome any enemy, conquer anything, but force me to work at a dull, routine task and gradually I lose all poetic vision."

"Why did I almost die of rage when I heard popular songs in my teens? Why have I always got sick of every job I've ever had? Because there is a devouring evolutionary appetite in me, a growing need to take life seriously. A church is needed. A monastery. Four walls. Something to symbolise that I take life many times more seriously than others.

"Death to the half-livers. The evolutionary appetite in me demands a seriousness that is far from this stupid civilisation. The day must come when I'm hailed as a major prophet, when my devouring need for seriousness will inspire thousands of others to spit on this civilisation of football pools and public houses, and demand a new way of life."

"It's odd, but I haven't yet settled back and said to myself:

'Well, you've made it at last.' This is the time every young writer dreams about. Scott Fitzgerald is supposed to have stopped strangers to tell them: 'My first book has been accepted.'

"And no doubt some young ambitious men of genius might read my life avidly one day. I simply work on, make plans to finish this book, then the novel, and never stop to tell myself: 'This is what you dreamed about . . . your opportunities are unlimited now.'

"A happy letter from Mum this morning, sending me the family's congratulations. Mum's letter cheered far more than the congratulations of friends in London. It used to be a dream of mine that I'd be able to show her a large cheque for my first book. It makes a great difference to know I can get into print and make people take notice of me. It means I can get on with the more practical work of world-bettering, while striving to achieve a wider understanding of the needs of our civilisation than any statesman has done so far. To be eventually Plato's ideal sage and king.

"Yesterday I bought a magazine on James Dean and meditated on this peculiarity of our age . . . the hysteria and success worship which has made me so successful, as it made Dean. It will take a long time before people will understand my feelings about this success. It is inflated. Yet I *am* the major literary genius of our century. Interesting this Dean worship. I've always wanted to be worshipped. But I'm not willing to pay the price of death.

"I must live on, longer than anyone else has ever lived. I am the most serious man of our age. Will-power and seriousness are the same thing. What is the purpose of a journal if not to reflect one's life as in a mirror, to detach one from it, yet this happens to me less and less of late.

"I suppose fame has made the difference. When I began a journal in 1947 I had nothing to record but ideas that needed clarifying, inner states that needed examining. I had nothing much to record, but I wanted to become more conscious of myself and to talk to myself about the things I felt to be important. I talked to myself for lack of a sympathetic audience. I felt that I had rescued my life from meaninglessness.

"Now I am dogged by lots of minor problems that come as a consequence of my fame, and hardly ever go deep enough into myself to really face how human they are. So the Outsider's life tends to be a struggle between real problems and mere human problems. His job is to conquer the human problems.

"How extraordinary that my fame should have corresponded

177

with that of James Dean, Elvis Presley, Bill Haley, Lonnie Donegan.

"I wonder whether it wouldn't be best to stop making public appearances? I'm sick of the rabble, the people who need to sneer and pull down serious writing."

Not astonishingly, such public circus acts of superiority aroused impatience, irritation and derision. These reactions were intensified by the news leaking that Wilson had sent postcards to two daily papers announcing his return from the horsewhipping-hunt (photographs of them reinstalled in Notting Hill), by literary definitions such as the one in the New York *Times Book Review* where Wilson declaimed opaquely: "Great writing is a combination of the microscopic and the telescopic . . . Third rate writing is all microscopic . . . the usual microscopic social documentation with its debts to Dos Passos, Faulkner, Tennessee Williams and Arthur Miller", by his pompous letter to George Devine, director of the Royal Court Theatre, when his play *The Death of God* was rejected last September, by a three-man committee consisting of Devine, Lord Harewood and Ronald Duncan, who told the *Daily Express:* "It shows he has no talent of any kind." Wilson issued the letter to the Press:

"Dear George,
"Thank you for the return of my play 'The Death of God'.
"Your attitude in the accompanying letter arouses a question that is by no means of interest to me alone, and I would be grateful to hear an explanation of it.
"A year ago, you asked me to lunch to ask me to write a play for the Court. You explained that you were anxious to persuade young writers to approach the theatre, and asked me to treat the Court as a 'country club'. You told me that any play I chose to write would be 'kicked and pushed around' until it was stageworthy, and, if it was not, that you would give full and sympathetic advice on its failings. You gave the impression that the Court would be a sort of midwifery centre for young writers.
"Now, after spending three months writing a play *for you,* and delaying writing a novel in order to do so, I receive the play from you with a brief note stating it is 'not dramatically alive', and thanking me for letting you see it *first*—this last word implying that I wrote it for a lark, and have started sending it the round of managers, you being the first.

178

"The question I would like to ask is: what has happened to your attitude in the course of a year? I am a busy writer with a great deal to do and you know that I regarded the play as practically commissioned by you. If you can send back my play with a brief rejection slip, what are other young writers to think—writers who are writing 'on spec', with the hope that the Court will give them a better deal than any other theatre. I know four others who are writing plays to send to you at the moment. You must agree that, on the surface, it looks as if the Court has simply lowered its standards all round since those idealistic days of its beginnings. You were certainly under no obligation to accept my play, but I would have supposed that you were very clearly under obligation to give me a full account of its faults. It is, after all, a first play— the first, I hope, of many.

"I feel that, since its beginnings, the Court has contributed very little to providing a 'new drama' with the sole exception—a considerable one—of discovering John (Osborne). This is not your fault. But what does worry me is that, with your present attitude, you cannot expect your writers to flock to your doors. That *is* your fault.

"I would be grateful and relieved if you could point out that I am being thoroughly unjust to you: for I am in complete in agreement on one point—that the business of creating a new theatre *is* in the hands of young writers. (Sgd.) Colin Wilson."

The age was changing its mind about 'bearing up' Colin Wilson. Support was perceptibly being withdrawn from the major literary genius of our century, and many of the things being printed about him were not in the least flattering. A public opinion poll among *Daily Mail* readers supervised by Henry Fairlie had a category for Comic of the Year—and there was Colin Wilson, along with Kruschev, Lord Hailsham and Tommy Steele. In a 'humorous' Alphabet of the Arts in *Books and Art* 'W' stood for Wilson, Colin—"A self-confessed genius who has already written two of the funniest books of the generation. He is greatly addicted to Shaw and a fashionable party-game this Christmas will consist in everyone present writing down what they imagine Shaw would have thought of *him*." In *The Observer* Maurice Richardson, conducting an imaginary TV programme, unkindly wisecracked: "Our next question comes from Victor Gollancz. He asks: 'Will the Brains Trust give their considered opinion of

179

Colin Wilson as a publisher's property?' Connolly, would you start us off?" And in his collection of short stories *A Bit Off The Map*, published in October 1957, Angus Wilson, showing no gratitude at all for Colin Wilson's dedication of *The Outsider* to him, drew in the title story a reminiscent portrait of a coffee bar messiah named Huggett ("The Crowd's not the same as the Angry Young Men which you read about. Someone said it was and Huggett got very angry, because it's by Love and Leadership that the Will works. And all these Angry Young Men believe in democracy and freedom and a lot of stuff that Huggett says just get in the way of real thinking".).

Yet these were only pea-shooters. The bombardment from the big guns came when *Religion and the Rebel* appeared on October 21, 1957. In a rather tense atmosphere of apprehension, Gollancz had taken the single precaution of obtaining a pre-publication endorsement from Sir Herbert Read that he considered this to be a better book than *The Outsider*, but this time not a single word of blurb appeared on the dove-grey jacket. Sir Herbert's brave words proved no armour-plating whatever against the howitzer attack that followed.

To obtain the full measure of the slump in Wilson's prestige, we must recapitulate for a moment to the reception given to *The Outsider* just seventeen months before. Kingsley Amis had wrinkled his nose at it in *The Spectator*, and, saying he would risk being written off as a spiritual wakey-wakey man, remarked: "I find Mr. Wilson's book a disturbing addition to the prevailing anti-rational mode, feeling as I do that one is better off with too much reason than with none at all. I hate the idea of the kind of people who may already hanker after behaving like Stephen Daedalus being persuaded that there is fashionable authority for doing so." *The Times Literary Supplement* used the words "charm" and "interesting" but was generally reserved in its approval. But everywhere else it was hallelujah. We have already seen the assessments given by *The Listener*, Toynbee and Connolly. There was also Mary Scrutton in the *New Statesman* who, despite making some criticism of its style and its inaccuracies, decided finally that the book was "really important".

After *The Observer's* review of *Religion and the Rebel* I heard some cruel things said about Toynbee and those who could not get off the bandwagon quickly enough when it began to appear that they were being taken for a ride by a kind of mad-dog philosopher. Certainly Toynbee's public renunciation was rather uncomfortably melodramatic, but on the other hand he was the only one who had the courage to go back on to the same platform and expose himself to the turncoat charges that were duly made. He could not have been more emphatic. Under the heading UNHAPPY SEQUEL he began by retrospectively redressing on *The Outsider* —"an interesting and praiseworthy book for a number of quite different reasons . . . [but] clumsily written and still more clumsily composed"—whereas *Religion and the Rebel* "is a deplorable piece of work", "vulgarising rubbish-bin", "inferior", "deeply depressing" and so on. Finally he conceded: "This is all very rude and unpleasant" but he insisted that he was still spiritually on Wilson's side.

Far worse was on its way. Connolly did not return to the subject in *The Sunday Times,* where Raymond Mortimer deputised. In a long and careful article Mortimer said that he personally had found *The Outsider* unreadable, but its success was due to the book "expressing a state of feeling that is obviously widespread". Wilson's "muddleheadedness" was inexcusable, but his chief quarrel with him was that he was not angry enough. "Indifferent to human suffering and injustice, except when the victims are his fellow-Outsiders, Mr. Wilson is at his silliest when he dishes out half-baked Nietzsche. An English Luther or Hitler? Should we be shivering in our shoes? I think Mr. Wilson is aping Shaw's use of self-praise as the simplest form of advertisement. He does not appear to have any of Shaw's other talents; but because so many readers have taken him seriously, I have been trying to do so myself. The attempt was foredoomed to failure."

In fact *The Times Literary Supplement* did take *Religion and the Rebel* seriously and took a full page to do so, at last rather sadly deciding that there had been a decline from *The Outsider.* Janet Adam Smith in the *New Statesman* dealt with this "highly embarrassing affair" very acidly, and finally expressed her preference for Jimmy Porter over the Outsider, "even if he is equally weak on logical reasoning." In *The Spectator* A. J. Ayer's review was headed FOLIE DE GRANDEUR, and although he claimed to find "the signs of megalomania more distressingly apparent", his tone was one of cold contempt.

Wolf Mankowitz snapped up the opportunity of another round and in the *News Chronicle* dealt with the matter with bare knuckles—"the midget Leicestershire Zarathustra", "very bad writer", "a chilling picture of a monstrously precocious boy living out his lonely fantasies of genius, of saint-hood", and: "Among the psychotics, psychopaths, schizophrenics, mystics, visionaries and others who believe that 'the answer to the Outsider's problems is not a simple one, such as getting himself psycho-analysed', there will surely be a ripple of horribly excited anticipation at the next move by Mr. Wilson and his select few genius friends. Perhaps it will be a movement towards the unification of Outsiders everywhere into a great *Reich* of the spirit." (Below the article David Holloway, editor of the books page, printed an announcement: "From now on the phrase Angry Young Man will not be used on this page in any context whatsoever").

Cooler, but even more devastating, was Maurice Cranston's appraisal in *The London Magazine:* "He has written it in terms appropriate to an audience of apes and spiritual lepers; he has set his sights at the lowest intellectual and moral level."

Actually, all the above was relatively polite against the reception *Religion and the Rebel* received in the United States—and *The Outsider* had not by any means stunned everyone: the *New Yorker* then called Wilson a "backwoods revivalist of blood-chilling consistency". In *The New York Times Book Review* John W. Aldridge (Visiting Professor of English at Queens College) said roundly of *Religion and the Rebel:* "By less charitable American standards Mr. Wilson is quite simply brash, conceited, pretentious, presumptuous, prolix, boring, unsound, unoriginal and totally without intellectual subtlety, wit and literary style." *Time* Magazine gave the subject their needling treatment, with Wilson's photograph captioned "Egghead, scrambled", and a headline THE TOHU-BOHU KID. Recalling Joy's father's: "Aha,

Wilson, the game is up!", the story continued: "With this volume, Wilson's game of intellectual hooky is certainly up . . . sequence of unblinking non sequiturs, half-fashioned logic and firm disregard for the English language." They quoted from his last chapter: "If life did not pervade space and time, the universe of matter would be *tohu bohu*, complete chaos", and commented: "As for the present state of Colin Wilson's mind and thought— *tohu bohu*."

The Tohu-Bohu Kid was not himself around to give interviews and issue statements at this traumatic time. He had earlier vanished from Notting Hill and was living—and writing hard—in a farm cottage near Mevagissey, Cornwall, and did not even appear at the *Declaration* party a week before *Religion and the Rebel* came out. To some extent it could be argued that the savaging he received almost amounted to a self-inflicted wound but in fact he seemed to have taken the mass attack rather well. Over the telephone he told a *News Chronicle* gossip-writer: "The opinions expressed by critics have been mostly fair, and some very good. It is very encouraging for a young man like myself to find various book critics running over themselves to get in a 'first line'—good, bad or indifferent—about what I write." Victor Gollancz in a wave of pessimism advised him to abandon full-time writing and find a job, but Wilson stuck to seclusion, breaking it only with a long letter to *The Times Literary Supplement* to discuss a somewhat abstruse definition of existentialism raised by their reviewer, but referred only obliquely in his last paragraph to all that had happened: "In conclusion, let me admit that I feel that the term 'Outsider' has outworn its usefulness; I shall henceforth abandon it. I hope I can persuade Britain's journalists to follow suit. I have always considered my two critical books as a prelude to creative work, and therefore as essentially incomplete in themselves."

However the matter did not rest there. There was a little rally of sympathy and support from people who, while not necessarily sharing Wilson's views, took the view that he had had a raw deal. In the same issue of the *Literary Supplement* appeared a letter from Sir Herbert Read explaining his statement that he considered *Religion and the Rebel* a better book than *The Outsider* to be relative, as he was not on record as having said that *The Outsider* was a good book. But, he continued, "after the unreasonable success of *The Outsider* a reaction was inevitable, and I expected it. I did not expect it would be so unfair—unfair to the youthful fervour of Mr. Wilson, unfair to his essential modesty, unfair to his effective style and unfair to his passionate seriousness. Dismayed by the avalanche of unfavourable reviews that has fallen on *Religion and the Rebel*, I have looked at it again. My opinion is not changed. It has all the virtues that recanting reviewers found in *The Outsider* and fewer of the faults they missed. It is far from being a perfect book (as Mr. Wilson would be the first to admit); but those readers who were impressed by *The Outsider* should not be too ready to accept the opinions of those reviewers who feel they have to make public amend for the brash enthusiasm of seventeen months ago."

Marghanita Laski also was fascinated by the *volte face*. "Surely literary history can show no other example of such a major effort to destroy a very bad book as in the case of *Religion and the Rebel*," she wrote also in the same issue. "What is the cause of this extraordinary phenomenon? Certainly, some of the reviewers seem to be using Mr. Wilson as a scapegoat for their own shame at having been so profoundly impressed by his first book. But in the case of most, the scale of vituperation seems disproportionate to the apparent cause. One has the impression that however silly Mr. Wilson's ideas, they are felt to constitute a real and important danger; the cumulative effect of the reviews is a loud cry of 'Retro Sathanas'. So it does seem worth asking to whom and why Mr. Wilson's ideas are so dangerously attractive, and what more valuable pabulum is to satisfy the hunger they have apparently fed."

The most carefully analytical of other letters protesting against the ganging-up came from Dr. James Hemming, the psychologist. To the *New Statesman* he wrote:

"Janet Adam Smith and others who join the chorus to sneer at Colin Wilson protest too much. Can it be that they are afraid of this new style of attack upon snug preconceptions?
"Wilson with his own cocksureness, probes painfully at three

established cocksurenesses of our day—the Ayer brand of linguistic philosophy, traditional Christian theology, and the Marxist interpretation of history. The response of those challenged is, regrettably, irritation: Wilson is an upstart who presumes to speak with the authority of his own convictions; he is a megalomaniac, a fascist; his definitions are woolly; he can't write. Mr. Wilson's case, as it emerges from *The Outsider* and *Religion and the Rebel,* is ignored. Those who admonish Mr. Wilson to start thinking haven't even bothered to think for themselves.

"As I see it, Wilson's case is this: (1) Life is manifest in evolution by the extension of consciousness; (2) Man feels within himself the yearning to become more conscious—more alive; (3) At any period in history, the *status quo* is accepted by the unthinking, but a minority is always pressing ahead in the direction of increased consciousness. These are the Outsiders; (4) Each one of these, in his individual experience, painfully outgrows the *status quo* and finds himself thwarted by a sense that life as it is manifested in his society is only half-life. A sense of triviality and futility overwhelms him, often quite suddenly and unexpectedly; (5) People caught in this confusion and despair may find themselves restored to hope by a visionary experience through which a new direction is imparted to their lives; (6) We are today at a stage in our civilisation when Outsiders multiply and the *status quo* fails more and more to satisfy the deeper yearnings of man; (7) The retreat into Christian orthodoxy, 'Crosstianity', and the escape into linguistic rationalism can, in the end, only increase futility and despair because they exclude too much of man's experience; (8) Existentialism offers a way forward because it can embrace the whole of human experience while still leaving a way open for further advance; (9) The insights and attitudes of existentialism will need to be communicated through ritual and ceremony if they are to influence society and not be limited in their effects to the Outsiders. . . . True he has not stated his case in as many words—that is not his method at present—but it is there plain enough. His critics should have dealt with it instead of fuming around like middle-aged ladies at a vicarage tea-party into which an uninvited tramp has strayed."

So what is the value of Wilson's dissent? Has he really hacked his way through to a new existentialist base, from which further explorations of the spirit may start, as Dr. Hemming suggests? Or is he the muddle-headed menace that so many other experts seem so suddenly to have recognised him as?

185

For a start, it is nonsense to claim, as many reviewers did, that *The Outsider* was all right and *Religion and the Rebel* all wrong. As is, I think, quite obvious, *Religion and the Rebel* is a continuation of *The Outsider*—they are the halves of one book—and in fact Wilson has himself told me that he wanted them published complete in one volume, but was persuaded to issue them separately. To pretend that virtues belong to one half and vices to the other is dishonest: what faults and virtues are present are implicit within the entire framework of the two books.

Yet there is this important difference: between completing the first section and starting the second Wilson had been exposed to the giddy experience of mass attention, and in *Religion and the Rebel* he has been emboldened by this experience to state with thumps on the table, attitudes that were hinted at more tentatively in the first. In *Religion and the Rebel* Wilson himself states candidly: "My admiration went to a certain idea of cold brutality of intellect." That is (to me, at any rate) a repugnant state of mind, and I suspect that was at the root of the coat-turning of many men of good will who had not perceived that "cold brutality" in *The Outsider:* they tended to rationalise their awakened dislike by applying to the second book literary or academic standards they had not previously employed, and expressing their revulsion in those terms.

To a considerable degree the rapture about the author's age and hard-luck story in the case of the first book, and the vilification of the second, caused the significant, essential fact to be overlooked, that, as Dr. Hemming pointed out, Wilson is not only expressing his dissentience against "three established cocksurenesses of our day", but he is proposing a fresh idea of man's position in the universe, even if he is doing it in a cocksure way. Why Wilson seems to me obligatory reading today is that, without conventional training (probably because of that) at university, he has half instinctively fumbled his way through to a *European* attitude that is almost unique among our post-war rebels. I have no intention of attempting to summarise *The Outsider* and *Religion and the Rebel*, since they are themselves attempts at summarising—or crystallising—a vast range of human experience of a particular kind, the visions and suffering of those in search of salvation. Yet what I believe should not be ignored is that although Wilson's research may often have been weirdly distorted and blinkered, he has forced himself up out of the cosy insularity of English letters (really like someone lifting himself by his own shoelaces) and looked at the terrain of European thought, and he knew in undertaking his task that there was no way of avoiding the 'sensationalism' of which the post-war French existentialists were so often accused. In other words, Wilson understood what Guido Ruggiero meant when he said: "Existentialism treats life in the manner of a thriller." If it believes its own premises, it has to.

Quite plainly Wilson says: "The Outsider is a man who has awakened to chaos". This seems to me the simplest of propositions—and the inference that naturally follows, that most of us, uneasily but blearily aware of the nearness of that chaos, turn away our eyes to dead manageable things, and our attention away from the disturbing person who insists that truth must be faced. The Outsider, he says, is not a crazy, mixed-up kid; nor a bored bank-clerk. He is a symptom of a dying culture, of a civilisation in a state of decay—he is a "frustrated man of genius—the same type as the angry and frustrated young man whom James Dean has made fashionable in the Fifties". But he is driven by something greater than his own personality to delve deeper, to escape the surrounding confusion and reach the power that he senses exists within him, which of course may be interpreted as a religious problem, the eternal search for God.

In spite of all the gestures of intellectual revolt, Britain still remains infuriatingly innocent of the facts of life: our younger intelligentsia live less in an ivory tower than in a self-contained flat. Wilson is one of the few among them who have taken into account such men as Sartre, Camus and Beckett, and the German Hermann Hesse, and who have tasted the deep vein of Continental nihilism and pessimism. Yet in the last analysis Wilson's view of life is that "for all its torture and uncertainty it is divine" —even though he knows logically that the pessimism he has described in both books implicates the whole human race. "Civilisation cannot continue in its present muddling, short-sighted way, producing better and better refrigerators, wider and wider cinema-screens, and steadily draining men of all sense of a life of the spirit," he says. Although "it would be merely silly to speak of 'remedies' ", he finds in the end reasons for hope and optimism, the solution being for the individual Outsider to continue trying "to bring new consciousness to birth".

Wilson's diagnosis of our disorientated society should be read because while often contradictory it is also adventurous and relevant, and I am going to predict that in five years' time, long after these recent incestuous squabblings have been forgotten, *The Outsider* and *Religion and the Rebel* will still be in and out of the public libraries all over the country, and will quietly be increasing and formulating thought. However, I hope they will never be swallowed whole, I hope that they will be read to be criticised—because, after supporting Wilson up to this point, I too now depart from him.

It is not Wilson's pessimism that bothers me at all—that seems to me comparatively mild and justifiable as far as it goes. It is his reasons for optimism which are not only morally unacceptable but which should be seen not to be accepted. After Mankowitz, Mortimer and others had charged him with Hitlerian strong man yearnings, Wilson seemed to steady up. He described himself to me as a "socialist", and said he detested cruelty and injustice. I am not disputing those claims, merely pointing out that, as far as I am aware, it was the first time he had made them—and this was after *Religion and the Rebel* appeared.

Meanwhile, there, in that book for evermore, are described attitudes that, if the book was honestly written, you have to accept as being his honest opinions. What does he say? He says that Sartre's doctrine of 'commitment' is essential. The Outsider hates modern civilisation for its materialism: therefore he must not flee from it into an ivory tower, but *"seek power over it"*. Again: he must "strive to become a moving force behind society; to acquire power for one's fellow men by becoming a power among them". Even more nakedly: "the Outsiders must achieve political power over the hogs". And at the end of his Introduction there is

188

the final, ominous implication that he has other activities fixed
with a glittering eye. He was glad, he says, to have the books published—"but their publication was not an essential part of my
purpose. I am not necessarily a writer. The moment writing ceases
to be a convenient discipline for subduing my stupidity and laziness, I shall give it up and *turn to some more practical form.*"
(My italics.) During a speech at a meeting of the Shaw Society in
April last year, he remarked: "Hitler began as an outsider. An
outsider is capable of directing his will by his imagination. Ninety-
nine per cent of society are insiders led by outsiders."

In an essay published in 1950, just before the present cultural
revolt took hold, Storm Jameson said that during the Thirties—
"a time of generous anger, and of growing bitterness"—if you
looked at the names on the anti-fascist pamphlets and manifestos
littering your desk, you would have thought that all the young
English writers and poets were solidily in one camp. In fact, she
observed, there were a few people insisting that the political crisis
was not the simple one of angels v. devils, and T. S. Eliot refused
to sign the round robins—"not, certainly, because he had any sympathy with fascism. But because he had looked closer into the darkness than had most writers. . . The rottenness went deeper. . .
That same liberal humanism in whose name we were protesting
had itself betrayed the dignity of man. It had allowed itself to be
defeated by the inhuman forces of a mechanical civilisation.
Liberals were still talking about the dignity of man in a world in
which man had long since lost most of his dignity and most of his
freedom."

It is all very well for Storm Jameson, at this extent of retrospect,
to look back upon the Thirties and pick subtly at the fine threads
of partisanship, but I am not a bit convinced that Eliot's reason
for standing aloof was not a detestation of socialism and
egalitarianism more than sorrow at the way he had been let
down by liberal humanism. Upon occasions of acute danger, and
in the face of huge human issues, there are always only two sides,
and the niceties must be jettisoned. Things really *do* become black
or white. That is not the myopia of the moronic. It is the simpli-
fication that has to be made, and the furthest qualification that the

189

intellectual dare attempt in these circumstances is to act *in defiance*—in the sense that, as things are politically in this country, the vast amount of votes the Labour Party would collect from the intelligent, anxious electors would be, I suspect, anti-Conservative votes.

Of course how Wilson labels himself is not much guidance: it is the conduct of his argument that must be judged for itself. For Wilson, Eliot is a constant reference point, the intellectual battery from which he charges himself. Despite Storm Jameson's plea, there is a tone of 'classic inhumanism', a cold disgust and despair about humanity, contained in all Eliot's distinguished writings which reflect the royalist-authoritarian attitude. Whereas Beckett's conviction of damnation leads him to throw in his lot utterly with the remnants of human feeling, Eliot's has led to abdication, self-immolation to the Mother Church ("Teach us to sit still"). Nietzsche of the superman ideology, T. E. Hulme, the Imagist poet, with his loathing of the ideas of "progress" and his taste for despotism, and Spengler and his power morality—these have been three of the philosophies upon which Wilson has fed himself. These are the philosophies which he repeatedly translates into modern terms with such remarks as: "The average man needs to believe in a saviour as a child needs to believe in Santa Claus," an observation which is not only arrogantly pompous but demonstrably inaccurate in pagan Britain where Godfrey Winn can solve your problems for you on TV.

I believe Colin Wilson made a valuable contribution when, with the eyes and the voice of a young man of the Fifties, he formulated a post-war philosophical attitude in Britain by putting an original mind to diagnosing the spiritual condition of the time. His solution—or the means he proposes for reaching a solution—is not for me, and I hope won't be for most other people here.

In Britain today there is the curious placidity, the half-living, that maddens Osborne and drives the Outsider further into isolalation. There is no outward pressure of urgency, of crisis, of imminent terror, of being on the "pain threshold", that the world situation might seem to justify. But is the period really so poisoned that the public who was instantly contacted by *The Outsider* was

one of hitherto unidentified, unrecognised anti-humanists? —
whose hearts leaped joyfully to read "Humanism is only another
name for spiritual laziness", which is exactly the sort of slogan
any sweat-shop industrialist or any corporate state commissar
would use as sanction for bullying and controlling.

It may indeed be true that man has long since lost most of his
dignity and most of his freedom, but it would be folly, and rather
frightening folly, to throw out what is left of the humanistic ideal
too, for if Britain were filleted of that you would be more likely
to get a Western Germany, power-driven, disparately rich, materialistic and ruthless, rather than a whole population with "fire in
the head", lifted to a higher intensity of living.

Still — there is the situation. The excitement that Wilson's books
have caused may be symptomatic of a vacuum in our society, one
which sufficient intensity of 'feeling' of the wrong sort, whipped
on by the shrill emotionalism of the Osbornes and the Andersons,
might fill with a new mystical absolutism of the extreme right-
wing.

Even more disturbing — curiously enough, for it had a negli-
gible sale and could not be taken seriously — was Bill Hopkins's
novel *The Divine and the Decay* which was published in November 1957, a month after the *Religion and the Rebel* débâcle.
Throughout Wilson's writing, despite its brashness and want of
precision, there is a general dynamic synthesis: you know what
he is getting at, and although there is an ugly look about some of
the methods he seems prepared to use, you can accept the ultimate
object, which is, fundamentally, a richer spiritual life for man.
The Divine and the Decay was bad luck on all concerned, Wilson
particularly, for it was an embarrassing disclosure of how fine is
the division between the Outsider's upward-strivings and the
vicious claptrap of the 'leader'-type saviour.

In his autobiographical notes at the beginning of this section
Wilson mentioned meeting Bill Hopkins in Paris in 1953, and
how they talked about "the literature we intended to create".
Later, in London, their relationship became closer. In the few
months before *The Divine and the Decay* came out, Wilson did
his best to excite interest in his friend's first novel. But I fear it was

191

a disservice he did him, for again he overdid it in a ham-handed way. Wilson threw his genius cloak over Hopkins. In the tape-recorder interview in *Books and Art* he said "Hopkins has no reputation—yet", and added: "But before the year is out his name will be known all over England." Following this Hopkins was interviewed by a *Sunday Express* reporter, who asked him if he was a genius.

"That," replied Hopkins, "is a very difficult, almost impossible question to answer. But if a mark of genius is going where others have not been, writing about subjects others have not touched upon, then I suppose you could call me a genius." The story ended: "Hopkins dreads the thought he might be lionised like Colin Wilson."

He need have had no fears on that score. Although such bosh as the above cannot have been of any assistance to him, I fear that his novel would have been roasted in any event. It certainly was roasted. Although there is an unwritten law of charity among critics to deal gently with a first novel, most of them waived it in this case.

The Divine and the Decay is about a man named Plowart, a fanatical and peevish power-drunkard, who has come to stay on a Channel island while his party boss is being hatcheted to death in London, a crime Plowart has instigated in order to seize leadership of the New Britain League, a fascist *cadre*.

Plowart conceives himself in world terms as a dictator, believes in "the purity and truth of violence", and keeps in his suitcase a pin-up gallery of pictures of history's tough guys—Attila, Genghis Khan, Bismarck, Hitler, Lenin, and the rest. He meets Claremont, Dame of the Island, beautiful, enigmatic and intuitive, a sort of radio-active Twinkletoes, whom he glumly rapes (the dullest rape scene in literature) and attempts to deprive of the secret of how he may unify his schizophrenic soul and thereby attain the power to achieve his destiny. In an attempt to divert his obsessions into a less menacing course than murder and tyranny, Claremont tries to lure him to his death. Ritualistically they strip naked and swim into the boiling tide-race. She drowns. He survives, for he is indestructible.

The power-war and its effect upon men is a fascinating subject and, although timeless in its application, of especial importance in this age. Also, although Hopkins was indulging in more wild talk when he implied that he is the first writer to investigate this theme, it is true that it receives strangely little attention from the younger novelists engrossed in nearer, domestic scenes. It is a subject that still needs attention, for *The Divine and the Decay*, while certainly serious—positively long-faced—in its approach, is ludicrous in its result.

The story is soaked in phosphorescent paint, aglow with allegory and fantasy, its characters are weirdies to the last superman, and Plowart particularly is a sad clown. *The Times* likened the writing to that of Amanda Ros, and that is often so—"I shall take the wheel of Mankind's charabanc". The book is as clogged and murky as the inside of a thorn thicket. All the same, there is a force and passion in the book, which comes through even Plowart's absurd blather—this kind of silly, sick stuff: "They had fallen prey to absurd philosophies like humanism, to social systems like democracy, to ludicrous virtues like compassion. . . . But in their forties they became drunks, homosexuals, drug addicts, sex maniacs or aimless drifters" (Why wait till forty to become a sex maniac?) and: "Humanity is nothing at all. . . . The only people who take it seriously are sentimentalists."

If Hopkins were trying to ridicule the unbalanced fanatic type of power-seeker, you might, while wishing he had stopped short of making him such a crackpot whose grotesqueness invalidates any reality or relevance, sympathise with his motive. Regrettably it seems likely (you can't say it is clear, because nothing in this apocalyptical peasouper is clear) that he is the mouthpiece for the author's beliefs. As this is always an arguable assertion, I went to *Declaration* again to see if there I could find reason for thinking that Hopkins was projecting Plowart as a horrid warning. On the contrary, in his contribution entitled "Ways Without A Precedent" there is only confirmation of the opposite. There he writes: "There is something maniacal about a really desperate man that welds him into a total unity and he becomes an embodiment of a single idea. . . . Desperation is the only attitude that

G

can galvanise us from this lethargic non-living of ours. . . . The examples can only be set by fanatics advancing beyond the arena of human experience and knowledge."

Unfortunately during the past thirty years mankind has suffered too many attempts of this kind of advance "beyond the arena of human experience and knowledge" by power-men who think "humanity is nothing at all".

In a newspaper interview Hopkins stated that he intends to launch a political party in a few years' time. In an autobiographical sketch he sent me he amplified this ambition:

"What I want is the dissolution of all political parties. What I want to see is an assembly of 640 of the most able and intelligent men and women of the state INDEPENDENTLY debate the merits of every issue laid before it. I want to see an end of professional politicians and the beginning of the versatile citizen who commands a vision of every part of his own society. I want to form a political party of individuals who will dissolve the Commons from within when it has achieved a majority of seats. My religious belief is in the Glory of Man—but the Glory is to the most highly developed and most highly disciplined of men, not to one and all simply because we share the same fleshly appearances. I hate that socialist emotional claptrap. If I can drive my mind and spirit far enough I think I can achieve a state of power and omniscience that is the quintessence of the artist. . . . In my present mood society will have no alternative but to listen, and when it listens it will be influenced."

I have spent some space on Hopkins—who at the time of writing is in Hamburg working on a second novel *Time of Totality*—because although all this may be thought to be puerile poppycock he is getting a public platform, he is getting books published and that presumes an audience. It ought to be recognised that what would have seemed quite impossible fifteen years ago—even five years ago—is happening. A cult of fascism has grown among a generation who were babies when Europe's gas-chambers were going full blast, a set of under-privileged romantics in the coffee bar network, more formidable than Angus Wilson's Huggett and The Crowd, who get their kicks in a low pressure culture from wishful thinking about torture, pain and killing. We seem to be on the edge of a new romantic tradition which is sanctifying the bully as hero. It is exceedingly strange, and profoundly disturbing, if the dissentience (the 'anger') in our present semi-socialised compromise welfare society is going to swing retrogressively to the discredited and hateful system of murder gangs and neurotic mysticism which perished in its own flames. We know that there is political boredom and apathy in Britain, that the drive seems lost and the blood runs thin. Can it be so intolerable that it is creating an ardour for the corrupt vigour of fascism?

The third name that is linked with Wilson and Hopkins in our native existentialist movement is Stuart Holroyd. His book *Emergence From Chaos* was published in June 1957. In the blurb his publisher (Gollancz, who also published Wilson) rather disingenuously exclaimed: "What has caused the extraordinary success of Colin Wilson's *The Outsider?* The most important factor is probably this—that the very young author (his youth is important) attacks contemporary 'humanism', and argues that the way out of present predicaments must be, in some form or another, a religious one. In arguing this (rightly or wrongly) he has clearly spoken for a great public. And now comes a very different type of book with, nevertheless, a similar message: and it is important to note that Mr. Holroyd has been in no way influenced by Mr. Wilson. *Emergence From Chaos* was well under way before *The Outsider* was begun."

No, but it is also important to note that Mr. Wilson was influenced by Mr. Holroyd. As he reveals in *Religion and the Rebel*, it was from Holroyd that he got the idea of "dashing off" *The Outsider*, and as they are close friends there is no doubt, nor any point in concealing the fact that they have influenced each other.

Holroyd is the youngest of the trio (Hopkins was twenty-nine when *The Divine and the Decay* came out) and this fact was again brought out with a theatrical drum-roll on the dust-jacket: "It was Colin Wilson's age—twenty-four—that made *The Outsider* so specially interesting. Was his thought, people asked, typical of that of the youngest generation of writers (not that, as he has himself made clear, he was claiming anything of the kind)? In this connection, we were fascinated to learn, what we had no idea

195

of when we accepted his manuscript, that Mr. Stuart Holroyd, author of the present book, is only twenty-three."

I got the impression that the critics were not so thunderstruck by this as they were supposed to be (the *Economist* remarked testily that "before we all succumb in awe before these prodigies" it is salutary to remember that Gilbert Murray was twenty-three when he was appointed Professor of Greek at Glasgow) but *Emergence From Chaos* received fair and careful attention. There was nothing of the gee-whizzing that greeted *The Outsider*. It was discussed seriously as was the due of the serious book that it is.

Emergence From Chaos is a philosophical work, a study of six poets in their relation to the spiritual upheaval of the contemporary world. Through their art, he argues, these men—Dylan Thomas, Whitman, Yeats, Rimbaud, Rilke and Eliot—found a religious way of attaining self-transcendence, and Holroyd uses them to illustrate his own case for a new religious "unitive life". In his introduction he says: "The modern poet's world is chaotic within and without. The spiritual chaos which prevails everywhere in our time and which manifests itself equally in indifference to religion on the one hand and fanatical embracing of substitute religions on the other, may have had its cause in political and economic conditions, but its effects have been far reaching and have profoundly influenced the mental life of modern man. The poet is always the most sensitive register of contemporary sensibility, and in this book I have tried to show how a number of poets have reacted to the modern predicament, what means they have used, and to what extent they have succeeded in emerging from the chaos into which they were plunged by the accident of their birth."

The book also, he makes clear at the outset, is a propagandist attack on humanism. In his chapter "The Renaissance of Destiny" he has this to say: "At a time like the present, when tremendous psychological forces are at work reducing men to a common level, religion alone can save the individual human personality from submergence. By this I do not mean that the Church can do it, but rather that a man having a genuine religious attitude to life will be immune to the levelling process." If the solution were as simple as that there really would be cause for celebration, but unfortunately Holroyd overlooks the fact that the "levelling" that I suppose he would agree is personified in the Soviet Union and, at a more richly material level, in the United States, is possible because of a pseudo-religious conviction within individual citizens of those nations that they *do* live in a spiritual state—in the grace of Communism on the one side and the American Way of Life on the other. Holroyd inevitably draws attention to this yawning fallacy in his book by declaring at the start: "Religion is not so much man's attempt to know God as his attempt to know himself. . . . Religion is not justified by its truth but by its efficacy . . . a religion is anything that a man can live by. . . ." That is a theological solecism which impairs his entire argument, for a man's religion can only become truly a religion when he passes from reason into faith and believes his God to be objectively true.

The superiority of Holroyd's book over Wilson's is that it is exact and carefully developed, whereas *The Outsider* was often slipshod and excited; its superiority over Hopkins's is that, whereas they are in agreement in believing that the source of all spiritual power is not external circumstances but inner dedication (the Act of Will, or, really, Kierkegaard's "Truth is subjectivity"), it is lucidly written and Holroyd is not possessed to the point of incoherence by the daydreams of political action that obsess Hopkins, or at least his character Plowart.

Holroyd was born in Bradford, Yorkshire, son of a working-class father (milkman, taxi-driver, commercial traveller) and a middle-class devout Methodist mother. He attended Arnold School, in Blackpool, and was expected to take the Oxford and Cambridge scholarship, but he decided to escape the academic atmosphere, and got a job with the local repertory company as an actor and stage manager. He left after a year, when they turned down his first play, and came to London to try and live by writing. He worked as a table-cleaner in a Corner House and in coffee-bars, and did a variety of odd jobs, and in 1956—while he was writing *Emergence From Chaos*—enrolled at University College to study philosophy under Professor A. J. Ayer. Then he found, he has told me, that "detached analytical philosophising was anathema to me. After a year I'd had enough of the scope and method of philosophy, and felt that the other two years of my degree course would only pile on intellectual lumber."

Holroyd has no compulsion towards Sartre's "engagement". He has told me:

"I lack it but don't 'feel the lack' of it. Political commitment can only serve to narrow down your vision, whereas the most important thing for the writer to do in our time is to achieve a comprehensive vision, to take everything into himself and there give it organisation, shape, unity. I don't feel to be lost in the dark, to be a 'rebel without a cause'. I confront the complexity of the contemporary world with the belief that the only way out of it is *through* it. We must take it into ourselves. It seems to me that anyone who accepts a political solution chooses to go round instead of through. My fundamental belief that no lasting or significant change can be effected from above but must come from below as the expression of a new sense of life, makes me sceptical of all action on the political level. The writers of the Thirties, and also some of the post-war writers, were too obsessed with the idea of their responsibility *to* society to take upon themselves the far greater responsibility *for* society and for its future. In the present decade the writer's responsibility *to* society is the responsibility of communicating a deeper sense of life, his responsibility *for* society is that of having the vision and the courage to create new foundations for belief. These two activities are not separate and distinct, but for their fulfilment we require a race of philosopher-artists such as Nietzsche predicted would one day appear in the world."

There appears here to be an altogether more objectively altruistic attitude, but it should not be thought that Holroyd is basically any less violent in his opposition to humanism, his opposition to the entire concept that man is capable of living by his own capacity, what Bertrand Russell defined as The Good Life, "one inspired by love and guided by knowledge," which is, really, no matter how manipulated and warped it has become, the concept upon which all present-day Western society is based. It immediately becomes obvious that Holroyd is as severe as the others (although for more complex and devout reasons than Hopkins) in his rejection of Christ's precepts of mercy and compassion, and especially of the traditional interpretation of holiness. "The popular idea of the saint, is like most such ideas, a half-truth. Gentleness and concern with the welfare of his fellow-men are not inevitable qualities of the saintly man," he writes. And: ". . . Nietzsche felt a great antipathy for the saintly man and considered him to be the most degenerate, weak-spirited and parasitic specimen of the human race."

In his *Declaration* essay, "A Sense of Crisis", he writes: "A man may be uncharitable, intolerant and self-centred, and still be profoundly religious." He finds a more authentic religious attitude in Rimbaud's deliberate demonism: "I succeeded in extinguishing within myself every human hope. . . . I summoned the executioners, that, dying, I might bite their rifle-butts. I summoned all plagues, to choke me in sand and blood. Adversity was my God. I sprawled in the mud, and dried myself in the air of crime." Remarks Holroyd: "Why did he wish to experience hell? Because he wished to explore himself thoroughly and knew that certain regions of the human soul are accessible only by way of extreme and violent experience."

In other words it is a *sense of sin* that these religious dissentients find lacking in the post-war world, and therefore redemption. This becomes clearer when Holroyd speaks directly of what he believes to be the metabolism of religious feeling: "The congenital optimism of the Humanist attitude has been severely shaken in this twentieth century. The faith in progress is still very strong, but here and there individuals have been waking up and asking, Where is it all leading to? And the answers which the more far-sighted of them have been constrained to give to this question have brought the Devil back into our world with a vengeance. The vision of evil has returned into modern art. And when these negative elements, the vision of evil, disillusionment and the sense of the vanity of life, have been ripened in the solitude of the human heart, there emerges out of them something positive and rejuvenative, namely the authentic religious attitude." In *Declaration* he asks: What is the main root of the degeneration in this age? and answers: "The humanist-scientific culture which has dominated the European scene for the last three hundred years, and infected all branches of thought, political, philosophical and aesthetic, with its poison."

Certainly one wishes that the question Where is it all leading to? was being asked more urgently and by more of his generation of writers. Holroyd is now working on a book entitled *The Despair of Europe* which he intends as a survey of the collapse of the moral order in Europe, which, if it did not happen precisely then, became evident at the outbreak of the 1914 war—since when, he maintains, three threats have overhung the consciousness of modern man: death, meaninglessness and condemnation.

What distinguishes the Wilson group from most of the other dissentients of the Fifties is that not only are they attacking the old philosophical structure, but they are doing so because they have examined it in a European context and have condemned it as inadequate. They see the ramifications of our social ills, not merely the local symptoms of a fall in gold reserves, or inflation, or diminishing imperial power, or this year's suicide rate, or the National Health bill of millions of pounds for tranquillisers. At the same time this conscientiously "cosmic eye" vision—Holroyd's insistence that "we must take it into ourselves"—brings about the complete ignorance of detail that I pointed to in Wilson's case, and there are in all the vast diagrams in which this group have chosen to work immense empty spaces of naïvete and inexperience.

What never seems to occur to them is that others who decline to accept their call to arms for a new militant religious aristocracy (which is actually a vision of the mediaeval monastery's high, invulnerable walls dominating the village from its hilltop) are also dismayed by the spread of contented barbarism. Of course it is true that throughout all the towns and cities of Britain there is a snack-bar level of well-paid zombie-life, that the People's Capitalism has produced Hoggart's "spiritual dry rot amid the odour of boiled milk", a soggy, sterile existence. Of course one can appreciate that Bertrand Russell, the Emmanuel Goldstein of the Wilsonians, is deficient in imagination, in the poetry of the senses that W. B. Yeats meant in the lines the Wilsonians love to quote:

A levelling, rancorous, rational sort of mind
That never looked out of eye of a saint
Or out of a drunkard's eye.

Of course man falls short of perfectibility; human virtue is less than pure; freedom and happiness are contingent upon more than the public ownership of the means of production.

Yet when you read (in Holroyd's *Declaration* piece): "The alternative is to acknowledge that government is an art which should be in the hands of an expert minority, and at the same time to make the system fluid enough to prevent power falling into the hands of self-interested demagogues," you realise that you are face to face with a political simpleton. Furthermore, you realise, despite their reading and their eagerness to span the widest range of ideas, geographically and historically, how insulated and stunted has been the experience of these Welfare State boys. They dismiss democracy, representational government, and the attempt to honour the dignity of man through social legislation that is the inspiration behind our system, without any apparent knowledge of the history of individual dedication, courage and idealism that went into the making of it. They must know, if only from their own families' histories, about such conditions as mass unemployment, Means Tests, malnutrition, Jarrow, strikes, insecurity and privation, slumps and slums. Yet I wonder if they would understand the baffled derision they would arouse in any well-paid industrial worker today, with a New Town house full of comfortable over-stuffed furniture, a telly and several strong warmly-clothed children, if they told him his life had been "poisoned" by humanism and that he had "lost his feeling of uniqueness"? They must be at least vaguely aware of the barb-wire, Thought Police compounds, castor-oil and rubber truncheons, racialism and slave-camps that filled all the atmosphere of Europe with fear. Yet I wonder if they would understand the anger of an adult who lived through that, and was embroiled in a war sanguinely fought to expunge those things, when they portentously recommended to him government by "expert minority" and the privilege of glory for "the most highly developed and most highly disciplined of men"? The aspects of modern life that sicken and horrify these dissentients may indeed be symptoms of the end of the era of liberal optimism, the decline of the West, but an insurrection by a will-power 'religion' could only wreck what might still survive and become vital again. Some dynamics are more dynamic than others, but they are not necessarily better. I am sure that the Wilsonians would regard Brecht as an old fuddy-duddy, full of pathetically antique sentimentality, yet although Brecht's loathing for commercial civilisation towered above theirs in rhetorical fury, his love for all life was generous and warm: he never doubted that man is indestructible—because man is not a machine geared obsessively to one purpose.

Praise the grass and the beasts who live and die near you!
See!
How the grass and the beast live like you
And must also die like you!
Praise the tree that from carrion grows up rejoicing to the sky!
Praise the carrion.
Praise the tree that devoured it.
But praise the sky too!

Despite the height at which the Wilsonians set their sights, their refusal to become bogged down in immediate surrounding questions, I am not sure that the hesitant, groping answer found by Thomas Hinde's Larry, the lost soul in the mid-century undergrowth, is not better: "It's just the sense of the importance of struggling." Finally I quote at the Wilsonians some words of their arch-enemy Russell which hold steadfast the ethic which, although applied too seldom, endures as a standard: "We are sometimes told that only fanaticism can make a social group effective. I think this is totally contrary to the lessons of history. . . The world needs open hearts and open minds, and it is not through rigid systems, whether old or new, that these can be derived."

Now the Nineteen-Fifties near their end. The decade began by attempting to graft on to itself a personality from earlier periods, a flourish of Edwardianism gingered up with a shot of the Roaring Twenties, but it has matured into a powerful distillation all its own, an extract of the essence of this surpassingly strange situation in which most of human society is in a state of physical well-being hitherto unequalled and on the brink of a mass nervous breakdown hitherto impossible.

Deliberately or unconsciously an age is expressed in artistic terms, and this is the situation in which the post-war writers of Britain are involved, this sense of living an illusory easy life in a world overhung by a primed nuclear device. It is precisely this inner apprehension and inadequacy which permeates present-day British writing, which has brought about the disestablishment of the older intellectual leaders and a new "movement" which fumbles with the authority it has appropriated.

The limitations of a book of this kind are obvious. What I have been attempting to do in the preceding pages is to isolate and examine a condition of dissentience which has become recognisable during the past ten years or so, which has grown out of the post-war situation and has also helped to produce this period's distinctive flavour. In an undertaking such as this there is an inevitable arbitrariness. I have sought this element of dissentience

203

in the work of the new generation of writers, but I have tried to avoid bending the pattern of the cultural revolt to premeditated theories, to exclude all that did not honestly seem to be within those terms of reference.

The consequence is of course that some of the best writers now at work have been either referred to only in passing or omitted altogether. I am thinking here of such mature, professional crafts-men of confirmed distinction as James Hanley, C. P. Snow, Anthony Powell, Gwyn Thomas, Henry Williamson, T. H. White, L. P. Hartley, P. H. Newby, Graham Greene, William Sansom, Laurence Durrell, Rose Macauley and J. D. Scott, and of younger writers of either clearly outstanding talent or exceptionally bright promise such as Brendan Behan, Frank Tuohy, Mervyn Jones, John Coates, Gerald Hanley, Colin MacInnes, Patrick Anderson, Doris Lessing, Christopher Arnold, Brian Glanville, Emyr Humphreys, William Golding and Francis King. All of these share a quality of ability that certainly is not possessed by all of the people to whom space has been devoted earlier in this book. But, for my purposes, one or other of two things are missing from the above: the sense of having been specifically sparked by circum-stances of this period or the sense of specifically influencing the mental mood of this period. This applies even to Mervyn Jones's thoughtful and accurately contemporary *The New Town* and to Colin MacInnes's brilliant, warm and wise novel about London's new coloured population, *City of Spades*. Sensitive to the climate and the times though these and many of the others are, they have an independence of the time and place in which they are writing, they are writers of a more traditional vein—whereas all those associated with the Angry Young Man idiom, these Anglo-Saxon existentialists and delinks, the I Like It Here boys and the "Method" leftists, are *part* of the scene.

Yet here is the central paradox within the "movement" of the Fifties: involved though they are in their individual love or hate relationships, so few of the new dissentients have taken true cogni-zance of their surroundings. Huge areas of our society, particu-larly the industrial life of the nation and the industrial popula-tion, who seem to be understood and served only by sections of

THE END OF INNOCENCE

the popular Press, continue to be largely ignored by the new writers. Theirs seems, in its different way, almost as narrow, egocentric and contracting a view of British life as was that of the old gang—the indigenous niggling narcissism of British writers whom Sartre lumped together as "the young ladies' orchestra". If you accept that a novel's function is to be the image of the society it draws its life from, it is precisely there that the new writing fails—because of its fragmentation. The novels and the plays are like jigsaw pieces whose total picture is an enigma. They deal with the plight of the individual, often movingly, often amusingly, but rarely with any whole sense of precedent or synthesis, and the major direction that is now discernible is getting the individual fitted snugly into the class structure, forcing the Establishment to accept the new intake on its own terms.

A drab sort of personality-cultism has become fashionable in the Fifties, and, while apologising for bringing the name up again, it is depressing to see how the half-baked symbolism of that broody bravo James Dean has soaked through into the 'serious' side of the new literature—the same suppurating exhaustion of a spiritual deadbeat on the road to nowhere. Of course that is the vital problem of our present civilisation: the dehydration of the personality, the sucking dry of human juices, the creation of Priestley's "permanent audience fixed in a consumer's attitude". But a writer does not illuminate the problem by turning it in upon itself, by giving it a tainted smartness, a cheap rebel-without-a-cause allure. Too much modern writing is busy glamourising this condition without genuinely caring about its causes. The old convention, when it mattered less, was the brilliant, eccentric artist versus the dull, stodgy bourgeoisie. The new convention is the psychopath versus the brainwashed. It is used as a gimmick and dangerously obscures the real dilemma.

Certainly the new writing is not all diamonds and gold leaf, but on the other hand the Fifties is turning out to be the most actively creative decade in Britain since the Twenties—far more so than the Thirties, which despite its atmosphere of sincerity and serious endeavour creaked with 'automatic' writing: the outcome of political cheer-leading and party-lining which produced much

205

unadmirable joycamp poetry and literature, that conscientious period of John Grierson and the dedicated romantics of documentary films, of Ralph Fox's *The Novel And The People,* of W. H. Auden's embarrassing experiments in the blues idiom. Whatever criticisms can be made of the current dissentients they are an innovating, restless talent, and it should not be forgotten how direly that was needed. I do not share Colin Wilson's optimism that this TV-and-paperback age is about to burgeon "a great literary renaissance", but let it not be forgotten that only a few years before the cultural revolt broke out the really big sellers were by men who had escaped from a *Stalag* or crossed the South Pacific on a balsa log, and I personally find it cheering that now a play such as *Look Back In Anger* and a book such as *The Outsider* can attract huge audiences. Also it does seem that, introverted and diffuse though much of the post-war work is, it has more of a dynamic than that being done by the corresponding generation of any other nation.

In France there seems to be in process a parallel metamorphosis, the death of the literature of the aristocracy and leisured middle-class, but among critics there is disappointment and anxiety that most of their Angry Young Men—the urgent voices of the late Forties, such at Dutourd, Vailland, Robbe-Grillet and Nimier—seem to have lost impetus. In America there has only just begun to be one. The tutorial middle-aged have had to change the traditional tune. Now it is not bathtub gin, petting parties, bobbysoxers, swoon-kids, reefer-smoking and jitterbugging that are lamented—it is the sobriety of America's high school and college youth. There the quietism, which in Britain at higher educational level derives from the prevailing climate of linguistic philosophy and Sir Lewis Namier's view of history, is wider and more negative. Intellectual apathy, neutralism, and a deliberate disavowal of enthusiasm seem to have become the characteristics of the American campus. Last year a little bubble of reaction appeared to be blowing up against that quietism and against what has been described by Elmer Rice as "the industrialisation of the writer—he is no longer creating . . . he writes to specification in the same way that a building contractor would order so many tons of steel girders". This revolt crystallised in an outlandish novel *On The Road* (due out here this spring) by Jack Kerouac, the self-nominated spokesman for what he has named the "beat (short for beatific) generation". The beats appear to be a minority of separatists, in *On The Road* a rootless gang of jukebox hobos, penniless religious rakehells, who hurl around the American continent in stolen or borrowed cars, or their own hotrods, listening to bop wherever they can dig it, chasing not only girls but the illusion of living: they shout "Yes!" to every experience, they are the ones "who are mad to live, mad to talk, mad to be saved, desirous of everything at the same time, the ones who never yawn or say a commonplace thing, but burn, burn, burn like fabulous yellow roman candles". Kerouac claims that the beat movement is part of the revival of religious mysticism predicted by Spengler "in the late moments of Western civilisation", and beat-mystic Philip Lamantia, explaining to TV-interrogator Mike Wallace the meaning of his lines:

> Come Holy Ghost, for we can rise
> Out of this jazz

said: "Christ invites everyone, including the outcasts. So there's no contradiction at all between Christ and a bebopper and a hipster."

America's beat generation hardly corresponds to the French Outsider, with his dulled imperviousness, nor to Britain's delinks, yet there is a similar international pattern perceptible: that of the social dissentient who is searching for moral coherence and religious belief. In France he has also been given the name of the Deserter (by Henri Thomas) and the Objector (by Michel Vinaver). It is in Britain that his identity and hostility have been expressed most vividly and forcibly—yet still in a purely parochial way.

Orwell used to point out in the middle Forties that no-one in Britain could really know what European politics were all about— not in the feeling-in-the-belly sense—because all their knowledge of that nightmare world of secret police, censorship of opinion, torture and frame-up trials was at several removes. Orwell, with his unique gloom at that time, looked forward and saw that "the democratic vistas had ended in barb-wire", and was the only writer I know of who could summon the courage—or hopelessness—to say then, when Utopia, a bit bedraggled and shrapnelnicked, was being dragged in by the scruff of the neck: "Since about 1930 the world has given no reason for optimism whatever. Nothing is in sight except a welter of lies, hatred, cruelty and ignorance, and beyond our present troubles loom vaster ones which are only now entering the European consciousness. It is quite possible that man's major problems will *never* be solved."

Following that, there is a certain melancholy logic and sequence to be derived from recalling François Mauriac's words about the writer's relationship to the tragedies of his times in an interview with Philip Toynbee last autumn, twelve years later. "Nobody can be forced to enter this horrible political battle of our time," said Mauriac. "Everybody has the right to prepare for his own death. The only decent alternative that I can see to this is to enter the battle and to engage oneself as I have done."

We may now be in the thick of some of the preliminary problems Orwell predicted, but Britain still is in that insulated state of mind that diluted the terrors of the Thirties by the time they got over the Channel. In Europe, it always seems to me, the very same perplexities are felt like a lash on the bare skin; here our seat is padded in the traditional public school way. By the time they reach Britain ideas and intellectual argument are muddied, as if they got too shaken up in transit.

Last year Albert Camus published *The Fall* and in France there was an instant electric response to the new postulates of this man who occupies a position of responsibility and authority that is unimaginable for a writer here, and far beyond the zone of influence Colin Wilson briefly believed he had created for himself. With four novels and two plays as his credentials, Camus, who is still a young man, has become the spokesman for his generation with his lucid exploration of the human conscience. In *The Outsider* and *The Plague* Camus displayed mentally the integrity and stamina that he displayed physically as a Resistance man. *The Myth of Sisyphus* was the statement of ultimate conflict— the man whose reason disavows the God that he must admit to himself is his only hope of redemption. Withheld from divine

grace by the reason that tells him it is the only way out of despair,
Camus seems now to be cutting purposively through the undergrowth towards a solution. The point I am making is that Camus's
endeavours to find the spiritual imperatives he needs are watched
with sharp attention and understanding in France, by Catholics
as well as by agnostics and ex-communists, because there is the
wide belief that the moral decisions he reaches will be valid and
right for his contemporaries.

Can you imagine anything like that happening in Britain, even
in these past few years when the individual writer has had more
publicity and a bigger audience for his views than perhaps ever
before? What is absent here is respect, and the newcomers must
accept that one reason why they don't receive it is because of the
disregard most of them have for the real conditions of misery and
frustration and bewilderment, a disinterest in discovering the
authentic sources of what satisfactions and fun are to be had. For
most of them—even if they do weave in some coffee bar atmosphere and a disorientated junior lecturer or two—the Fifties
remain virgin land.

You have, when assessing our Young Angries, to attune your ear
to anger's full octaves. In the period that followed the end of the
first world war appeared such books as Henry Williamson's *The
Pathway*, Robert Graves's *Goodbye To All That*, Richard Alding-
ton's *Death of a Hero*, and Siegfried Sassoon's *Memoirs of an
Infantry Officer*. All these were post-war angry young men, angry
at the huge swindle into which they and their generation had
gone with such careless enthusiasm and perished, angrier still at
the mental war-attitudes of the civilians and politicians, and the
books they wrote were passionate with the compulsion to tell
England what they had seen and experienced, what a fraud was
the home-front version of the Western Front, what no-one at
home yet knew: that the old world had ended. Since then in our
lifetime the reasons for grief have been too big and pervading to
be disregarded, and beside them no amount of snivelling and
petulance and rattling of the play-pen is going to carry much
weight. You have to set your measurement of despair against the
crags Beckett has climbed, and of hope beside that which always

soars out of Brecht's anatomy of corruption. You have to decide about the importance of a novelist's conception of moral issues by relating them to those in which all of the Western World is involved, not only London, or a cathedral town, or the Potteries. You have to take into account a universality that perhaps cannot be found here.

"Can man survive? This is *the* question, this is *the* anguish, of our age," wrote Storm Jameson in *The Writer's Situation* eight years ago. At that time Miss Jameson felt that a writer's job was to "insist upon the value of values", and finally she was able to reaffirm the faith of Andrè Malraux—certainly no optimist—in the "resurrection and everlasting life of Europe".

I don't know what answers Miss Jameson would give today. Then she came to the conclusion that: "What we need now may be just that insolent irresponsibility, the contempt for safety and comfort and riches, the passionate delight in freedom, the curiosity, the blind hunger for experience and new knowledge, of the mediaeval wandering scholar. . . . The temptations to write for the most glittering rewards ever offered to writers are enormous. Perhaps the only new method is to take vows of poverty and simplicity and refuse bribes." Despite their superficial likeness to the mediaeval wandering scholar I fear I can see no sign of any of the post-war rebels, the French *clochard,* the American "beat generation", or the British delink, rising to that high ascetic standard of conduct—or even of ideals.

However one *knows,* without being able to produce statistics, what a diffuse but profound influence a work of art can have—I am thinking now of the artistic conversions that such American films as *Winterset* and *Grapes of Wrath,* a play like *Awake and Sing,* the Hemingway stories and Dos Passos's newsreel novels had on my generation who were leaving school just before the Hitler War broke out. So perhaps chemical things are now happening to produce more outward looking, greater alertness to not only the surface eddies of the Fifties, but to the deeper currents. I am not here prescribing what sort of writing we *should* be getting, only remarking on the sort we *aren't* getting, for what cannot fail to strike anyone who looks around at the contemporary dissentient scene is not only the triviality of some of the emotion but the sparseness of constructive ideas. Despite an aggressive and bold manner, the prevailing spirit is often self-seeking and insecure. I dread that I shall sound like a lectern-beating prize day speaker lamenting the death of the lust for adventure, but there is a suspicion that the cultural revolt is petering out into withdrawal and safeplaying: pity is solicited only for the individual who 'hasn't made it'. Even in many of those who rail against the present there is an implicit repining for the past (e.g. Osborne, but also a good deal of the 'new conservatism' in poetry and criticism) and little enthusiasm for moving imaginatively forward. Political idealism, as we have seen, is either quixotic or is regarded as futile, or as a rather loathsome disease, and the inevitable frustration comes through in a form of anarchic unrest. 'Inspiration' and the rejection of reason seem to be the way out of scepticism chosen by both the emotional left-wingers and the Wilson right-wingers. Anarchic unrest can be a healthy productive state of mind, but at this mid-century moment it seems to impel the individual not to construct new standards but to try to adapt the old society to his own liking. It is almost like a counter-revolution by the sons of the White Russians.

I have been trying to think how this decade will look to someone in 1984 evaluating its culture and its mood from an examination of the writing and public utterances of its young intellectuals. I think that he will see a sensitive, emotional, intelligent but wretchedly neurotic society, obedient to protocol beneath the exhibitionist 'rebelling', and obsessively class-conscious. For this seems to me to be the most ironical paradox of all. Britain put itself through a straightening-out process of democratisation and economic levelling, and has come out at the other end with many of the old values still intact, in a different place and slightly exacerbated by the disruption, which might be likened to trying to flatten a bump in linoleum: when you look round it's heaved up behind you, and anyway the pattern is exactly the same. The alacrity with which the U and non-U vogue caught on for a while in the middle Fifties was a demonstration of the continuing eagerness of the British to belong to the right set, to have the rubber-stamp of approval upon our accent and manner of behaviour, not at all costs to be a MIF (milk in first) which is the middle-class version of a square. Finally the distinguishing subtlety was to have the inside appreciation that the most non-U thing in the world was to use the phrase non-U, and this was carried further, as described in Roger Longrigg's *Switchboard,* into a whole alphabet of caste code letters. For numbers of the besieged middle-classes this passing fancy seemed to contain the prayed-for promise that things were going to get better.

Aware now that *plus ça change, plus c'est la même chose,* welfare-succoured, reared into a society with a humanitarian ethic of decency and kindliness, in which 'good citizenship' has been propagated as the criterion of conduct, the new dissentient may be starting to suspect that this is an artificial placidity which has no link with the larger crises of vanishing individuality in an over-organised bureaucratic civilisation, and the even bigger commination of nuclear war. The writer, like all of his age, has been conditioned to respect and adhere to the man-of-centre ideal who might be represented as a £16-a-week steady, pipe-smoking artisan with a safe job in the local works, a New Town house with a primrose front door, an attractive wife and two 'kiddies', and a life well balanced between the TV set and the neatly-tended garden. The dissentient does not necessarily live in these circumstances (although it is surprising how many *do,* with just a little thicker topping of culture) but he has the picture always before him as the hub of present-day civilised life. If he deviates or carries his opinion through into rejection, it is like stepping off a warm, well-lit stage, where the convector-fire burns brightly and the 'contemporary' armchairs form a tight, safe circle, into the outer darkness—he is instantly one of those lost souls in search of his cards of identity.

So, ambivalent and uncertain, the new writer's hero tends to fall into either of two already rather stylised forms, both of which are self-centred in its literal egocentric meaning. He is either the expedient conformist, a single-minded success boy, conserving all his energies for swarming up the ladder (financial rather than

212

social) and with none to spare for footling idealistic pursuits, or he is the rebel, the Angry Young Man.

The go-getter is no new type, either to society or fiction, but the difference in the post-war model is that, although driven by ambition, envy and greed in the good old ruthless Trollope way, he has no admiration or liking for the class he is gatecrashing. He wants its advantages and privileges, but its conventions look to him to be wet, lah-di-dah and stupid. He has no wish to be assimilated. He merely wishes to kick the Wendy house out of the way and take over.

The rebel at least keeps his distance, but no political affiliations are possible for him; he has no wish "to lash the vice and fallacies of the age". He has no sense of 'otherness' because his personal rancours occupy his introversion. Not reprovingly but quite objectively I mention that among the writers and prominent intellectuals—Priestley, Toynbee, Gollancz, Alex Comfort and John Berger—who earlier this year took an active part in the anti-H-bomb campaign there was not a single one of the younger well-known dissentients. The reason that this type of post-war adventurer refuses to throw his militancy in support of any of the accepted political or religious movements is because he is unconvinced that there is any ideal left to be worked for, and suspects that anyway all of the party vested interests, who are piqued because he won't throw in with them, would twist him.

It seems to him to come down to this: Marx was a fraud. Freud never really worked. The revolution was sold-out. Utopia turned out to be a cross between a giant post office and a Fabian summer school. The new dissentient reads the lengthy analyses that appear in the political weeklies and the trans-Atlantic literary journals, all of which argue from the assumption that ours is "a society in a state of transition". That is the key phrase: the ready-made theory that although the omelette is still liquid it will soon be nicely cooked and looking just like the other one. The inference to be drawn is that progress continues, all these restless odds and ends will form up and fall into their proper stations, and dear old England will be just as she always was, proud, eccentric and patchily prosperous.

I doubt if there is a single one of the younger intellectuals who thinks that is anything but pathetic nonsense. The talk on the one hand of becoming a Third Force, and on the other of being *Great* Britain again with the old lion roaring, has no perceptible effect whatsoever upon him. To him it does not seem that this is "a society in transition". It seems to him a nation in regression whose tensions have gone slack, whose muscles have failed, whose dynamic has forever gone. The condition is that of decadence. He does not see a frontier-minded population thrusting aside old ideas to find new and better patterns of living. He sees a corpse, pumped full of a formaldehyde of welfarism to preserve the illusion of life.

In a situation that appears as extreme as this there are only three possible courses. You throw in your hand and go over to the "shiny barbarism"—of course, as an intellectual, you don't actually participate but merely move on to its higher income group periphery—and, having done this spiritual bunk, you see the time out in the family circle, where there are always your review copies to read, the hi-fi, the children, and the appurtenances of the furtive cultivated mind, the only lack being a future. This is really the most pessimistic course. Or, if you see the underlying stagnation and believe there is still time for fresh springs to be channelled in, you set about it. That is the rarest activity of all in current writing. Much commoner are the half-way housers—those who hate the death-warmed-up Britain of today but who, having no positive ideas, lose their nerve and just fulminate. That is a very unhappy position to be in.

It is this stricken lack of confidence that gives much modern British writing its specific overtone of a sort of shaky defiance. No matter how complex a paradigm the writer considers his art to be—or how simple a job to do—it is fed and nourished by the community he lives in. If he hates it, there is an obligation upon him to say why and try to justify that hate. But the overall impression left from a study of the work of the post-war dissentients in all its variety is a lack of confidence in their dissentience, an uncertainty about their position in society and the purpose of their rebellion—so they bluster to cover up the self-doubt.

A text book definition of the angry young man of today, both the fictional hero and his real-life creator, might be: a state of talent largely surrounded by indecision. It is at that point that we find the apprentice writer (for, after all, even with a best-seller or two and some thousands of pounds to the good, that is what anyone in his thirties still is) in Britain in the late Fifties. There is a panicky feeling that the old points of reference have been lost — gone is the basic conviction of the strength and decency of the common people everywhere, the assumption that there must be material progress and that material progress would naturally produce spiritual progress. There are those who would like to return to the womb of socialist simplicities, those who want to be rid of those old moral encumbrances, and the rest see no reason for faith in either undertaking and are displaced and empty of the sense of social fitness.

There is now among Britain's dissentients an ominous atmosphere of the end of the party: the fun and games are over, all the excitement and the popping of Beaujolais corks, the glad-hands and the introductions all round. The barricades have been flattened; barring a few stubborn pockets of resistance, the enemy territory has been occupied. They are, as has been widely and repetitively stated, the inheritors and the new spokesmen.

Whatever happens in Britain in the next twenty-five years, humanity at large isn't dead yet and, barring the obvious occurrences that could swiftly accomplish that, may by then be groping through into the clammy light of dawn. Obviously this is one of history's big traffic jams, with all the combined turbulence of new forces of philosophy, religion, politics and science boiling up against the banks of hardened obsolete thinking, of prejudice, fear and mistrust, and there is no telling yet where or when the break through might come, and how the world map of civilisation will then look.

Yet whatever change in shades of emphasis and degree of direction may be brought about by new parties in power, the root situation will not change. Historically Western civilisation has come to the managerial stage. Society, whatever the banners of its various governments, will remain for our lifetime and our

215

children's, complex, centralised and depersonalised. Apparently at opposite political poles, the deadly similarity of the new ethic can be seen in two powers which dominate the world today, the U.S.A. and the U.S.S.R. This is becoming the century of the Organisation Man, the well-adjusted, hedonistic, orthodox, committee man, bred to serve the faceless paternalistic corporations which interlock throughout the modern world, whether they are called General Motors or the Lenin State Tractor Plant. However much it may be argued whether 'engagement' is right or wrong for the artist in specific political issues, there can be no dispute about his function within the wide context of our time. It is the duty of everyone sensitive to the situation to help to humanise the machine we have to live in; it is, because of his own nature, the particular duty of the artist to exalt the human spirit, to glorify the full meaning that the free personality can have, and to work to improve—or even just maintain—communication between those who have stayed free.

The post-war dissentient may feel anger or disgust at the local symptoms of these great changes, but he too rarely attempts to see them wholly—in their relation to the bigger metabolism that is in process. Now he may have to. He could not have had a more generous welcome, more attention, a better Press. He has had no cause to make the complaint that has been the genuine unhappiness of so many of his predecessors—lack of an audience. Now he has obligations to fulfil.

On the last page of *Lord of the Flies,* William Golding's novel, the twelve-year-old leader of the desert island castaways suddenly weeps "for the end of innocence, the darkness of man's heart". That is the situation that our post-war writers must acknowledge and deal with. In this technologically triumphant age, when the rockets begin to scream up towards the moon but the human mind seems at an even greater distance, anger has a limited use. Love has a wider application, and it is that which needs describing wherever it can be found so that we may all recognise it and learn its use.

216

index

217